# High Crimes and Misdemeanors in Presidential Impeachment

# High Crimes and Misdemeanors in Presidential Impeachment

*H. Lowell Brown*

HIGH CRIMES AND MISDEMEANORS IN PRESIDENTIAL IMPEACHMENT

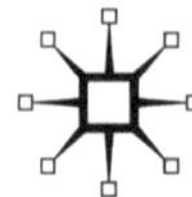

Copyright © H. Lowell Brown, 2010.



First published in 2010 by
PALGRAVE MACMILLAN®
in the United States—a division of St. Martin's Press LLC,
175 Fifth Avenue, New York, NY 10010.

Where this book is distributed in the UK, Europe and the rest of the world, this is by Palgrave Macmillan, a division of Macmillan Publishers Limited, registered in England, company number 785998, of Houndmills, Basingstoke, Hampshire RG21 6XS.

Palgrave Macmillan is the global academic imprint of the above companies and has companies and representatives throughout the world.

Palgrave® and Macmillan® are registered trademarks in the United States, the United Kingdom, Europe and other countries.

ISBN: 978–0–230–62135–0

Library of Congress Cataloging-in-Publication Data

Brown, H. Lowell.
   High crimes and misdemeanors in presidential impeachment /
H. Lowell Brown.
      p. cm.
   Includes bibliographical references.
   ISBN 978–0–230–62135–0 (alk. paper)
      1. Impeachments—United States—History. 2. Johnson, Andrew, 1808–1875—Impeachment. 3. Nixon, Richard M. (Richard Milhous), 1913–1994—Impeachment. 4. Clinton, Bill, 1946– —Impeachment.
   I. Title.

KF5075.B76 2010
342.73'062—dc22                                        2009017695

A catalogue record of the book is available from the British Library.

Design by Newgen Imaging Systems (P) Ltd., Chennai, India.

First edition: January 2010

10 9 8 7 6 5 4 3 2 1

Printed in the United States of America.

# Table of Contents

# Preface

The U.S. Constitution provides that the president and other civil officers of the federal government may be removed from office upon impeachment by the House of Representatives and conviction by the Senate of treason, bribery, and "other high Crimes and Misdemeanors" (Article II, Section 4). The offense of treason was defined in the Constitution (Article III, Section 3) and bribery was an offense well established in common law. In contrast, however, no authoritative definition of "high crimes and misdemeanors" was provided either in the Constitution itself or in the debates of the Framers at the constitutional convention. As a consequence, the meaning of high crimes and misdemeanors—and in particular whether evidence of criminal conduct is required—has been a matter of controversy since the first impeachment and trial of Judge John Pickering in 1804 (chapter 2) and continuing through the impeachment and trial of President William Jefferson Clinton (chapter 4).

In order to discern what the Framers intended when they adopted high crimes and misdemeanors as grounds for the removal of the president from office, it is necessary not only to look at the debates at the convention and in the state ratification proceedings but to consider as well the usage of high crimes and misdemeanors in British parliamentary impeachments (including the impeachment of Warren Hastings, Governor General of India, which was occurring at the time of the federal constitutional convention) and by the legislatures of the colonies and states preceding the convention, all of which informed the conceptual thinking of the Framers concerning presidential impeachment. It is likewise necessary to view the impeachment debates in the larger context of the Framers' aspirations and anxieties regarding the office of president that they were creating. This is the focus of chapter 1 and it is from these various sources that emerge the understanding of high crimes and misdemeanors as conduct in the discharge of the office of the presidency amounting to an abuse or overreaching of the powers of that office and an understanding that high crimes and misdemeanors were to be reserved for only the most grievous official conduct that poses a direct threat to the constitutional order of government.

Official misconduct described by Alexander Hamilton as being "injuries done to society itself."

The Framers left to the Congresses the task of giving concrete substance to high crimes and misdemeanors. Thus, the impeachment proceedings that have been instituted beginning with the "State Trials" of Senator William Blount, Judge Pickering, and Justice Samuel Chase, in which a number of the Framers themselves participated, are instructive. This is the focus of chapters 2 through 4.

The impeachments and trials of President Andrew Johnson (chapter 2) and President Clinton (chapter 4) and the proceedings of the House Judiciary Committee concerning the presidency of Richard M. Nixon (chapter 3) each reveal the struggle of the legislators to marry the implications of high crimes and misdemeanors with their critiques of presidential misconduct. Regrettably, this struggle has often been obscured by partisan ardor.

However, having conceived of impeachment as a remedial, political process rather than a punitive, judicial proceeding, it is doubtless that the Framers anticipated controversy whether recourse to such an extreme measure was warranted. Nevertheless, although there has not been unanimity, when viewed in the context of the circumstances that have led to the three presidential impeachments, there is consensus that high crimes and misdemeanors must arise from the official acts of the president (in contrast to misconduct in the president's private affairs) and must amount to a breach of faith with the Constitution that is so grave (whether or not the conduct is also criminal) that there is no alternative to removal by the Congress of the elected head of state.

# Author's Note

In undertaking this journey of discovery, the author has benefited from the kindness of many people. Professor Robert Allison, of Suffolk University, Charles W. Blau, Esq., of Dallas Texas, and Professor Michael J. Gerhardt, of the University of North Carolina School of Law, have been generous with their time and gracious in their criticism in reviewing the manuscript. However, the author is most deeply indebted and grateful to Professor Eric Schickler who guided the work while at Harvard University and who has continued to provide counsel and encouragement since his return to the University of California at Berkeley.

The author also wishes to express his thanks to Nancy Giachinta, of Raymond, Maine, who typed draft upon draft of the manuscript with good humor and without complaint.

But it is to my wife, Ella, that I owe my greatest debt of gratitude and thanks for her unfailing support, and for her belief and confidence. It is to her that this book is dedicated.

H. Lowell Brown
Falmouth, Maine

# 1

# Original Meaning

When the constitutional convention considered the question of presidential impeachment, and as grounds therefore "high crimes and misdemeanors," the delegates had a breadth of experience upon which to draw. Impeachment, as derived from English parliamentary practice, had been advocated by Josiah Quincy and John Adams even before independence as a means of holding the crown's colonial government accountable for what they believed were abuses of official authority. The arguments of Quincy and Adams were grounded firmly in English parliamentary impeachment history as reported by Cobbett, Hatsell, Howell, Salmon, and Selden. This practice established high crimes and misdemeanors as referring to the official misconduct of public officials in derogation either of their offices of trust or of an act of Parliament, or otherwise as being contrary to the interest and security of the nation.

English impeachment practice was also vividly before the delegates as the impeachment of Warren Hastings unfolded during the convention. The Hastings impeachment was clearly impressed on the mind of George Mason, author of the high crimes and misdemeanors provision, and of other delegates as well.

Thus, conceptually, the meaning of high crimes and misdemeanors was drawn from English impeachment practice and from the American experience with impeachment both before independence and in the states thereafter. To the delegates, impeachment was, as Hamilton wrote in Federalist 65, "a national inquest into the conduct of public men" and "high crimes and misdemeanors" were offenses that arose "from the abuse or violation of some public trust" that were "injuries done immediately to society itself."

One of the most remarkable features of the interlocking authorities created in the U.S. Constitution is that the highest officers of the executive and judicial branches of the federal government can be removed from office by the third, coordinate branch, the legislature, by impeachment in the

House of Representatives and conviction in the Senate. As grounds for this extraordinary proceeding, the Constitution provides that "the President, Vice President and all Civil Officers of the United States shall be removed from office on impeachment for, and conviction of, Treason, Bribery, or other high Crimes and Misdemeanors."[1] However, the meaning of high crimes and misdemeanors has proved to be elusive and has been a source of partisan controversy. Neither the language of the Constitution nor the record of the debates in the constitutional convention provides a conclusive definition of what the Framers had in mind.

Unlike "treason," which the Framers defined in Article III, Section 3, and "bribery," an offense established in both common and statutory law, the meaning of high crimes and misdemeanors was not specified either in the Constitution itself or in the debates. This lack of specificity was not oversight on their part, however, because the Framers recognized that impeachment was a political process, and not simply an adjudicative proceeding. The Framers thus adopted a phrase, high crimes and misdemeanors, with a long history of parliamentary usage in Britain, which had been imported to the American colonies, by which governmental officials had been held to account for the conduct of their public offices.

In light of this historic usage, high crimes and misdemeanors had a commonly understood meaning for the delegates that was independent of the words themselves. When viewed as part of the larger debate concerning the nature of the presidency itself, what emerges from the debates at the constitutional convention and at the state ratification conventions is the understanding that by adopting high crimes and misdemeanors as grounds for presidential impeachment, the president could be removed for abuse of the powers of office and in that way the Republic would be protected from the arbitrariness of an "elected monarch" and the constitutional order would be preserved.

## Impeachment at the Federal Constitutional Convention

On September 11, 1786, commissioners delegated from Delaware, New Jersey, New York, Pennsylvania, and Virginia met in Annapolis, Maryland to consider "the trade and commerce of the United States" and in particular "how far a uniform system in their commercial intercourse and regulations might be necessary to their common interest and permanent harmony." The delegates reported their "earnest and unanimous wish, that speedy measures be taken, to effect a general meeting, one of the States, in a future Convention, for the same, and such other purposes, as the situation of public affairs, may be found to require." The delegates pointed out that "important defects in the federal government" had been generally acknowledged and had led to their meeting. It was the delegates' assessment that those defects were "of a nature so serious, as…to render the situation of the United States delicate and critical, calling for an execution of the united virtue and wisdom of all the members of the confederacy." The delegates recommended that the states appoint commissioners "to meet at Philadelphia on the second Monday in May next, to take into consideration the situation of the United States, to devise such further provisions as shall appear to them necessary to render the constitution of the Federal Government adequate to the exigencies of the Union."[2]

The delegates assembled in Philadelphia on Friday, May 25, 1787.[3] However, the Virginia delegation had already been at work since May 17.[4]

*The Virginia Plan*

On May 29, 1787, Edmund Randolph, the Governor of Virginia, introduced a series of eleven resolutions that became known as the Virginia Plan.[5] This proposed plan of government had been formulated by the delegation during the preceding twelve days, based largely on Madison's preconvention preparation.[6] The Virginia Plan served as the basis for much of the convention's deliberations.[7]

The debate on impeachment was entwined with the convention's creation of the office of the presidency.[8] Although the presidency was without precedent in the colonial experience, a central predicate of the revolution had been rebellion against what was viewed as arbitrary power exercised by a distant monarch through his delegated governors and appointed "placemen."[9]

In light of that history, the delegates labored to prevent the institution of an elected "republican monarch,"[10] while investing the office with authority sufficient to counterbalance that of the Congress. Impeachment became the avenue of last resort to ensure "the Republic would not have to resort to revolution to remedy executive abuse of power."[11]

The plan called for the establishment of a "national judiciary" composed of "one or more supreme tribunals, and of inferior tribunals to be chosen by the National Legislature." These courts were to have jurisdiction, among other things, over "impeachments of any National Officers."[12]

The delegates resolved into a Committee of the Whole House in order "to consider the state of the American union." On Friday, June 1, the Committee of the Whole took up the Virginia Plan's seventh resolution concerning the national executive. With respect to the length of the executive's term in office, Madison proposed that the term be for seven years, with no eligibility for reappointment. Gunning Bedford, a delegate from Delaware, opposed the seven-year term because the country could be "saddled" with an unfit executive if, after assuming his office, "it should be found on trial that he did not possess the qualifications ascribed to him, or should lose them after his appointment." Bedford argued that even impeachment would not provide a remedy under those circumstances because "an impeachment would reach misfeasance only, not incapacity."[13] Madison observed, however, that "to prevent a Man from holding an Office longer than he ought, he may for malpractice be impeached and removed," although he would not be subject to removal "for any ineligibility."[14]

The report of the Committee of the Whole was made on June 13. The report contained a provision that the "national executive" was to be elected by the legislature for a single, seven-year term and would be "removable on impeachment and conviction of malpractices or neglect of duty."[15]

Debate on impeachment continued the following day after John Dickinson of Delaware raised the question of impeachment "on the request of a majority of the legislatures of individual states." George Mason of Virginia felt that "displacing an unfit magistrate" was "indispensable" in view of "the fallibility of those who choose, as well as by the corruptibility of the man chosen." Hugh Williamson and William Davie, both from North Carolina, later moved that provision for removal of the executive "on impeachment and conviction of malpractice or neglect of duty" be added to the president's proposed term of office, and delegates agreed.[16]

*The New Jersey Plan*

An alternative to the Virginia Plan was put forward by William Paterson, Governor of New Jersey, on June 15. The proposal became known as the New Jersey Plan.

The New Jersey Plan contemplated the removal of the "federal executive" upon application of "a majority of the Executives of the several states."[17] The New Jersey Plan also called for the establishment of a federal judiciary whose jurisdiction extended to hearing and determining "in the first instance on all impeachments of federal officers."[18]

*The Hamilton Plan*

A third plan of government was offered by Alexander Hamilton on June 18. The Hamilton Plan also contemplated removal of government officers, including senators, by impeachment. Under the Hamilton Plan, federal officials would be subject to impeachment and removal for "mal-and corrupt conduct." The trials of impeachments were to be held before the judges of the "superior court of Law of each State."[19]

Despite vigorous debate of the New Jersey and Hamilton Plans, the Virginia Plan, which included provision for removal of the executive upon impeachment and conviction of malpractice or neglect of duty, was reported out of the Committee of the Whole on June 16, to be taken up by the convention. The question of removal was debated on July 20.[20]

Charles Pinckney of South Carolina and Governeur Morris of Pennsylvania took the position that the chief executive should not be subject to impeachment. Instead, the executive's culpability should be left to the voters to decide, while those who had acted with the chief executive would be subject to prosecution. Morris argued that the chief executive could not commit a criminal act "without coadjutors who may be punished" and if the chief executive were reelected, "that will be sufficient proof of his innocence."[21]

Mason immediately responded that "no point is of more importance than the right of impeachment should be continued." Mason emphasized that no one should be above justice, particularly "that man … who can commit the most extensive injustice." Mason stated "When great crimes were committed he was for punishing the principal as well as the Coadjutors."[22]

Although Mason had supported election of the executive by the national legislature, there was "the danger of their being corrupted by Candidates," and to Mason, "this furnished a particular reason in favor of impeachments while in office." Mason asked rhetorically, "shall the man who has practiced corruption and by that means procured his appointment in the first instance, be suffered to escape punishment, by repeating his guilt?"[23]

Benjamin Franklin of Pennsylvania also opposed the motion of Morris and Pinckney to eliminate presidential impeachment. Franklin argued that retaining the impeachment clause was favorable to the president because impeachment provided a means for the adjudication of misconduct. As Franklin observed, "What was the practice before this in cases where the chief Magistrate rendered himself obnoxious? Why, recourse was had to assassination in which he was not only deprived of his life but of the opportunity of vindicating his character." Thus, Franklin concluded, "It would be the best way therefore to provide in the Constitution for the regular punishment of the Executive where his misconduct should deserve it, and for his honorable acquittal when he should be unjustly accused."[24]

Morris conceded that there was misconduct in office that would warrant impeachment. It was Morris' view that "corruption and some few other offenses to be such as ought to be impeachable." Morris was also of the view that "the cases ought to be enumerated and defined."[25]

To Madison, it was "indispensable" that provision be made for "defending the Community against the incapacity, negligence or perfidy of the chief Magistrate." Madison also observed in this regard that the executive "might lose his capacity after appointment. He might divert his administration into a scheme of peculation or oppression. He might betray his trust to foreign powers." The proposed limitation of the executive to a single seven-year term of office would not provide sufficient security against such eventualities.[26]

Concern was expressed by several delegates that investing the legislature with impeachment power would disturb the balance of powers among the three branches of the federal government. Pinckney argued that impeachment would be "a rod over the Executive" that would "effectively destroy his independence." Agreeing with the earlier comments of Pinckney and Morris, Rufus King of Massachusetts contended that the executive "would be periodically tried for his behavior by his electors, who would continue or discontinue him in trust according to the manner in which he had discharged it." Accordingly, King said, like the legislators, the executive "ought to be subject to no intermediate trial, by impeachment." In any event, King felt that impeachment of the executive by the legislature "would be destructive of his independence and of the principles of the Constitution."[27]

Randolph was sympathetic to the risk to executive independence posed by the threat of legislative impeachment. Randolph suggested, as had Alexander Hamilton, that a forum of state judges be convened to try impeachments rather than empowering the legislature to do so. Nevertheless, Randolph strongly favored impeachment. Randolph noted that "the Executive will have great opportunities of abusing his power, particularly in time of war when the military force, and in some respects the public money will be in his hands." Like Franklin, Randolph expressed the concern that "should no regular punishment be provided, it will be irregularly inflicted by tumults and insurrections."[28]

According to Madison, Morris was persuaded by the debate and became "sensible of the necessity of impeachments." Observing that even King Charles II had been bribed by Louis XIV, Morris agreed that "The Executive ought therefore to be impeachable for treachery" and for "Corrupting his electors." Morris' view was that as to the latter offenses, the executive "should be punished not as a man, but as an officer, and punished only by degradation from his office." However, Morris shared the concerns expressed by Pinckney and King that great care had to be exercised to ensure that impeachment would not make the executive dependent on the legislature.[29]

Removal of the executive by impeachment and conviction was approved by the delegates in a vote of 8 to 2, Massachusetts and South Carolina voting in the negative.[30] The resolution concerning establishment of the executive was brought before the convention on July 26. As adopted, the resolution provided that the president was "to be removable on impeachment and conviction of malpractice or neglect of duty."[31] The matter was referred to a committee for detailing the Constitution.[32]

The Committee of Detail presented its draft of the Constitution to the convention on August 6. Under the Committee's draft, the executive would be subject to removal upon impeachment by the House of Representatives and conviction in the Supreme Court for "treason, bribery or corruption."[33] There was no explanation for this change.

Debate on the Committee's draft commenced on August 7. It was not until September 8, however, that debate resumed on the provision for presidential impeachment.[34]

When the clause providing for trial of the president by the Senate for treason and bribery came up for debate, George Mason questioned why the grounds for impeachment were restricted to treason and bribery only. Mason contended that "Treason as defined in the Constitution will not reach many great and dangerous offenses." Mason cited as an example the charges against Warren Hastings, the former Governor General of India who was the subject of impeachment proceedings in the English Parliament at the time, noting that "Hastings is not guilty of Treason."[35] Mason also noted that bills of attainder "which saved the British Constitution" had also been forbidden under the proposed constitution and therefore, it was "the more necessary to extend the power of impeachments." Mason moved that "maladministration" be added as grounds for impeachment of the president and Elbridge Gerry, of Massachusetts, seconded his motion.[36]

Several delegates objected to the addition of maladministration as grounds for impeachment. Madison argued that "so vague a term" would be "equivalent to a tenure during pleasure of the Senate." Morris also argued that removal for maladministration was superfluous because "an election every four years will prevent mal-administration."[37]

Mason immediately withdrew maladministration as a ground for impeachment and in its place substituted "other high crimes and misdemeanors against the State." Without further debate, the delegates approved "the question thus altered."[38]

That there was virtually no debate or discussion concerning Mason's substituted language strongly suggests that the phrase "other high crimes and misdemeanors against the State" had a generally accepted meaning to the delegates.[39] Mason's reference to the Hastings' impeachment proceedings that were ongoing in England reflected the delegates' awareness of English Parliamentary procedure, as popularized by the Hastings case.

The convention delegates were also familiar with impeachment, which had become an established procedure in the states during the colonial period and, as a consequence, provision for impeachment of state officials had also been included in the majority of the postindependence constitutions of the states. One of the most notorious of the colonial impeachments had been brought against Chief Justice Peter Oliver in the Massachusetts colony for high crimes and misdemeanors.

## Precedents for Impeachment

In the decade preceding independence, impeachment was one means by which the colonies sought to address abuses of official authority and to assert their autonomy. In 1766, the lawyers of South Carolina petitioned the English Governor, William Bell, to permit the courts to hear cases without the requirement of royal stamps because the lack of stamps had forced the courts to close. Although Governor Bell had granted their petition, the Chief Justice, Charles Shiner, another royal appointee, refused to hear cases without the necessary stamps.

When the courts reopened on March 3, 1766, Justice Shiner dissented from the decision of his fellow justices to allow cases to proceed. In view of Shiner's intransigence, the colonial assembly requested the newly appointed governor, Charles Montagu, to remove Shiner. With the concurrence of his council, Governor Montagu suspended Shiner until instructions could be received from England. Shiner's death resolved the controversy.[40]

Contemporaneously with the Shiner affair, the colonial assembly in New Jersey challenged the fitness of another royal judge. On June 18, 1767, the assembly summoned Chief Justice Frederick Smyth to appear and answer charges that he had solicited special compensation to hold court in one of the counties in New Jersey during the summer months.

The assembly relied on its authority over judicial compensation to support its action, which was not otherwise specifically authorized by statute or by the colonial charter. Although Smyth had been appointed by the crown and served at the pleasure of the King, Smyth appeared before the assembly. Ultimately, the assembly showed leniency and Smyth was not removed.[41]

A contest over control of judicial compensation would catalyze a monumental conflict between the crown prerogative in the colonies and the coalescing movement for independence. The focus of the conflict was the question of whether the judges of the Superior Court of Massachusetts would accept compensation from the English civil list, and the result was the impeachment of Chief Justice Peter Oliver for high crimes and misdemeanors.

*The Impeachment of Chief Justice Peter Oliver*

The issue had arisen in 1771 when reports first circulated that Hutchinson was to be compensated from the civil list rather than by the colonial assembly.[42] Although the issue subsided after a strong protest was lodged by the assembly, the controversy returned virulently in the summer and fall of 1772 when it was confirmed that Hutchinson and the Superior Court Judges were to receive crown salaries.[43]

Royal compensation of the judges was viewed by many as a threat to the independence of the judiciary and a challenge to the liberty of the colonists as free Englishmen under the royal charter.[44] Hostility was first ventilated at the town meetings held in Boston on November 2 and Cambridge on December 14, 1772. However, through the labors of the committees of correspondence, Boston's *Votes and Proceedings*, which describe the compensation as a "plan of despotism" that was "rapidly hastening to a completion…under a constant, unremitted, uniform aim to enslave us," was communicated throughout Massachusetts and beyond.[45]

There followed a momentous debate in the General Court and the popular press concerning English versus American constitutionalism and the sovereignty of Parliament. In each debate, the legal and historical scholarship of John Adams played a central part.

In addresses to the General Court on January 6 and March 6, 1773, Governor Hutchinson argued that because there could not be two sovereign authorities governing the colony, the authority of Parliament was supreme.[46] The assembly, assisted by John Adams, countered that it was the royal charter establishing the colony that defined the liberties and immunities of the subjects in the colony, and accordingly, the charter was not subject to subsequent restriction and limitation by Parliament.

Adams expanded on this thesis that the charter (and thereby, the General Court) was the sole source of authority over the governance of the colony, in the second of the great constitutional debates of 1773 between Adams and Major General William Brattle that arose from Brattle's advocacy of crown salaries for the judiciary at the Cambridge town meeting on December 14, 1773, and in the *Massachusetts Gazette*.[47] This controversy over the authority of Parliament ripened into a crisis when the chief justice of the Superior Court, Peter Oliver, refused to renounce his crown salary and was impeached by the Massachusetts assembly.

Following the adjournment of the General Court by Governor Hutchinson on March 6, 1773, four judges of the Superior Court accepted only half of the salary provided for them by the assembly with the expectation that the remainder of their salaries would be paid by the crown.[48] When their action came to the attention of the assembly in June, explicit statements of their intentions were required on threat of impeachment.[49] By September 1773, all of the judges, with the prominent exception of Chief Justice Oliver, had declared their intentions to accept only the salaries appropriated by the assembly.[50] Oliver, however, submitted a lengthy statement setting forth his reasons for not complying with the assembly's direction that the judges eschew compensation from the crown. When Governor Hutchinson rejected the call for Oliver's removal by the assembly, popular hostility focused on Oliver, threatening even his physical security.[51]

At this time, Adams was invited to dine with Samuel Winthrop. At that dinner, Adams was asked by one of the guests whether he had any thoughts on "escaping this snare." Adams replied that he agreed with the others present that "petitions and remonstrances to King or Parliament will be ineffectual" and that "nothing but force will succeed." Nevertheless, Adams suggested as an alternative, "I would impeach the judges."[52] Adams explained that "our House of Representatives have the same right to impeach as the House of Commons has in England and our governor and council have the same right and duty to receive and hear impeachments as the King and House of Lords have in Parliament."[53]

Adams recorded in his diary that he had explained that "there had been precedents enough, and by much too many, in England" for such a proceeding and that impeachment "was a dangerous experiment at all times, but it was essential to the preservation of the constitution in some cases that could be reached by no other power but that of impeachment." Adams had also explained that the authority for impeachment derived from the charter's guarantee of "all rights and privileges of Englishmen" and thus, "if the House of Commons in England is the grand inquest of the nation, the House of Representatives is the grand inquest of this province, and the council must have the powers of judicature of the House of Lords in Great Britain."[54]

Following Adams' remarks at dinner, several people came to his home to discuss his impeachment proposal. Among his visitors was Joseph Hawley who served on the committee in the assembly that had been formed to address the Oliver issue. Adams provided Hawley with several treatises on English parliamentary proceedings. According to Adams' diary, he told Hawley that "judicature in Parliament was as ancient as common law and as Parliament itself. That without this high jurisdiction it was thought impossible to defend the Constitution against princes, and nobles, and great ministers, who might commit high crimes and misdemeanors which no authority would be powerful enough to prevent or punish."[55]

When the Assembly was informed on February 22, 1774, by Governor Hutchinson that he would not consult the council concerning Chief Justice Oliver, the Assembly resolved to impeach Oliver.[56] Hawley's committee was given the task of drafting the articles of impeachment and, according to Adams, Hawley insisted that the committee consult with Adams.[57] On February 24, 1774, "Articles of Impeachment of High Crimes and Misdemeanors" against Chief Justice Peter Oliver were adopted.

In the articles, the Assembly reiterated its authority over the Superior Court by virtue of the charter of King William and Queen Mary. The Assembly also reiterated its authority to impose "proportionable and reasonable Assessments, Rates and Taxes" for the support of the Superior Court. However, the Assembly said, "many evil-minded persons" had misconstrued the charter "to introduce and establish another Form of Government and a new Mode of supporting the executive and judicial Officers of Government" and had procured through falsehood an act of Parliament "for the defraying of the charges of the Administration of Justice" in the colonies.[58]

The Assembly charged that Oliver had declined to accept the salary appropriated to him pursuant to the charter and instead had accepted a crown salary "with Design to subvert the Constitution of this Province...and to introduce into the said Court a partial, arbitrary and corrupt Administration of Justice." In the view of the Assembly, the crown salary "cannot fail to have the Effect of a continual Bribe in his judicial Proceedings," and by his acceptance of the crown salary "he hath betrayed the Corruption and Baseness of his Heart and the sordid Lust of Covetousness: In Breach of his Engagements to rely solely on the Grants of the General Assembly, necessarily implied and involved in his accepting said Office."[59]

The Assembly charged that Oliver's acceptance of the crown salary was a violation of the "Constitution of this Province" and of the "natural and most essential Rights of the People,"—the rights of "appropriating their own Property" and of "Judging the Merits of their own Servants." Further, by his "Defiance and Contempt" of the sentiments of the assembly, Oliver had "Wickedly and Perversely endeavoured to continue and increase the Discontent and Jealousies of this People."[60]

In his letter to the House declaring his intentions to accept the crown salary, Oliver had claimed that his previous salary granted by the assembly had not been sufficient to maintain his family. This too constituted grounds for impeachment because in asserting that claim, Oliver had "ungratefully, falsely and maliciously labored to lay Imputation and Scandal upon his Majesty's Government, insolently and contemptuously insinuating, that by the Parsimony, Injustice and Ingratitude of the said Government, in with-holding from him and adequate and due Reward for his Services as a Justice."[61] Thus, Oliver had "misrepresented and traduced this Government and endeavoured to alienate the Hearts of his Majesty's Leige People of this Province from his Majesty, and set a Division between them; to introduce into said Court a partial and corrupt Administration of Justice, destroy the present Form of Government of this Province, and establish an arbitrary and tyrannical Government in its Stead."[62]

Stripped of the rhetorical flourishes, the high crimes and misdemeanors for which Justice Oliver was impeached were: 1) disagreement with the construction of the Massachusetts charter proffered by Adams (in his debate with General Brattle) and the Assembly (in the debate with Governor Hutchinson) vesting sole authority over the judiciary in the Assembly; and 2) defiance of the will of the Assembly that the only compensation that the judges could lawfully accept was that which was appropriated by the Assembly. What emerges from the Oliver affair is that impeachment was seen as an essentially political proceeding in which the legislature could challenge what were perceived as *ultra vires* acts by coordinate authorities—in Oliver's case, the judiciary. It is also clear that the high crimes and misdemeanors with which Oliver was charged were not private acts but rather derived from the way in which he had conducted his public office.

The Oliver affair also resolved itself politically without a trial before Governor Hutchinson and the council. Although Governor Hutchinson again refused to act,[63] jurors first in Boston, Charlestown, and Worcester, and then throughout Massachusetts refused to be sworn. The court did not sit again until a new one was appointed by the colonial government following the battle of Lexington in 1775.[64]

It is significant that the high crimes and misdemeanors with which Oliver was charged were not "true crimes" at common law. Rather, they could be considered "state crimes" arising from Oliver's violation of the constitutional duties and obligations of his public office under Massachusetts charter, at least as the charter was construed by a majority of the assembly.

It is clear also that the impeachment of Oliver was simply an episode in the larger constitutional struggle between the Parliament and colonial legislature of Massachusetts. Thus, from its beginnings in colonial America, impeachment was a political rather than a judicial proceeding in which the legislature sought to redress what were considered to be abuses or usurpations of authority.

In formulating his impeachment strategy against Chief Justice Oliver, Adams drew heavily on treatises and collections of the parliamentary judicature of England.[65] Adams' researches also formed the basis for his pamphlet *Thoughts on Government*, which was circulated among the colonies. Among those influenced by *Thoughts on Government* was George Mason of Virginia.[66] Mason was the principal author of the Virginia Constitution, which provided for the impeachment of "the governor, when he is out of office, and others offending, against the state, either by mal-administration, corruption, or other means by which the safety of the state may be endangered." Mason was also the proponent of high crimes and misdemeanors as a grounds for impeachment at the federal constitutional convention.[67] It seems clear, as well, that other delegates to the convention were familiar with the place of high crimes and misdemeanors in British parliamentary practice.

### *Parliamentary Impeachment in Great Britain*

Both Josiah Quincy and John Adams relied on British Parliamentary precedent to support their assertions of legislative authority over what they and other like-minded revolutionaries viewed as the abuses of the crown's representatives in the colonies. British legal scholars of the seventeenth and eighteenth century had commented on impeachment by the House of Commons and their work was well known to lawyers in the colonies.[68] Sir Matthew Hale, in his treatise *Pleas of the Crown*, described the Commons as "the grand inquest of the nation."[69] Similarly, William Blackstone, in his equally prominent *Commentaries on the Law of England*, described the jurisdiction of the Parliament as "the supreme court in the kingdom, not only for the making, but also for the execution of laws…the method of Parliamentary impeachment."[70]

According to Blackstone, impeachment had derived "from the constitution of the antient Germans" but the English constitution had "much improved upon the antient model imported hither from the continent." Impeachment, however, was an extraordinary procedure in a number of respects. To Blackstone, impeachment by the Commons and trial by the Lords was a departure from the general rule that "the union of the legislature and judicial powers ought to be most carefully avoided." The departure was a necessary one because "a subject, entrusted with the administration of public affairs, may infringe the rights of the people, and be guilty of such crimes, as the ordinary magistrate either dares not or cannot punish."[71]

Thus, it was both the nature of the offense and the standing of the offender that necessitated prosecution and adjudication by the two houses of Parliament. In respect of the nature of the offense, Blackstone noted that the "first and principal" offense against the public, which he described as "Misprisions and Contempts affecting the King and Government," was that of "mal-administration of such high officers, as are in public trust and employment."[72] These offenses, he wrote, were "usually punished by the method of Parliamentary impeachment," in contrast to other public wrongs that were adjudicated in the courts.[73] It was also because the impeachable offense was one against the public at large—that is, an infringement of the rights of the people—that in Blackstone's view precluded the Commons from sitting in judgment "because their constituents are the parties injured."[74]

Writing in 1777, another prominent commentator on English law, Richard Wooddeson, observed in his Vinerian Lectures at Oxford that although "all the king's subjects are impeachable in parliament," it was "such misdeeds, however, as peculiarly injure the commonwealth by the abuse of high offices of trust, are the most proper, and have been the most usual grounds for this kind of prosecution." In that regard, Wooddeson said, "if a lord chancellor be guilty of bribery, or of acting grossly contrary to the duty of his office, if the judges mislead their sovereign by unconstitutional opinions, if any other magistrate attempt to subvert the fundamental laws, or introduce arbitrary power, these have been deemed cases adapted to parliamentary inquiry and decision." Likewise, he said, "where a lord chancellor has been thought to have put the seal to an ignominious treaty, a lord admiral to neglect the safeguard of the sea, an ambassador to betray his trust, a privy counselor to propound or support pernicious and dishonorable measures, or a confidential adviser of his sovereign to obtain exorbitant grants or incompatible employments; these imputations have properly occasioned impeachments; because it is apparent how little the ordinary tribunals are calculated to take cognizance of such offences; or to investigate and reform the purity of the state."[75]

Blackstone was also of the view that the ordinary courts were not suited to sit in judgment of a person charged by Parliament. As he wrote, "but before what court shall this impeachment be tried? Not before the ordinary tribunal, which would naturally be swayed by the authority of so powerful an accuser."[76] Instead, the Commons, "which represents the people, must bring its charge before the other branch, which consists of the nobility, who have neither the same interests nor the same passions as popular assemblies." Thus, to Blackstone, it was "proper that the nobility should judge, to insure justice to the accused; as it is proper that the people should accuse, to insure justice to the commonwealth."[77]

Wooddeson agreed with Blackstone that trial of impeachments was properly before the Lords, but for somewhat different reasons. To Wooddeson, the subject matter of the impeachments (i.e., abuses of powers "to the extensive detriment of the community"), were not suitable for "ordinary tribunals." That, together with the dignity of the Commons as the "grand inquest of the nation," required that trials be held in the other legislative branch. Thus, he wrote, "It is certain that magistrates and officers entrusted with the administration of public affairs may abuse their delegated powers to the extensive detriment of the community, and at the same time in a manner not properly cognizable before the ordinary tribunals. The influence of such delinquents, and the nature of such offenses, may not unsuitably engage the authority of the highest court, and the wisdom of the sagest assembly. The Commons, therefore, as the grand inquest of the nation, become suitors for penal justice and they cannot consistently either with their own dignity, or with safety to the accused, sue elsewhere but to those who share in the legislature."[78]

It should be noted, as well, that accusations of misconduct by impeachment differed from those by "appeal." Blackstone noted that an appeal, "when spoken of as a criminal prosecution, denotes an accusation by a private subject against another, for some heinous crime, demanding punishment on account of the particular injury suffered, rather than for the offense against the public."[79]

In contrast, impeachment represented an accusation of an offense against the public by the Commons itself. As Sir Matthew Hale observed, "Appeals were nothing else but accusations, either of Capital or Criminal Misdemeanors, made in the Lords House by particular Persons; but Impeachment is made by the Body of the House of Commons, which is equivalent to an Indictment *pro Corpore Regni,* and therefore is of another Nature than Accusation or Appeal."[80] Impeachment has also been seen as the means by which the rule of law was enforced against those whose proximity to the crown might otherwise afford them immunity from prosecution in the courts.[81]

## *The Early Impeachments*

The first parliamentary trial appears to have taken place at Shrewsbury on September 30, 1283, when David, the brother of Llewellyn, was tried on a charge of treason. According to Sir James Fitzjames Stephen, "The sheriff of each county was to return two elected knights, and the governing bodies of twenty cities and boroughs were to return two representatives for each. Eleven earls, ninety-nine barons and nineteen other men of note, judges, councilors, and constables of castles were summoned by special writ." Judgment was rendered by a "body chosen from the justices of the *Curia Regis* under John deVaux." Stephen noted that "the assembled baronage watched the trial as his peers, and the Commons must have given a moral weight to the proceedings."[82]

Stephen cited several other early examples of parliamentary trials. In 1291, the Archbishop of York was prosecuted for having purchased "a debt that was owed to a Jew who had been banished and whose debts had been forfeited to the King."[83]

In 1350, in what Stephen described as "a remarkable though anomalous proceeding," Sir Thomas Berkeley was called before the King and the Parliament to answer for the murder of Edward II who had been in his care. Berkeley denied knowledge of the circumstances of the King's death and claimed that he had been elsewhere and in such ill health that he had no recollection of any of the events, although he had assigned trusted guards and officers to protect the King. Berkeley was acquitted.[84]

Both Stephen and Henry Hallam considered the proceedings against Richard Lyons, William Ellis, John Peake, William Lord Latimer, and John Lord Neville in 1376 to have been "the earliest impeachment in the full sense of the word."[85] Each was charged with fraud against the King. They had loaned money to the King "upon usurious contracts." They had also bargained "with the King's creditors, to take off the sums due them upon small advance" and had committed "many other extortions, deceits and oppressions." Commons requested that the articles of impeachment be heard "by the judges and other lords in London and other suitable towns" and the King agreed to do so.[86]

Over time, the Commons assumed the role of accuser of public wrongs. As noted by John Hatsell, in his treatise *Precedents of Proceedings in the House of Commons*, toward the end of the reign of Edward III, "the House of Commons took upon themselves the character of accusers…of persons charged with treason and other high crimes and misdemeanors against the state."[87]

Hatsell also observed that the conduct underlying these early impeachments involved public offenses representing abuse of office. Hatsell wrote that "the crimes for which, during this period from 1376–1450, the Commons impeach, are misdemeanors, committed by persons engaged by the crown, either at home or in its foreign possessions—mal-administration of justice, and extrajudicial conduct in the judges of the realm."[88]

Consistent with Hatsell's view, in 1386, Michael de la Pole, the Earl of Suffolk and Chancellor of England, was impeached by the Commons of high crimes and misdemeanors for misconduct in office. De la Pole was charged with having defrauded the King while acting as chancellor by having "purchased of our lord the King lands, tenements and rents to a great value…at much smaller value than really they were worth by the year, in deceit of the king."[89]

De la Pole was charged with other misuses of his office as well. Funds that were to be "expended in a specific manner guarding the sea," were not. De la Pole was charged with having promised the Parliament to assist in improvement of the realm, "yet it was not done, and that by default of him who was the principal officer or minister." Further, funds that had been granted by Parliament for the relief of the City of Gaunt had not been expended by de la Pole for that purpose and as a consequence, "the said City of Gaunt lost and also a thousand marks of the said money."[90] De la Pole was convicted by the Lords and his land was confiscated.[91]

There do not appear to have been any impeachments in the 162-year period between 1459 and 1621.[92] This hiatus has been attributed to the ascension of the judicial power of the privy council, exercised through the Court of the Star Chamber, and to the "immense increase of royal power during the Tudor period," exercised by the King through bills of attainder.[93]

*The Assertion of Parliamentary Prerogative*

The economic crisis in England during the reign of James I led the Parliament to revive impeachment as a vehicle for attacking the monopolies that had been established under the royal grant. Particular focus was placed on the patent for manufacturing gold and silver thread, which was thought to have contributed to the depression in the English cloth industry.[94] In 1621, Sir Henry Yelverton, the Attorney General, was charged by Commons with high crimes and misdemeanors arising from his misuse of office in connection with the effectuation of a monopoly in gold and silver thread.

The monopolists Sir Giles Mompesson and Sir Francis Michell were impeached,[95] as were those in government who were seen as having authorized the grants including Sir Henry Yelverton.[96] Yelverton was charged with having "advised the patent of Gold and Silver Thread to be resumed into the king's hands, conceiving the same to be a monopoly" and having "advised the patentees to proceed by contract with the king." It was further charged that Yelverton had caused "diverse persons" to be imprisoned "for refusing to enter into bonds to restrain their own trade."[97] Yelverton was found guilty by the Lords. He was fined and imprisoned in the Tower.[98]

For the Parliament that met in 1624, the impeachment power became the vehicle for "an assertion of the responsibilities of ministers to Parliament" in contrast to the Tudor view that "ministers were responsible to the sovereign alone."[99] Among the most significant actions in this regard was the impeachment of the Lord Treasurer Lionel Cranfield, Earl of Middlesex, who had managed the finances of James I. As Henry Hallam observed, "the wrath of the commons was justly aroused against that shameless corruption, which characterizes the reign of James beyond every other in our history."[100]

In the case of the Lord Treasurer Middlesex, who was impeached by Commons in 1624 of the high crimes and misdemeanors of corruption in office, it was charged that he had used his position in the "Office of the Wardrobe" to procure "gifts and discharges of great sums of money which he received for the execution of that place and for the queen's funeral." Commons also alleged that Middlesex had misused his position by "taking advantage of his office to purchase large claims due to the king at an inadequate price and then compound the payment of even that price, to the great loss of the king, and to his own profit."[101] Middlesex was charged with having been derelict in his duties, as well, in that he had "allowed the Office of Ordinance to go unrepaired, though money was appropriated for that purpose, and allowed contracts for greatly needed powder to lapse for want of payment."[102] Middlesex was convicted by the Lords and was stripped of his offices, fined, and imprisoned in the Tower.[103]

The impeachment power was next employed to express the Commons' displeasure with abuses during the "eleven years of tyranny," between 1629 and 1640, during which Parliament had not been convened.[104] This displeasure was clearly revealed in the proceedings against Judge Robert Berkeley, and eventually against the other eleven judges of the Law Court, in 1640.

Judge Berkeley was impeached on charges of "high treason and other great misdemeanors" having to do with rulings upholding the King's authority over several revenue measures that Commons claimed had "traitorously and wickedly endeavoured to subvert the fundamental laws and established government of the realm of England…by traitorous wicked words, opinions, judgments, practices and actions."[105]

The first of these judgments and opinions related to the King's authority over the production and sale of corn, including the price. Commons charged Berkeley with having upheld the authority of the King under a statute enacted during the reign of Henry VIII to grant "licenses and dispensations" for the growing and selling of corn, "and thereby great gain might be raised to his majesty." It was the view of the Commons that it was "manifest by the said statute, corn is none of the victuals thereby intended." Thus, Commons charged that Berkeley's ruling upholding the King's authority "was contrary to law, and to the plain sense and meaning of the said statute and contrary to his own knowledge." It was further alleged that Berkeley had rendered this opinion "with the purpose and intention that the said unlawful charge might be imposed upon the subject."[106]

Berkeley was also charged with similar misconduct in upholding the King's authority over the manufacture of soap, which was the basis for the organization in 1632 of the corporation of soap boilers by Baron Richard Weston, the Lord Treasurer and Earl of Portland. Under that scheme, the King was paid a royalty on all soap manufactured by the corporation. Soap that was manufactured by others who were not members of the corporation was subject to condemnation. As a consequence, the King was able to tax (in the guise of the royalty) all the soap manufactured in England.[107] Sixteen soap makers had been prosecuted before the Court of the Star Chamber for "pretended offenses…touching the making and uttering of soap and using the trade of soap makers." The charges against Berkeley arose from his handling of their case.[108]

According to the charges by the Commons, Berkeley had stricken the defendants' answers to the charges and had suppressed evidence favorable to the defendants. Commons characterized these rulings as having been "contrary to law and justice, and contrary to…Sir Robert Berkeley's own knowledge." By reason of these rulings, Commons said, "Defendants were sentenced in the said court of the Star Chamber to be committed prisoners…and disabled from using their trade of soap makers…and deprived of their trade and livelihood."[109]

Third, Berkeley was impeached for upholding the King's authority to raise revenue through assessments for national defense. Historically, port cities had provided ships for the King's use in time of war. Over time, in lieu of providing ships, seaports provided funds for the purchase of ships and this practice became known as "ship-money."[110] In 1634, a call was made to provide ships with which to subdue the pirates. This call for funds was extended the following year to include in-land counties, as well. By 1636, it had become clear that the ship-money assessments were a permanent, general tax. In 1637, ship-money writs were challenged in the Law Courts.[111]

Berkeley was impeached for having sided with the King that "the charge of the defense ought to be borne by all the realm in general." Berkeley was also criticized for barring argument on the legality of ship-money and for his statement in that regard that "there was a rule of law and a rule of government that many things might not be done by the rule of law, might be done by the rule of government." As the King was above criticism, Berkeley and others became the focus of what were considered abuses of governmental powers and were said to have given the King poor advice thereby abusing the King's trust.[112] Although the Lords invited Commons to present the case against Judge Berkeley,[113] the record does not reflect the outcome of the proceedings.

Similarly, Edward Herbert, the Attorney General, was impeached by the Commons on February 15, 1642, for having instituted proceedings on the instructions of the King against six members of Parliament for their part in passage of the Grand Remonstrance in 1641.[114] Herbert was charged with the high crimes and misdemeanors of acting "contrary to his oath and duty of place," by having "falsely, scandalously, and maliciously" published articles of high treason against Lord Kimbolton, a member of the House of Lords, and five members of the House of Commons: John Hampden; Arthur Hasterling; Denzil Hoiles, John Pym, and William Strode.[115] Herbert was acquitted by the Lords after the King sent a letter to Parliament absolving Herbert of guilt.[116]

Also during this time there was what has been called the "altar controversy" in which particular importance was attached to the placement of the communion table in churches. The issue was whether the altar should be located "tablewise" in the center of the church, accessible by the congregants, or "altarwise" at the east end of the church where it was raised and separated from the congregation by a rail.[117] The altar controversy was the product not only of the antagonism to the Church of Rome but also represented a sharp division in the Anglican Church over the increasing influence of Puritanism and the liturgical value of ceremony. The controversy was fueled by the critique of William Laud, the Archbishop of Canterbury, and was the predicate for the impeachment of Bishop Wren in 1640.

The bill of impeachment against Bishop Wren for high crimes and misdemeanors was comprised of twenty-five articles arising from his administration of the church. Seven of those specifications involved the placement and ceremonial use of the communion table. Four of the articles addressed his suppression of the preaching of sermons. The remaining articles attacked his actions in regard to the aggrandizement of the clergy and parish personnel.[118] Once again, however, the record does not indicate what, if any, further action was taken by the Lords.[119]

### *Impeachment during the Civil War*

The civil war against Charles I, which began in the spring of 1642 and ended with his execution in January 1649, resulted in impeachments as Parliament asserted its will against the crown and punished those who were in opposition. The growing schism in the church between the Puritan movement and the episcopacy also resulted in impeachments.

In a series of impeachments for high crimes and misdemeanors lodged in 1642, various nobles were prosecuted for the actions on behalf of the King and against the will of the Parliament. Sir Edward Dering and Richard Spencer were impeached for having sponsored a "Kentish Petition to Parliament" with the intention of raising "commotion and sedition among the people and to have awed the Parliament."[120] The Lord Mayor of London, Sir Richard Guerney, was charged with publishing "illegal proclamations, containing in them matters of dangerous consequence, and contrary to the votes of both Houses of Parliament," and with having endeavored "to raise tumults and discords…to make an increase the differences between his majesty and the Parliament." Guerney was also charged with having disobeyed the directive of Parliament to set aside stores of arms and ammunition in the city.[121] Relatedly, Sir Thomas Gardiner was impeached for using his influence on the mayor and council of London to raise funds and outfit a military force of 200 men to fight on behalf of the King of Scotland. Gardiner too was charged with having worked "to bring the parliament, city and the whole kingdom into disorder and confusion."[122] Lastly, four justices of the peace in Leicester County were charged with having resisted arrest by Parliament with the assistance of 300 armed men "in contempt of justice, and to the high affront and scorn of parliament."[123]

Later, in 1648, Sir John Maynard was impeached for treason "and other high crimes and misdemeanors" after Maynard attacked Parliament with an armed force and assaulted "the person of the speaker and divers members of both houses attending on the parliament." Maynard was also charged with raising an army of 18 regiments and commandeering 4000 muskets and 400 barrels of gun powder "to be employed and used for the army and arraying of the said Reformado officers and soldiers…to be employed for the destruction of Parliament's army."[124]

The civil war altered the dynamics of Parliament's relationship with the King. Although liturgical formality and suspicion of the Roman Church's influence remained part of the political subtext,[125] the focus of impeachments by the Commons returned to the accountability of the elite for misuses of office.[126]

*Impeachment for Maladministration and Misuse of Office*

In an initiative that would later inform the American conception of impeachment and of high crimes and misdemeanors, Parliament asserted it's authority over finance to inquire into the conduct of governmental affairs and administration. In 1665, Parliament established the "appropriation of supply" and in 1667, Parliament instituted the Commission of Public Accounts. In furtherance of this initiative, the impeachment power was employed by the Commons as a vehicle for inquiring into the conduct of government officials. During this period of parliamentary activism in the second half of the seventeenth century, there was a dramatic increase in the number of impeachments. However, in many cases, the charges were thinly supported and were motivated primarily by a desire to remove ministers and judges whose politics and policies were out of favor. Consequently, it was often left to the Lords to temper the ardor of the Commons.[127]

In 1668, Peter Pett, a commissioner of the Royal Navy, was charged by Commons with having failed to bring a ship, the *Royal Charles*, to a place of safety despite having been ordered to do so by the Duke of York and as a consequence the *Royal Charles* and other ships were lost to the Dutch invaders. Pett was also charged with having obstructed the defense against the Dutch invasion by having employed naval ships "for the carrying away of some of his own particular goods," by refusing to provide "the number of tools required, notwithstanding he had sufficient quantity in his majesty's stores," and by providing inferior lumber to be used for "platforms and batteries to oppose the enemy."[128]

Vice Admiral Sir William Penn was also impeached in 1668 for high crimes and misdemeanors relating to thefts from captured prize ships. The Commons charged that Penn had conspired with others to embezzle goods from two captured Dutch ships, thereby defrauding the King.[129]

In 1675, Commons impeached the Earl of Danby, who was the Lord High Treasurer of England, for "Offences, Crimes and Misdemeanors of a Very High Nature," relating to his stewardship. Danby was charged with "exposing his majesty's treasure and revenue to private bargains and corruptions" and "laying aside the chancellor and under-treasurer of the exchequer, and other officers whereby the usual and safe government of his majesty's affairs relating to his revenue, and all checks and comptrolls are avoided." It was alleged that Danby had converted funds from the Irish reserves "to his own private advantage" and had "procured great gifts and grants from the crown, whilst under great debts by warrants signed by himself." These charges were subsequently dropped.[130]

However, a second impeachment was brought against Danby in 1678 on charges of "High Treason and Other High Crimes, Misdemeanors and Offences," arising from his secret diplomatic dealings in the French court.[131] It was charged that Danby had "traitorously encroached to himself regal power, by treating in matters of peace and war with foreign princes and ambassadors, and giving instructions to his majesty's ambassadors abroad, without communicating the same to secretaries of state, and the rest of his majesty's council…against the express declaration of his majesty and his majesty's parliament." Commons alleged that Danby had negotiated a treaty with the French that was disadvantageous to the English for which "he did endeavour to procure a great of sum money from the French king."[132]

The administration of the Navy again came under scrutiny with the impeachment in 1680 of Edward Seymour, a member of Commons and treasurer of the navy. Seymour was charged with the high crimes and misdemeanors of misusing funds appropriated to the navy, in that Seymour had loaned to the army funds appropriated to the navy and had failed to pay merchants providing stores to the navy.

Seymour was also charged with misuse of his office for personal gain by receiving a salary over and above his compensation as speaker, which had continued to be paid to him during the prorogation of Parliament. It was also alleged that Seymour had embezzled goods from a Dutch prize ship.[133]

The Commons continued to address official corruption in the 1695 impeachment of the Duke of Leeds, who was president of the Privy Counsel. Leeds was charged with having accepted payments from a group of merchants in order to procure a charter for training in the East Indies.[134] While the Leeds case was pending, the Commons resolved that "The offer of any money, or other advantage, to any member of Parliament, for the promoting of any matter whatsoever, depending or to be transacted, in Parliament, is a High Crime and Misdemeanor, and tends to the subversion of the English Constitution."[135]

Impeachments for high crimes and misdemeanors were instituted in 1701 against three members of the Privy Counsel: The Earl of Orford, Lord Summers, and Lord Halifax, for corruption and for mismanagement of their public offices. Orford was charged with abusing his position as paymaster and receiver general of the navy" to embezzle "considerable sums of money, and great quantities of wine, oil, and other provisions for the fleet," as well as the proceeds from the sale of prize ships.[136]

Along with Orford, Summers and Halifax were impeached for their role in advising the King to enter into a treaty with France, which the Commons considered "dishonorable to his majesty, highly injurious to the interest of the Protestant religion," and which "manifestly tended to disturb the general peace of Europe, by altering the balance of power therein." Sommers and Halifax were also charged with procuring for themselves grants of land and revenues belonging to the crown.[137]

In the case of Henry Sacheverell, a priest in the Anglican Church, impeachment for high crimes and misdemeanors was invoked to condemn the defiance of a resolution of Parliament and thus defiance of Parliament itself. In 1705, Parliament adopted a resolution celebrating the installation of King William III and Queen Mary, providing that anyone who suggested that the church was in danger under their administration "was an enemy to the Queen, the Church, and the Kingdom." The resolution was subsequently issued as a royal proclamation. Thereafter, Sacheverell delivered a sermon at St. Paul's Cathedral condemning the "Happy Revolution" and the toleration of religious dissent supported by the Whig government,[138] and stating that the church was "in a condition of great peril" under the reign of Queen Mary. Sacheverell also contended that the Queen's administration "tends to the destruction of the constitution." Sacheverell was convicted by the Lords.[139]

There was a series of impeachments for high crimes and misdemeanors in 1715 arising from the prosecution of the war with France. The first of these was the impeachment of the Earl of Oxford, who was the Lord High Treasurer and a member of the Queen's Privy Council. Oxford was alleged to have conducted secret negotiations with France in which he had aided the French. He was also alleged to have frustrated the prosecution of the war by instructing the Duke of Ormand (who would also be impeached) to avoid engaging the enemy and by sending instructions to the Queen's representatives calculated to cause dissension among the allies. Oxford was further charged with having used his influence to favor the French in the peace negotiations.[140]

The second of these impeachments involved the Duke of Ormand who had commanded the English forces in the Netherlands. Ormand was charged with high crimes and misdemeanors for having provided information to the French concerning strategy, as well as the number and movement of troops. When it was learned that Ormand had absconded to France, he was attainted by the Parliament and never returned to England.[141]

The high crimes and misdemeanors charged against Viscount Bolingbroke paralleled several of the charges lodged against Oxford. Bolingbroke was charged with having disclosed the Queen's instructions to the French during the peace negotiations at Utrecht. Bolingbroke was also alleged to have given other assistance to the enemy. Bolingbroke was attainted along with Ormand but was later pardoned.[142]

The last of these impeachments relating to the war with France was that of the Earl of Strafford, who was also impeached for high crimes and misdemeanors. Strafford was a member of the Privy Council and had served as the Queen's "ambassador extraordinary to the States General [the Netherlands] and…one of her plenipotentiaries to treat with the ministers of France" at Utrecht. In that capacity, it was alleged that Strafford had counseled the French to be intransigent in negotiations and had advised the French on ways to create dissention among the allies. It was further alleged that Strafford had attempted to alienate the Queen from the "illustrious House of Hanover" and had advised the Queen that peace should be made with France despite the prospect of additional military victories over the French army. Commons charged that as a consequence of this advice, the French King was the "absolute master of the negotiations of the peace." The record does not reflect further proceedings in this matter.[143]

Finally, in 1725, Commons impeached the Lord Chancellor of Great Britain, the Earl of Macclesfield, for high crimes and misdemeanors relating to his abuse of office. Macclesfield was charged with "corruptly and extorsively" accepting payments in exchange for appointing individuals to a variety of public offices. Macclesfield was also charged with dereliction of his official duties in failing to arrest and remove a master in the Court of Chancery who had embezzled funds and by intimidating other masters of the court into paying for the defalcation. Macclesfield was found guilty by the Lords and a fine of £30,000 was imposed. Nevertheless, he appears to have been in full favor of the court afterwards.[144]

### The Significance of English Impeachment History to the Framers

The revival of the medieval process of impeachment in the mid-seventeenth century occurred during a watershed in relations between Parliament and the crown, as Parliament asserted its prerogative to inquire into the conduct of the government departments.[145] In contrast to the Tudor period, during which attainder was the preferred means of displacing ministers who no longer enjoyed the confidence of the crown, during the reign of the Stuarts, impeachment became the means by which the highest of officials of government could be made accountable to Parliament.[146]

Impeachment, or the threat of impeachment, became a powerful means for Parliament, and the Commons in particular, to assert control over the administration of government and to hold to account those who, acting under color of their offices, had abused their authority. Sir Robert Walpole remarked in the early eighteenth century that while it was accepted that the King could do no wrong, "at the same time it is no less certain that the ministers of state are accountable for their actions, otherwise Parliament would be but an empty name."[147] Thus, the impeachment power allowed at least some level of control over the conduct of government to be exercised by the Parliament and enlarged the standards to which officials could be held beyond the offenses ordinarily cognizable in the courts.[148]

Impeachment was also a means by which Commons could assert indirect influence over the crown since public scrutiny and criticism of the actions of the senior ministers was a direct reflection on the King's conduct of the affairs of state. In this way, even royal authority admitted of some Parliamentary influence.[149]

Thus, as Parliament's power grew from the seventeenth to eighteenth centuries, the authority of Commons to impeach the loftiest officers of the King's government should be viewed as an essential element of the checks and balances underlying the British and subsequently the American constitutions. As has been observed, discretion to accuse those who have abused their power should not reside with the executive whose conduct is likely to be the subject of the accusation.[150]

Without question, English impeachment law precedent and the usage of Parliament of high crimes and misdemeanors informed and framed the conception of impeachment in the Constitution. The importation of this parliamentary device was not done wholesale, however. For example, attainder was barred under the Constitution. Instead, to the extent that the writings of Josiah Quincy and John Adams, both of whom were learned in eighteenth-century law, provide insight into the thinking of the Framers, it appears that the English impeachment process was viewed holistically and pragmatically, to be suited for use in the American frame of government.[151]

In Quincy's January 4, 1768, letter to the *Boston Gazette*, he described in summary the English parliamentary process of impeachment in the Commons and trial before the Lords. In providing this summary, Quincy relied primarily on the *Judicature of Parliament* by John Selden. Quincy's references to Selden and other authorities are generally for the purpose of providing an explanation or an example of a point of procedure.

To the extent that Quincy included citation to specific impeachment proceedings, it was to show the range of official conduct that was subject to impeachment. Quincy cited the impeachments of Lord Finch, Sir Robert Berkeley, and Lord Strafford as having been brought "for high treason in subverting the fundamental laws and introducing arbitrary powers." In like fashion, Quincy cited the proceedings against the Spencers for impeding counsel to the king";[152] Michael de la Pole "that he being chancellor, acted contrary to his duty"; the Duke of Buckingham, "for a Plurality of Offences"; the Earl of Oxford, "for exercising incompatible Offices"; and Lord Finch "for threatening other Judges to subscribe to his Opinions." Each of these brief characterizations appear to have been offered solely to support Quincy's contention that "no subject, however great and powerful, is beyond the reach of a strict examination into his conduct, or out of danger of a scourage for his crimes,"[153] and not as an analysis of what constituted an impeachable offense.

Similarly, in Adams' accounts of his role in the Oliver impeachment, Adams identified Selden's *Judicature of Parliament* and Hatsell's *State Trials* as the authority for his proposal to impeach Chief Judge Oliver and any of the other judges who accepted a crown salary. In his 1814 letter to William Tudor, Adams wrote that when Hawley visited him to inquire concerning the legal basis for impeachment of the judges, "I invited him into my office, opened the charter, and requested him to read the paragraphs that I had marked. I then produced to him that volume of Selden's works which contains his treatise on Judicature and Parliament, other authorities in law were produced to him, and the *State Trials*, and a profusion of impeachments with which that work abounds." Adams also reported that when Robert Treat Payne visited concerning the proposed impeachment of the judges, "[i]nstead of entering into particular conversation with him, I took him into my office, and showed him all that I had before shown to Major Hawley."[154]

It does not appear, therefore, that either the revolutionaries, who viewed the impeachment of colonial officials as a means of preserving their rights and their autonomy under their crown charters, or the later statesmen, who incorporated the process of impeachment into the federal Constitution, regarded the cases of impeachment in the English Parliament as representing a common law of impeachment from which impeachable offenses, or specifically that high crimes and misdemeanors, had evolved from and could be defined by reference to precedent. Indeed, it does not appear that Parliament regarded its own impeachments in that way either.

Instead, what does emerge from the history of impeachments in the seventeenth and eighteenth centuries, however, is the evolution of a power relationship between the legislative and executive elements of the English government. As a consequence of that evolution, Parliament, and in particular the Commons, could interpose itself into the conduct of state affairs, foreign and domestic, and could charge, and possibly remove, senior officials of the government based on their misconduct in office, either due to overreaching, abuse of authority, or self-dealing, each of which would constitute a high crime and misdemeanor. It was in this way that Quincy, Adams, and ultimately the Framers of the Constitution understood the meaning of high crimes and misdemeanors by a public official in Parliamentary usage.

Nevertheless, there was one English impeachment for high crimes and misdemeanors with which it seems clear that the Framers of the Constitution were familiar and to which specific reference was made at the constitutional convention in the colloquy concerning presidential impeachment that resulted in the adoption of high crimes and misdemeanors as grounds for impeachment. That matter was the impeachment of Warren Hastings, the movement toward which was widely reported in the months preceding the constitutional convention.[155]

### The Impeachment of Warren Hastings

Warren Hastings served as the first English governor general of India from 1773 until 1785. Hastings had been employed by the East India Company since 1750.[156] By 1772, the year of Hastings' appointment as president and governor of Bengal, the East India Company was on the verge of bankruptcy, due largely to the cost of wars with the Marathas and with Mysore. To provide support to the company, and thereby to protect British interests in India, Prime Minister Frederick North obtained passage by Parliament of the Tea Act, which would lead to open rebellion in the American colonies, and the Regulating Act, which greatly enlarged the authority of the governor of Bengal, giving him authority, albeit ill defined, over the other provincial presidents. Thus, Hastings became governor general for Great Britain, acting through the East India Company, in India.[157]

The colonial administration of India under Hastings was a matter of controversy in Britain. As the Select Committee of the House of Commons reported in 1783, "during the whole period that elapsed from 1773 to the commencement of 1782, disorders and abuses of every kind multiplied."[158]

Hastings himself was criticized personally for his administration. He was the subject of criticism for his conduct in the Maratha War (1775–1782) and the subject of scandal concerning the death of the Governor of Madras in 1777. The accumulation of huge debts owed to British creditors and the commencement of the second Mysore War in 1780 threatened the company's influence in Southern India. Hastings' military adventures were considered a dangerous distraction from the company's commercial activity.[159]

Edmund Burke, who led the impeachment movement, considered Hastings to be a despot who had destroyed India economically and socially.[160] Burke wrote to Lord Thurlow in 1784 that he was not an enemy of Hastings, personally, "But of some things I am certain. I know that the Country under his care is sacked and pillaged, and I know he is the Government." Nevertheless, Burke's animus toward Hastings had a personal dimension.[161]

It appears clear that Burke did not believe that impeachment of Hastings would be successful. In a letter to Phillip Francis in 1785, Burke suggested that he was motivated by a desire to make "the maximum impact on public opinion" and to generate "support for reform in the system of government in India."[162] It has also been suggested, however, that Burke wanted to damage Hastings' standing in the community such that Hastings would have no further role in the affairs of India.[163]

To that end, on April 4, 1786, Burke put forward the initial allegations of misconduct on the part of Hastings. There would ultimately be twenty-two charges. Among these allegations, as reported in the popular press, Hastings was charged:

1. With gross injustice, cruelty and treachery against the faith of nations, in hiring British soldiers for the purpose of extirpating the innocent and helpless people who inhabited Rohillas;
2. With various instances of extortion, and other deeds of maladministration against the Rajah of Benares;
3. With the numerous and insupportable hardships to which the Royal Family of Oude had been reduced, in consequence of their connection with the Supreme Council;
4. With impoverishing and depopulating the whole country of Oude, rendering that country, which was once a garden, an uninhabited desert;
5. With a wanton and unjust and pernicious exercise of his powers, and the great situation of trust which he occupied in India, in overturning the ancient establishments of the country, and extending an undue influence by conniving extravagant contracts, and appointing inordinate salaries;
6. With receiving money against the orders of the Company, the Act of Parliament, his own sacred engagements, and applying that money to purposes totally improper and unauthorized;
7. With having resigned by proxy for the obvious purpose of retaining his situation, and denying the deed in person, in direct opposition to all those powers under which he acted; and
8. With enormous extravagances and bribery in various contracts with a view to enrich his dependents and favorites.[164]

As Burke would later explain in his opening statement to the Lords on February 15, 1788, the crimes with which Hastings had been charged by the Commons, "were crimes, not against forms, but against those eternal laws of justice, which are our rule and our birthright: his offenses are not in formal, technical language, but in reality, in substance and effect, High Crimes and High Misdemeanors."[165]

In May 1787, the Commons formally impeached Hastings. The trial before the Lords lasted from February 1788 until April 1795, when Hastings was acquitted of all charges. In all, the proceedings, although sporadic, consumed nine years.[166]

But the flaws and faults of the Hastings impeachment were not before the delegates to the federal constitutional convention and are not germane here.

Rather, when Mason referred to the "many great and dangerous offenses" that would not fall within the definition of treason and the common understanding of bribery but would nevertheless warrant impeachment and removal, Mason cited the allegations then being made against Hastings by Burke and Sheridan. This colloquy led directly to the substitution by Mason of high crimes and misdemeanors, instead of maladministration opposed by Madison, as the means of describing the various forms of official misconduct that would not constitute treason or bribery but nevertheless would justify impeachment. Thus, the charges against Hastings arising from his service as Governor General of India provide insight into the thinking of the delegates.[167]

The high crimes and misdemeanors with which Hastings was charged in 1786 were not offenses under the criminal law, as Burke conceded. Instead, Hastings' "crimes" were actions taken under color of his public office that were in contravention of acts of Parliament respecting India; direct orders of the Court of Directors of the East India Company; treaty obligations; understandings with Indian provincial rulers; the best interests of the East India Company; and local Indian law. The charges against Hastings also involved abuses of his official authority, including: encouragement of revolutions against provincial governments; causing the death of a rajah; payment of "excessive salaries and emoluments" to subordinates; acceptance of gifts; and refusal to honor his resignation as governor general.[168] They were thus public offenses (in contrast to private conduct) resulting from his breach of the public trust that went to the heart of his service as a public officer.

*Impeachment in the States Following Independence*

The delegates to the federal convention could also draw on their own states' experiences with impeachment following independence. At the time of the convention, the constitutions of eight states made provision for some form of executive impeachment.[169]

The Constitution of the Commonwealth of Virginia, adopted on June 29, 1776, declared that "The Governor, when he is out of office, and others offending against the State, either by mal-administration, corruption, or other means, by which the safety of the State may be endangered, shall be impeachable by the House of Delegates." If convicted, "he or they shall be either forever disabled to hold any office under government, or be removed from such office *pro tempore*, or subjected to such pains and penalties as the laws should direct."[170] The principal architect of the Virginia constitution was George Mason.

The Virginia impeachment provision was incorporated in other state constitutions. On September 10, 1776, Delaware adopted virtually the same provision in its constitution.[171] Maladministration was also specified as the grounds for impeachment and removal in the Constitutions of North

Carolina on December 18, 1776;[172] New York, on April 20, 1777;[173] Vermont on July 8, 1777;[174] and South Carolina on March 19, 1778.[175] The State of Georgia, in the constitution adopted on February 6, 1777, provided simply that "every officer of the State shall be liable to be called to account by the House of Assembly."[176] Massachusetts, which had recognized the inherent right of its legislature to impeach Justice Oliver, included a provision in its constitution adopted in 1780, that "The Senate shall be a court, with full authority to hear and determine all impeachments made by the House of Representatives, against any officer or officers of the Commonwealth, for misconduct or mal-administration in their offices."[177]

A variety of impeachment proceedings had also been instituted in the states during the period between independence and the federal convention.[178] Official corruption, including bribery, extortion and self-dealing, was the most common grounds for impeachment.[179] Among those cases, the proceedings against Judge Francis Hopkinson in Philadelphia are particularly instructive.

Hopkinson had been a signer of the Declaration of Independence and was the Chief Justice of the Admiralty Court, as well as a leader of the revolutionary party in Pennsylvania. On November 22, 1780, an impeachment inquiry was instituted concerning charges that Hopkinson had authorized the sale of prize ships and cargoes prior to their lawful condemnation. Representing the lower house of the Pennsylvania legislature in the prosecution of Hopkinson were William Bradford, the Attorney General of Pennsylvania, and James Smith, who had also been a signer of the Declaration of Independence. Hopkinson was defended by James Wilson and Jared Ingersoll, both of whom would later represent Pennsylvania at the federal convention.

On December 8, 1780, Hopkinson was impeached for having solicited and received gifts in exchange for official actions including the sale of the prize ship *Charlotte* before it had been properly condemned. Following trial before the upper council of the legislature, Hopkinson was acquitted on December 26, 1780.

Despite finding him not guilty of the charges, it was noted by the legislature that had there been evidence of a quid pro quo between the payments received by Hopkinson and his official acts with regard to the *Charlotte*, "we would have been at no loss to have declared him guilty." The legislature also explained that absent evidence that Hopkinson's actions had been "willfully wrong," he could not be found guilty.[180]

During this period, impeachments had also been instituted for willful disregard of the commands of a coordinate department of government, as in the 1785 impeachment of Matthew Lyon in Vermont for refusal to produce documents relating to the seizure of loyalist property when called upon to do so by another government agency. Incompetence and inattention to duty were also common grounds for impeachment, although it was noted that, "no one was impeached without evidence of intentional neglect or total incapacity to perform official duties."[181]

Thus, when the delegates to the federal convention considered the proposals for removal of the executive following impeachment by the House of Representatives and conviction by the Senate, they did so informed by their experience and that of their state legislatures, as well as by their knowledge of impeachments in England as most recently exemplified in the impeachment of Warren Hastings. Unquestionably, the delegates recognized impeachment as a remedy to redress official misconduct by a public official in the discharge of the responsibilities of the office. It was this misuse of public office that the delegates described as treason, bribery, and other high crimes and misdemeanors warranting impeachment.

The views expressed concerning impeachment during the ratification debates, particularly those of Alexander Hamilton, are in accord.

## The Ratification Debate

It is both interesting and enlightening that despite sharp disagreements over the forum in which impeachments should be adjudicated and, indeed, as to the efficacy of impeachment *vel non*, there was harmony in the views expressed by the Constitution's proponents, the Federalists, and its critics, the Anti-Federalists, as to the nature of the grounds for impeachment. In fact, the basis for impeachment did not figure prominently in the ratification debate at all.[182]

Eleven days after the final adjournment of the constitutional convention, Tench Coxe wrote in favor of the Constitution to the *Independent Gazetteer* of Philadelphia, under the name "An American Citizen." In this piece (the second he had written), Coxe noted that the Senate's power of removal was limited with respect to the president: "They can only, by conviction on impeachment, *remove and incapacitate a dangerous officer*." However, in contrast to impeachment, Coxe observed that "the punishment of him as a criminal *remains within the province of the courts of law to be conducted under all the ordinary forms and precautions*, which exceedingly diminishes the importance of their judicial powers."[183]

In a pamphlet entitled "An Examination into the Leading Principles of the Federal Constitution," published in Philadelphia on October 17, 1787, Noah Webster, another proponent of the Constitution, also drew a distinction between the Senate under the Constitution and "the house of peers in England" and "the senate in Rome." Writing as "A Citizen of America," Webster pointed out that unlike the English and Roman bodies, senators were to be elected for a fixed six-year term and "may at any time be impeached for mal-practices."[184]

Pennsylvania's convention was the first to debate the merits of the proposed federal constitution and on December 12, 1787, Pennsylvania became the second state, after Delaware, to ratify the Constitution. Unlike Delaware, the debate in Pennsylvania had been robust.[185] On December 17, 1787, the views of the dissenters in the Pennsylvania convention were published in the *Pennsylvania Packet* of Philadelphia. Among the concerns expressed by the dissenters was that since the appointment of federal officers by the president were subject to the "concurrence of the senate," the appointees therefore "derive their offices in part from the senate" and as a result the judgments of the senators with regard to impeachment could be biased. One consequence of this bias, the dissenters opined, would be a tendency "to screen great delinquents from punishment."[186]

There was also the concern among the critics of the proposed constitution that too much power was to be concentrated in the president and the Senate, as exemplified in the treaty power that allowed the president to enter into treaties, which would become the law of the land even though the treaty may have been contrary to the prior law in effect, subject to ratification by two-thirds of the Senate. This issue was debated by Rowland Lowndes, an opponent of the Constitution, and Edward Rutledge, the brother of one of the Framers, in the South Carolina legislature on January 16, 1788. Rutledge cited impeachment as being the safeguard against abuse of their power. As reflected in the records of the debate, Rutledge argued that "if the president or the senators abused their trust, they were answerable for their conduct—they were liable to impeachment and punishment, and the fewer that were concerned in the abuse of the trust, the more certain would be the punishment."[187]

Impeachment as a remedy for breach of the public trust was also addressed in several of the *Federalist Papers* that, although they may not have been the most influential factor in the debate over ratification,[188] are nevertheless instructive as to original intent because their author, Alexander Hamilton, had played a leading role at the constitutional convention and had participated significantly in the fashioning of the impeachment provisions.

Writing under the name Publius in Federalist 65 Hamilton commented on the judicial character of the Senate sitting as a court of impeachment. In doing so, Hamilton opined on the nature of the offenses that would give rise to impeachment. Hamilton wrote: "The subjects of its jurisdiction are those offenses which proceed from the misconduct of public men, or, in other words, from the abuse or violation of some public trust. They are of a nature which may with peculiar propriety be denominated *political*, as they relate chiefly to injuries done immediately to the society itself."[189] Another leading Federalist, James Wilson, expressed this view as well.[190]

Although initially unsuccessful in obtaining ratification, the Federalists in North Carolina dominated the debate.[191] In that debate, James Iredell, a leading Federalist who would later be appointed to the Supreme Court by

President Washington, elucidated the character of the conduct that would warrant impeachment and removal of the president. During the debate on July 28, 1788, Iredell told the North Carolina convention that in contrast to Great Britain, in which only the advisor to the King is answerable for the misconduct in office, under the proposed federal constitution, "[n]o man has an authority to injure another with impunity," and thus, "[i]f the President does a single act, by which the people are prejudiced, he is punishable himself, and no other man merely to screen him." In that regard, if the president "commits any misdemeanor in office, he is impeachable, removable from office, and incapacitated to hold any office of honour, trust or profit. If he commits any crime, he is punishable by laws of his country, and in capital cases may be deprived of his life."[192]

Later in that same debate, Iredell stated that the impeachment power was intended "to bring great offenders to punishment. It is calculated to bring them to punishment for crimes which are not easy to describe, but which everyone must be convinced is a high crime and misdemeanor against the government." For that reason, the Constitution reposed the authority to impeach and remove the president in the Congress, "who represent the great body of the people," because "the occasion for its exercise will arise from acts of great injury to the community, and the objects of it may be such as cannot be easily reached by an ordinary tribunal."[193]

As had other Anti-Federalists, Samuel Spencer objected to the Senate's removal power because in essence, the Senate would be trying the president "for doing what they advised him to do, and which without their advice he would not have done." Under those circumstances, Spencer said that he could not "conceive therefore, that the president can ever be tried by the Senate with any effect, or to any purpose, for any misdemeanor in his office, unless it should extend to high treason, or unless they should wish to fix the odium of any measure on him, in order to exculpate themselves."[194]

Iredell responded to Spencer stating that, "when any man is impeached, it must be for an error of the heart, and not of the head. God forbid, that a man... should be liable to be punished for want of judgment. This is not the case here." Iredell cited, as an example, the making of an improvident treaty, a frequent Anti-Federalist criticism of the Constitution. Iredell explained that "if the President, with the advice of the Senate, should make a treaty with a foreign power, and that treaty should be deemed unwise, or against the interest of the country, yet if nothing could be objected against it but the difference of opinion between them and their constituents, they could not justly be obnoxious to punishment." Were that not the case, Iredell observed, "no man who regarded his reputation would accept the office either of a Senator or President."[195]

Of equal importance, Iredell observed that "[a] public officer ought not to act from a principle of fear."[196] As Iredell explained, "Were he punishable for want of judgment, he would be continually in dread. But when he knows that nothing but real guilt can disgrace him, he may do his duty firmly if he be an honest man, and if he be not, a just fear of disgrace, may perhaps, as to the public, have nearly the effect of an intrinsic principle of virtue."[197]

Under these circumstances, Iredell suggested that "the only instances in which the President would be liable to impeachment, would be where he had received a bribe, or had acted from some corrupt motive or other." Iredell also suggested that the president "must certainly be punishable for giving false information to the Senate."[198]

## Original Meaning

Thus, the view of impeachment that emerged from the ratification debates in both the state assemblies convened to consider the proposed Constitution and in the broadsides of the Federalist and Anti-Federalist partisans, was that impeachment served as the means by which the legislature could keep the coordinate branches of the government in check from overreaching their authority and through which federal officers (those described by Coxe as "dangerous officers" or by the Pennsylvania dissenters as "great delinquents") could be held responsible and punished for official misconduct.

Impeachment under the federal Constitution was to be (to borrow Hamilton's phrase) a national inquest into the conduct of public men. Impeachment was to address breaches of the public trust by public officers. Hamilton's conception of such high crimes and misdemeanors as being, in essence, political offenses relating chiefly to "injuries done immediately to the society itself," seems to have been generally held by constitutional protagonists and antagonists alike, and comes as close as any to a restatement of the original meaning of high crimes and misdemeanors.

After ratification, however, it was left to Congress to give substance to the Framers' worthy sentiments and aspirations. The tests of the newly created congressional impeachment power came quickly. Within ten years of ratification, Congress faced the impeachment of Senator William Blount as a consequence of his Western adventures. The Blount impeachment was followed in 1803 by the impeachment of the insane and infirm Judge John Pickering and in the following year by the impeachment of a Justice of the Supreme Court, Samuel Chase, for his unrestrained partisanship. These were the State Trials in which the contours of the impeachment power were clarified and high crimes and misdemeanors began to acquire meaning in the context of American impeachment.

2

# The Impeachment and Trial of Andrew Johnson

In the months after ratification of the federal Constitution, the Congress took up the establishment of the new executive departments. The debate concerning one of them, the Department of Foreign Affairs, is of interest because it was an occasion on which James Madison opined on the nature of impeachment under the Constitution and in particular, his views on what was meant by high crimes and misdemeanors.

The question was whether the secretary of foreign affairs would be subject to removal by the president.[1] The debate on this issue was a momentous one to Madison because, he said, "The decision that is at this time made, will become the permanent exposition of the constitution and on a permanent exposition of the constitution will depend the genius and character of the whole government."[2]

In contrast to the views he had expressed at the federal constitutional convention two years before, Madison framed the issue of removal as being the remedy for maladministration by those holding federal office. Madison stated, "The danger to liberty, the danger of mal-administration, has not yet been found to lie so much in the facility of introducing improper persons into office, as in the difficulty of displacing those who are unworthy of the public trust."[3]

Although Madison had objected to the specification in the Constitution of maladministration as a grounds for impeachment, it is clear that he viewed some level of maladministration to be the essence of the misconduct in office that would warrant removal of the president or a subordinate from office. At the constitutional convention, however, Madison had expressed the concern that impeachment for maladministration would upset the balance of power by rendering the tenure of the president subject to the pleasure of Congress. In the context of the debate over the removal power, however, Madison argued that maladministration, either in the form of continuing in office a person who was unfit or in the form of removing from office a person who was worthy to continue, was remediable through impeachment—of the unfit office holder in the first instance and of the president in the second.

Even a decade later, while the debates over ratification of the Constitution were still fresh and many of the Framers were still actively engaged in public affairs, Congress continued to wrestle with defining the conduct that would constitute high crimes and misdemeanors. Indeed, the period between 1797 and 1805 saw three impeachment trials in the Senate that would to a great extent define the contours of federal impeachment.

The first of what have been referred to as the State Trials involved William Blount, a U.S. Senator from Tennessee, who was accused of fomenting rebellion in the Spanish and French colonies of Florida and Southern Louisiana. The second was against John Pickering, a U.S. Judge, for intemperance and mental incompetence. The third State Trial also had as its object the unseating of a federal (and Federalist) judge, Samuel Chase, associate justice of the Supreme Court, for reasons of judicial partisanship.

The Blount proceeding established the principle that members of the U.S. Congress are not "civil officers" under Article II, Section 4 of the Constitution, and therefore, are not subject to impeachment and removal. Pickering, who according to his own son was both alcoholic and insane, was removed for being incompetent to hold office. Chase, however, proved not so easy to remove as had Pickering, and his acquittal, despite his own outspoken partisanship and the deep partisan divide in a Senate whose majority opposed him, demonstrated the wisdom of the Constitution's requirement of a majority of two-thirds of the Senate in order to convict.

## The State Trials

### *In the Matter of William Blount*

William Blount was a man of the eighteenth-century West. He was born in North Carolina on March 26, 1749. Blount speculated in land and other business ventures and when the policies of the colonial governor ran counter to those interests, Blount aligned himself against the British.[4]

Between 1782 and 1787, Blount served several terms alternatively in the federal and state legislatures. In 1787, Blount, who had become a Federalist largely in reaction to Shays' Rebellion, was appointed to be a delegate to the constitutional convention in Philadelphia. Although Madison suggested that Blount was not an enthusiastic signor,[5] Blount campaigned for ratification of the Constitution in North Carolina through the initial defeat to eventual success in 1789.[6]

In the meantime, Blount had increased his land holdings in North Carolina's western lands. Blount supported the movement to cede the land west of the Appalachian Mountains to the federal government. The accession was accepted and on June 8, 1790, President Washington named him governor of the territory.[7] In January 1796, Blount presided over the convention held in Knoxville to draft the state constitution. The following March, Blount was elected U.S. Senator by the newly formed Tennessee state legislature.[8]

Perceiving that the Federalists were unsympathetic to his financial interests in the western territory, Blount formally aligned himself with the Republicans in 1796. At that time, Blount's speculative investments in land had collapsed in part because of reports that Spain and France intended to reassert claims to western lands as part of their alliance against England. As a consequence, it appears that in November 1796, Blount joined in a plan put forward by John Chisholm, another Westerner, to engage, with the assistance of the native peoples, in hostile action against the Spanish in Florida and eventually against the French in Louisiana.

To succeed, their plan required the aid and support of the British. However, their plan would also violate the 1794 Neutrality Act, which provided that organizing a military expedition against a foreign dominion with which the United States was at peace would constitute a "high misdemeanor," punishable by three years imprisonment.[9]

On July 3, 1797, President Adams sent a message to the House of Representatives warning of "the critical situation of our country," and forwarding a collection of correspondence and other documents in order that "Congress might be enabled to form a more perfect judgment of it and of the measures necessary to be taken."[10] Among the documents forwarded to Congress were correspondence exposing Blount's involvement in the Chisholm conspiracy.[11]

On the strength of this evidence, the House of Representatives voted to impeach Blount on July 7, 1797, and instructed Congressman Samuel Sitgreaves to "go to the Senate, and at the bar thereof, in the name of the House of Representatives, and in the name of all the people of the United States, impeach William Blount, a senator of the United States, of high crimes and misdemeanors; and acquaint the Senate that this House will in due course exhibit particular articles against him, and make good the same."[12]

In the Senate, Blount denied authorship of the incriminating correspondence but two senators identified his handwriting. Accordingly, the committee empanelled to investigate the matter reported to the Senate that "your committee have no doubt that Mr. Blount's conduct has been inconsistent with his public duty, renders him unworthy of a further continuance of his present public trust in this body, and amounts to a high misdemeanor." On July 8, 1797, the Senate adopted a resolution that "William Blount, Esquire, one of the Senators of the United States, having been guilty of a high misdemeanor, entirely inconsistent with his public trust and duty as a Senator, be, and hereby is expelled from the Senate of the United States."[13] A short time later, Blount absconded to Tennessee, never to return.[14]

A committee of impeachment was empanelled in the House and on January 25, 1798, the committee reported five articles of impeachment against Blount.[15] Each of these charges arose from conduct outside Blount's duties as a U.S. senator, although in each instance it was alleged that his actions had been "contrary to the duty of his trust and station as a Senator of the United States, and against the peace and interests thereof."

The Senate formed itself as a "High Court of Impeachment" on December 17, 1798.[16] When the trial convened on January 3, 1799, Blount's attorneys, Jared Ingersoll (also a former delegate to the constitutional convention) and Alexander J. Dallas (who would later become the reporter of the decisions of the U.S. Supreme Court),[17] urged the Senate "not to hold jurisdiction of the said impeachment."[18] This would prove to be the dispositive argument in the Blount trial.[19]

Dallas contended on behalf of Blount that impeachment for high crimes and misdemeanors was restricted to official conduct. Dallas argued that while "ordinary penal laws" would apply to an offense regardless of whether the crime was committed by a public official or private citizen, "official offences can only be committed by public officers" and it would be contrary to the separation of powers to permit a court of justice to remove a public official. Impeachment was intended to preserve the independence of government departments and "to secure the people from abuse of executive authority." Thus, Dallas concluded, official offences alone were contemplated.[20]

Also on behalf of Blount, Ingersoll argued that "the only causes cognizable" in impeachment "are malconduct in office." Ingersoll noted that the "punishment" resulting from impeachment "is official … and therefore, peculiarly adapted as punishment for misconduct in office." Otherwise, Ingersoll argued, "offences not immediately connected with office" were best left to the courts. Citing the English authorities, Blackstone and Wooddeson, Ingersoll also noted that with respect to impeachment in England "all the writers speak of this power as intended only as useful in charges against officers for malconduct in office." Thus, Ingersoll said, "My argument is, that what in England is said to be the most proper, and has been the most usual, in this particular, is, by the Constitution of the United States, the exclusive ground of proceeding by impeachment."[21]

The House managers countered that impeachment served two objects: "first, to remove persons whose misconduct may have rendered them unworthy of retaining their offices; and secondly, to punish those offences of a mere political nature, which though not susceptible of that exact definition whereby they might be brought within the sphere of ordinary tribunals, are yet very dangerous to the public." According to the House managers these political offenses "in the English law, and in our Constitutions which have borrowed its phraseology, are called 'high crimes and misdemeanors.'"[22]

The debate on the nature of impeachable high crimes and misdemeanors was left unresolved by the Blount proceedings. A motion was offered on January 7, 1798, that Blount was a "civil officer" subject to impeachment and that his plea to the charges of high crimes and misdemeanors should be "overruled."[23] The Senate voted in the negative on January 10.[24] On the following day, the Senate adopted a motion stating, "The Court is of the opinion, that the matter alleged in the plea of the defendant, is sufficient in law to show that this Court ought not to hold jurisdiction of the said impeachment, and that the said impeachment is dismissed."[25] The Senate announced its judgment concluding the Blount affair on January 14.[26]

### *In the Matter of John Pickering*

On February 13, 1801, less than three weeks before the Federalists surrendered control to the Republicans, the Congress enacted the Judiciary Act. The Act corrected a number of deficiencies in the federal judiciary under the Judiciary Act of 1789, notably by expansion of jurisdiction of the federal courts. The Act also created new district and circuit courts, setting the stage for the notorious "midnight appointments" of judges by the outgoing Federalist President, John Adams.[27]

The incoming Republicans were angered by what they saw as a bald attempt by the Federalists to lay siege to the Republicans from an impregnable federal judiciary. In response, President Jefferson relieved the "midnight appointees," of their posts as federal attorneys, marshals, and other functionaries whose service was at the president's pleasure. Among the displaced was William Marbury whose appointment as justice of the peace for the District of Columbia was withheld by Jefferson and whose suit to compel James Madison, the secretary of state, to deliver his commission would result in the Supreme Court's great decision in *Marbury v. Madison*, establishing the authority of the federal courts to rule on the constitutionality of federal laws.[28]

While the *Marbury* case was percolating in the Supreme Court, Republican attention focused on what would now be described as a "soft target," District Judge John Pickering of New Hampshire. Pickering was a native of New Hampshire. He had distinguished himself during the revolution and was elected to the Continental Congress, although he refused to serve because of a fear of traveling over water. He was a leader of the movement to ratify the federal Constitution and was one of the drafters of the New Hampshire State Constitution. Pickering became chief justice of the New Hampshire Supreme Court in 1790. In 1795 he was appointed to the Federal District Court in New Hampshire by President Washington.[29]

At the time of his appointment to the federal bench, however, his mental and physical condition was deteriorating. He had been censured by the state legislature in 1794 due to his erratic behavior and absences from the court.[30] By 1803, Pickering was senile and a habitual drunkard, "a pathetic relic of a once honored and effective statesman."[31]

Albert Gallatan, Jefferson's Secretary of the Treasury, assisted by John Samuel Sherburne, the U.S. Attorney, had gathered evidence of Pickering's performance with respect to the seizure of the Brig *Eliza*.[32] On the basis of Gallatan's investigation, President Jefferson sent a message to the House of Representatives on February 3, 1803, containing evidence of Pickering's judicial conduct.[33] After receiving Jefferson's communication and the accompanying documents, the House voted to impeach Pickering in October 1802.[34]

On January 2 and 3, 1803, four articles of impeachment were authorized by the House. The first three articles related to Pickering's conduct of the trial concerning the seizure of the Brig *Eliza*.[35]

The articles of impeachment were presented to the Senate on January 4, 1804.[36] The Senate convened itself as a court of impeachment on March 2, 1804. Pickering did not answer the charges. Instead, his son, Jacob S. Pickering, submitted a statement in which he characterized his father as being insane and therefore incapable of "corruption of judgment" and not "amenable to any tribunal for his action."[37]

Not surprisingly, much of the debate in the Senate focused on whether Pickering's incapacity to serve as a district judge was sufficient grounds for impeachment. As Senator William Coke had pointed out even before the Senate trial had commenced, if impeachment required proof of a violation of law, "I know of no law that makes derangement criminal."[38] Senator Samuel White echoed this argument when the Senate debated the merits of the charges. White told his colleagues that although he was convinced of Pickering's guilt of the conduct alleged in the articles of impeachment, he could not find Pickering guilty of high crimes and misdemeanors, which was the sole basis for removal.[39] Senator James Jackson also stated that "Insanity is here a bar to all proceedings on impeachment," and he asked, "How shall we get rid of the judge?"[40]

This was the central issue, and the central flaw, in the Republican case of "high crimes and misdemeanors" against Pickering. While there was general agreement that Pickering had committed the acts set forth in the articles, even assuming that Pickering's conduct rose to the level of crime, his mental condition precluded his formation of the necessary *mens rea* and therefore, his criminality would be excused.[41] As one senator observed: "When the powers of reason and the sense of right and wrong are destroyed in the mind, that man can commit no crime. I will not say an insane man may not be removed from office but I say he cannot be convicted of crimes."[42]

To finesse the issue of whether Pickering had to be criminally responsible in order to be impeached, Senator Anderson proposed that the verdict be submitted to the Senate as guilty or not guilty "as charged," and not as to whether Pickering's conduct amounted to high crimes and misdemeanors.[43] Speaking in opposition, Senator Jonathan Dayton pointed out that the Senate was "simply to be allowed to vote, whether Judge Pickering was guilty as charged—that is, guilty of the facts charged in each Article—a yes or no. If voted guilty of the facts, the sentence was to follow, without any previous question whether these facts amounted to a high crime and misdemeanor." However, he also told his colleagues that "The constitution gave no power to the Senate, as the high court of impeachments, to pass such a sentence of removal and disqualification, except upon charges and conviction of high crimes and misdemeanors."[44] Notwithstanding the apparent constitutional insufficiency, by a party-line vote of 19 to 7, Pickering was convicted.[45]

However, due to the substantive and procedural flaws, the precedential value of the Pickering case is at best questionable. As Henry Adams later observed, "So confused, contradictory, and irregular were these proceedings that Pickering's trial was never considered a sound precedent. That an insane man could be guilty of crime, and could be punished on *ex parte* evidence, without a hearing, with not even an attorney to act on his behalf, seemed such a perversion of justice that the precedent fell dead on the spot."[46]


*In the Matter of Samuel Chase*


Within an hour of the Senate's conviction of Pickering, the Republican House of Representatives voted to impeach Samuel Chase, an associate justice of the U.S. Supreme Court and an outspoken Federalist.[47] Chase had been a revolutionary and a member of the "Sons of Liberty" in Maryland, opposing the Stamp Act and treating the royal governor and his Tory allies with "contemptuous defiance." His opposition to British colonial rule led to his election to the Continental Congress, where, contrary to the instructions given him by the Maryland legislature, he was an ardent supporter of the Declaration of Independence, of which he was one of the signers.[48]

Although he had opposed ratification of the federal Constitution, Chase had been a firm supporter of George Washington from their days in the Continental Congress, and he became a strident Federalist. After having served as chief justice of the Criminal Court of Baltimore, on January 26, 1796, Chase was appointed associate justice of the Supreme Court by President Washington.[49]

Chase was intemperate in his partisanship for the Federalist cause. As a circuit judge, Chase had presided over the treason trial of John Fries in April and May of 1800.[50] Chase also presided over the trial of James Thompson Callender for seditious libel under the Sedition Act in May 1800.[51] His conduct of these trials was controversial and it was said that among the Republicans "of all the Judges, no one was more hated than Chase."[52]

Then, on February 24, 1803, Chief Justice Marshall speaking for a unanimous Supreme Court announced the decision in *Marbury v. Madison*,[53] holding that the Supreme Court was vested with the authority to review acts of Congress and to nullify legislation as being unconstitutional. The Republican response was apoplectic.

Less than two months after Marshall had announced the *Marbury* decision, in an address to the Baltimore Grand Jury on May 2, 1803, Chase stridently criticized Jefferson and the Republicans for their attack on the judiciary.[54] With that speech, Chase again became the lightning rod for Republican hostility and distrust toward the Federalist judiciary. John Montgomery, a member of the Maryland state legislature and a Republican, witnessed Chase's address to the grand jurors. In an article published in the *Baltimore American* on June 13, 1803, Montgomery wrote that Chase should be impeached. Montgomery sent President Jefferson a copy of the *Baltimore American* article. Jefferson wrote to Joseph Nicholson, who was then deeply engaged in the Pickering impeachment, questioning whether "this seditious and official attack on the principles of our constitution and on the proceedings of a State" should be allowed "to go unpunished."[55]

Nicholson pondered the matter over the summer of 1803 but ultimately eschewed a leadership role in the impeachment effort.[56] In his place, the Republicans turned to John Randolph of Virginia, a man "whose lust for conspicuous leadership was insatiable."[57] It was a fateful choice because, as Henry Adams observed, "a worse champion…for a difficult cause could not be imagined."[58]

After almost a year, the House adopted eight articles of impeachment against Chase on March 12, 1804.[59] After Randolph apprised the Senate of the impeachment of Chase,[60] in a letter to John Adams, John Quincy

Adams remarked that "it was said at all events the articles charged against Mr. Chase were of high crimes or misdemeanors. This was not altogether true. For besides the frivolous nature of the charges contained in several articles, it is very remarkable that *one* of them, differing from all the rest, had omitted even the allegation of *evil intent*. It does not pretend to charge anything more than an error on a point of law."[61]

In this, the articles of impeachment reflected the Republican theory of impeachment, as articulated by the Republican leader of the Senate, William Branch Giles. According to Giles, it was sufficient that the Congress disagree with a decision of the Supreme Court to warrant impeachment of the justices.[62] Thus, in Giles' view, impeachment was not predicated on conduct that would be considered criminal. Indeed, Giles told Adams: "A trial and removal of a judge upon impeachment need not imply any criminality or corruption in him." Instead, Giles said, "a removal by impeachment was nothing more than a declaration by Congress to this effect: You hold dangerous opinions, and if you are suffered to carry them into effect you will work the destruction of the nation."[63]

Justice Chase submitted his answer to the articles of impeachment on February 4, 1805.[64] Chase contended that to sustain impeachment, proof of criminal conduct was required, which he denied committing.[65] He also disputed each instance of alleged misconduct.[66]

Thus, it was under two competing theories of the nature of impeachment and the meaning of high crimes and misdemeanors that the issue of the impeachment of Justice Chase was joined in the Senate. On the one hand, the House managers and their allies in the Senate leadership argued in essence that an impeachable offense could be nothing more than a difference of opinion or political philosophy between a holder of public office and the majority party in the Congress. Chase and his distinguished defense team argued to the contrary that only criminal conduct that could support an indictment would warrant impeachment and removal.[67] As Henry Adams observed, "The Senate became confused between these two views, and never knew on what theory it acted."[68]

The trial commenced before the Senate on February 9, 1805, and consumed nine days during which fifty-two witnesses testified.[69] Thereafter, the House and the defense presented eight days of summations.

Speaking for the House managers, Congressman George Washington Campbell drew a distinction between "such misdemeanors as would authorize a removal from office" and "such as are criminal in the ordinary sense of the word in courts of common law, punishable by indictment." Campbell told the Senate that "So far as the offence of the officer is injurious to society, only in consequence of the power reposed in the officer being abused in the exercise of his official functions, it is inquirable into only by impeachment." Campbell further observed that "though impeachable offenses are termed in the Constitution high crimes and misdemeanors, they must be such only so far as regards the official conduct of the officer." Thus, Campbell said, "Impeachment…may be considered a kind of inquest into the conduct of an officer, merely as it regards his office; the manner in which he performs the duties thereof; and the effects that his conduct therein may have on society." Even treason and bribery, he argued, "can only be inquired into by impeachment so far as the same may be considered as a violation of the duties of the officer…and not as the criminality of those offenses independent of the office."[70]

However, in a reversal that was as stunning as it was inexplicable, one of the House mangers, Congressman Joseph H. Nicholson, repudiated this interpretation of high crimes and misdemeanors that he himself had advocated in the Pickering impeachment and which was the basis of the House case against Chase. Despite Campbell's unambiguous statement that it was not necessary that an impeachable offense be "an indictable one," and that impeachment was an "inquest" into the execution of public office, Nicholson declared to the contrary that "We do contend that this is a criminal prosecution for offences committed in the discharge of high official duties, and we now support it, not merely for the purpose of removing an individual from office, but in order that the punishment inflicted on him may deter others from pursing the baneful example which has been set them."[71]

Chase's defense team—Robert Goodloe Harper, Joseph Hopkinson, Philip Barton Key, Charles Lee, and Luther Martin, whom one commentator described as a "brilliant phalanx of Federalist lawyers," argued that impeachment required proof of indictable crime.[72] Hopkinson argued that the plain meaning of high crimes and misdemeanors required proof of criminal conduct. He stated that "'Misdemeanor' is a legal and technical term, well understood and defined in law; and in the construction of a legal instrument, we must give to words their legal signification. A misdemeanor, or a crime…is an act committed or omitted, in violation of *a public* law, either forbidding or commanding it. By this test, let the conduct of the respondent be tried, and by it, let him stand justified or condemned."[73]

After his cocounsel had addressed the specific allegations of misconduct in the impeachment articles, Luther Martin reiterated Hopkinson's argument that criminality was necessary for impeachment and argued that "there are many crimes and misdemeanors for which a judge ought not to be impeached, unless immediately relating to his judicial conduct." Thus, Martin said, "there may be instances of very high crimes and misdemeanors, for which an official ought not to be impeached, and removed from office; the crimes ought to be such as relate to his office, or which tend to cover the person, who committed them, with turpitude and infamy; such as show there can be no dependence on what integrity and honor which will secure the performance of his official duties."[74]

The trial concluded on March 1, 1805, with the acquittal of Chase on all of the charges.[75] At the conclusion of the voting, Vice President Aaron Burr, who had presided over the trial, announced that "It appears that there is not a constitutional majority of votes finding Samuel Chase, Esq., guilty of any one article. It therefore becomes my duty to declare that Samuel Chase, Esq., stands acquitted of all the articles exhibited by the House of Representatives against him," and with that the Chase impeachment was concluded.[76]

The Pickering and Chase proceedings established impeachment as the means by which a federal judge could be removed notwithstanding life tenure, based on their conduct both on and off the bench. In Pickering's case, removal followed the Senate's conclusion that Pickering's behavior demonstrated that he was no longer capable of serving as a judge.

The effect of the Chase proceedings in giving substance to the phrase high crimes and misdemeanors is ambiguous. Chase's counsel had argued with great skill and passion that only serious criminal conduct that arose from official action and that directly reflected upon the suitability of the accused to perform a public office would support impeachment and removal. The House had impeached Chase on a much broader construction of the impeachment power and a correspondingly vague interpretation of high crimes and misdemeanors. While it seems to be a fair reading of events that the House's interpretation was solidly rejected by the Senate, an a fortiori conclusion that the contrary position put forward by the defense was therefore approved is not warranted either. This lack of clarity in the rule emerging from the Chase verdict is accentuated by the Senate's decision in the Pickering case, approximately a year earlier, which upheld removal of a judicial officer when no criminal conduct was even alleged. Instead, in the case of Pickering, the Congress resorted to the impeachment power to fill in an apparent gap between judicial tenure during "good behavior" and a judge who was no longer physically or mentally capable of discharging the responsibilities of his judicial office.

Nevertheless, while John Quincy Adams was correct that Chase's acquittal "arrested the career of political frenzy," he was prescient in his observation that the hiatus would only be "for a time."

In the fifty years that intervened between the failed Chase impeachment and the proceedings against President Andrew Johnson, Congress continued to engage in "Grand Inquests" into the conduct of civil officers. During this time, two federal judges, James Hawkins Peck[77] and West

H. Humphreys,[78] were impeached by the House. Following trial by the Senate, they were convicted of high crimes and misdemeanors and were removed. In 1834, President Andrew Jackson was censured by the Senate as a consequence of his veto of the charter for the Second Bank of the United States but the censure was subsequently expunged by the Senate in 1837.[79] President John Tyler's veto of a tariff extension bill in 1843 resulted in a resolution of impeachment being offered by John Minor Boots. The resolution was defeated.[80]

The nature of high crimes and misdemeanors continued to be a subject of discussion by scholars, some of whom had themselves participated in the writing of the Constitution and in the ensuing State Trials of Blount, Pickering, and Chase.

William Rawle was a prominent Pennsylvania attorney at the time of ratification. In his 1829 treatise on the Constitution, Rawle wrote that impeachment was necessary because "[t]he delegation of important trusts, affecting the higher interests of society, is always from various causes liable to abuse." However, the very nature of those abuses rendered them unamenable to prosecution in the civilian courts as ordinary crimes.[81] For that reason, in Rawle's view, the high crimes and misdemeanors that would warrant impeachment were not crimes in the ordinary sense, but were offenses that could only be committed by public officers. To Rawle, "the legitimate causes of impeachment…can only have reference to public character and official duty," and therefore, "Murder, burglary, robbery, and indeed all offences not immediately connected with office, except the two expressly mentioned [treason and bribery], are left to the ordinary course of judicial proceeding, and neither house can regularly inquire into them."[82]

James Wilson, who had been one of the principal Framers of the Constitution and the leading Federalist advocate for ratification in Pennsylvania, made a similar observation concerning Anglo-American impeachment in his well-known lectures on U.S. law. He wrote that "[i]mpeachments, and offences and offenders impeachable, come not, in those descriptions, within the sphere of ordinary jurisprudence. They are founded on different principles; and are governed by different maxims, and are directed to different objects."[83]

Wilson noted that in England, impeachments had been lodged against executive officers "for malversation in office, or what are called high misdemeanors." This conception of impeachment had been transplanted to the United States, such that "[i]n the United States and in Pennsylvania, impeachments are confined to political characters, to political crimes and misdemeanors, and to political punishments."[84]

Professor (and later, Supreme Court justice) Joseph Story also viewed impeachment under the U.S. Constitution as having been intended "to reach high and potent offenders, such as might be presumed to escape punishment in the ordinary tribunals, either from their own extraordinary influence or from the imperfect organization and powers of those tribunals."[85] Like Hamilton and Wilson, Story characterized impeachment as having been "designed as a method of national inquest into the conduct of public men."[86]

As such, Story wrote that Congress' impeachment authority was to be invoked, "over offences, which are committed by public men in violation of their public trust and duties." As these duties are often political, the impeachment power "partakes of a political character, as it respects injuries to society in its political character." For this reason, Story cautioned that the impeachment power must be "guarded in its exercise against the spirit of faction, the intolerance of party, and the sudden movements of popular feeling."[87]

Story also commented at some length on the nature of offenses constituting high crimes and misdemeanors that would warrant impeachment. He noted that because impeachment was intended to redress offenses that were political in character, impeachable offenses were not ordinary crimes. Instead, impeachable offenses "are founded on different principles…and require different remedies from those which ordinarily apply to crimes," a view he shared with James Wilson.[88]

Story made clear his view that not all criminal offenses should be considered impeachable offenses. He wrote: "It will not be sufficient to say, that in cases where any offence is punished by any statute of the United States, it may, and ought to be, deemed an impeachable offence. It is not every offence, that by the constitution is so impeachable. It must not only be an offence, but a *high* crime and misdemeanor."[89] Like Rawle, Story argued that even the most serious felonies would not warrant impeachment unless they arose from and were directly related to the discharge of official duty. That is because impeachment "is not so much designed to punish an offender, as to secure the state against gross official misdemeanors. It touches neither his person, nor his property; but simply divests him of his political capacity."[90]

Story also noted that there had been parliamentary impeachments founded on "purely political" conduct, "none of which is in the slightest manner alluded to in our statute book."[91] Story noted as well that in the Blount, Pickering, and Chase impeachments, "not one of the charges has rested upon any statutable misdemeanours."[92]

In 1858, James Kent observed in his highly regarded *Commentaries on American Law*, that as a means of preventing "abuse of the executive trust" by the president, the Constitution had "rendered him directly amenable by law for mal-administration." Kent noted that "The inviolability of any officer of government is incompatible with the republican theory, as well as with the principles of retributive justice." Thus, he wrote, if "neither the sense of duty, the force of public opinion nor the transitory nature of the seat, are sufficient to secure a faithful discharge of the executive trust," but instead, if the president uses the "authority of his station to violate the constitution or law of the land," then "the house of representatives can arrest him in his career by resorting to the power of impeachment."[93]

A contemporary of Kent, George Ticknor Curtis, also wrote that the "object" of impeachment was "to ascertain whether cause exists for removing a public official from office." Curtis stated that such cause was not limited to a violation of positive law, but instead, he wrote, "a cause for removal from office may exist, where no offence against positive law has been committed, as where the individual has, from immorality or imbecility or maledministration [sic], become unfit to exercise the office."[94]

In 1867, as the conflict between Andrew Johnson and the Radical Republicans focused on impeachment, an influential exchange of articles was published in the American Law Register by Professor Theodore Dwight and Judge William Lawrence (who as a congressman subsequently participated in the impeachment proceedings in the House). The White/ Lawrence exchange framed the issue of whether only criminal conduct was impeachable—an issue that would be a central focus of the Johnson impeachment proceedings.

The first of these articles, published in March 1867, was a lecture given by Professor Dwight entitled "Trial by Impeachment," a subject Professor Dwight observed in his introduction that had "recently assumed extraordinary importance."[95] The central thesis of Dwight's article was "There can be no impeachment except for a violation of law of Congress or for the commission of a crime named in the constitution."[96]

With respect to impeachments under the Constitution, Dwight argued that "the crimes to which it is to be applied" were left "to be settled by the general rules of criminal law." As there was "no common law of crimes" under U.S. law, thereby rendering English precedent "consequently not applicable," Dwight concluded that "unless the crime is specifically named in the constitution, impeachments like indictments can only be instituted for crimes committed against the statutory law of the United States."[97]

Judge Lawrence responded to Dwight in an article published in September 1867.[98] Judge Lawrence argued that rather than being limited to statutory crimes, impeachment was intended to reach "malfeasance, nonfeasance, and, in some cases, misfeasance."[99] In a pointed rejoinder to Dwight, Lawrence wrote that: "It is absurd to say that impeachment is here a mode of procedure for *the punishment of crime*, when the constitution declares its object to be *removal from and disqualification to hold office* and that 'the party convicted shall nevertheless be liable and subject to indictment, trial, judgment, and punishment, according to law,' for his *crimes*."[100]

Rather than being a procedure for the adjudication of crimes, as Dwight had contended, Lawrence characterized impeachment as "a means of removing men from office whose conduct imperils the public safety, and renders them unfit to occupy official position."[101] Lawrence noted that "misdemeanor" had different meanings in its usage in the common law, in parliamentary practice, and in its common sense meaning. In its parliamentary sense, misdemeanor "means 'maladministration' or 'misconduct' not necessarily indictable."[102] The Framers of the Constitution, he said, understood the parliamentary usage of the term high crimes and misdemeanors, which were "the words of the British Constitution which describe impeachable conduct," and therefore, the Framers "saw that the high court of impeachment took jurisdiction of cases where no indictable crime had been committed, in many instances, and there were then … 'two parallel modes of reaching' some but not all, offenders; one by impeachment, the other by indictment."[103]

Lawrence further disputed Dwight's conclusion that impeachment would lie only for treason, bribery, or a violation of U.S. statute, by pointing out that Dwight's construction "would lead to consequences the most ruinous and absurd."[104] Lawrence observed in this connection that "[t]here are many breaches of trust not amounting to felonies, yet so monstrous as to render those guilty of them totally unfit for office."[105]

Lawrence concluded by offering his own definition of an impeachable high crime or misdemeanor. It was Lawrence's view that "an impeachable high crime or misdemeanor is one in its nature and consequences subversive of some fundamental or essential principle of government or highly prejudicial to the public interest, and this may consist of a violation of the Constitution, of law, of an official oath, or of duty, by an act committed or omitted, or, without violating a positive law, by the abuse of discretionary powers from improper motives or for an improper purpose."[106] Lawrence's definition would be the basis of the House's impeachment of President Johnson as articulated by the principal manager, Benjamin Butler.

## The Impeachment of Andrew Johnson

### *The Run-Up to Impeachment*

The impeachment of President Andrew Johnson has been viewed as being emblematic of the struggle between the Executive and the Congress, and within the Congress itself, over the essential character and the course of

Reconstruction.[107] The controversy over how the defeated states of the Confederacy were to be treated, both legally and politically, had preceded the cessation of the Civil War. Indeed, the opposition to lenient treatment of the southern states had been so forceful among the radical element of the Republican Union party that even the reelection of Lincoln had been called into question.[108] When Andrew Johnson succeeded the murdered Lincoln on April 15, 1865, he became the inheritor of the controversy that would eventually consume his presidency in its vortex.

Johnson was not Abraham Lincoln. Johnson was from the South and had owned slaves himself. He had been a Democrat throughout his career and had broken with his party, not over the issue of slavery, but because he considered the secession of the southern states to have been treason. His armed opposition to the rebellion as military governor of Tennessee had ingratiated Johnson to the Republican Union party and secured him a place on the ticket with Lincoln, as a play for the support of the War Democrats in the North.[109]

Johnson had an uncertain constituency. He was seen as an enemy of Reconstruction by the Radicals.[110] Johnson was hated by his own party, which viewed his affiliation with Lincoln and the Union Republicans as a betrayal. Johnson was also viewed as a traitor to and an oppressor of his own state as the result of his service as the military governor of Tennessee. As a consequence, Johnson was not accorded the *gravitas* that Lincoln had, which had kept the Radical Republicans in check even though they did not embrace Lincoln's policies toward the South.

The fragile alliance between Johnson and the Radical Republicans ruptured when Johnson opposed the Fourteenth Amendment to the Constitution and vetoed legislation extending the life of the popular Freedman's Bureau.[111] Johnson contended that the legislation directly affected the rights of the eleven states of the former Confederacy who were not represented in Congress, as they were entitled to be under the Constitution.[112] The Radicals were frustrated in their effort to override Johnson's veto of the Freedman's Act and as one writer observed, "The thing was done. War was broken out and the first victory was the President's."[113]

The intense conflict between Johnson and the Radicals broke fully into the open when, in a speech on February 22, 1866, Johnson identified Thaddeus Stevens, Charles Sumner, and Wendell Phillips by name as being "opposed to the fundamental principles of this government" and as "laboring to prevent and destroy" those fundamental principles, "as were the men who fought against us."[114] In that speech, given from the portico of the White House during the celebration of Washington's birthday, Johnson directly addressed the Radicals stating: "I tell the opponents of the government…you are engaged in the work of breaking up the government by amendments to the Constitution."[115]

The next open clash between Johnson and the Radicals was over the Civil Rights Act of 1866. Although the act passed the Senate shortly after the Freedman's Bureau bill, there had been resistance in the House and the act was finally adopted on March 13. Johnson's veto message was delivered on March 27, and on April 6, the Senate was finally able to muster the two-thirds vote necessary to override the veto.[116] A similarly tortured path was followed in overcoming Johnson's opposition to the Fourteenth Amendment.[117]

Two days after Congress adjourned, white police officers attacked a convention of Radicals and blacks that had met in New Orleans for the purpose of proposing amendments to the Louisiana constitution that would grant suffrage to blacks. More than forty delegates were killed. Federal troops quartered nearby were not called to the convention hall until the riot was over. Johnson was blamed for having failed to protect the delegates from what was later described as a "massacre." For his part, Johnson accused congressional Radicals with complicity in planning the riot.[118]

At roughly the same time, Johnson spoke to representatives of several delegations to the recently concluded convention of the National Unionists in Philadelphia. Johnson used their meeting as an opportunity to criticize the Congress for hindering the restoration of the Union by excluding the southern states.[119] He told the delegates, "We have witnessed in one department of the government every endeavor to prevent the restoration of peace, harmony and union.... We have seen this Congress pretend to be for the union, when every step and act tended to perpetuate disunion and make a disruption of the states inevitable."[120] In this same vein, Johnson charged the Radicals with assuming despotic authority over the majority of their fellow Republicans.[121] Johnson's attack on the Congress and the Radical Republicans would become one of the articles in his impeachment.

Thereafter, Johnson made a tour of the northern states, which he called the "swing around the circle," in which he continued his attack on the Radicals. In Cleveland, Johnson again accused the Radical Republicans of preventing restoration of the Union. Referring directly to the Radicals, Johnson charged "this factious domineering party" with having "undertaken to poison the minds of the people."[122] This speech, too, was cited in the articles of impeachment.

The House also cited statements made in Chicago concerning responsibility for the New Orleans riot. Johnson once again charged that the riot had been "substantially planned" by the "Radical Congress." Johnson told his audience in Chicago that "every drop of blood that was shed is upon their shirts and they are responsible for it."[123]

Johnson and the Radicals clashed over the removal of federal office holders whose views accorded with those of the Radicals. To Johnson, the right to remove entrenched office holders was "a question of power." As Johnson explained, "Being in power, as they are, their object is to perpetuate their power." Johnson contended that his intention was to turn out those office holders who "have stayed home here five or six years, have held the offices, grown fat, and enjoyed all the emoluments of position." Johnson complained, however, that "when you talk of turning one of them out…they come forward and…pass laws to prevent the Executive from turning anybody out."[124] The legislation to which Johnson referred was the Tenure of Office Act, the alleged violation of which would be the predicate for several of the articles of impeachment.

The Radicals viewed the removal of these office holders as simply Johnson's replacement of loyal Republicans with individuals loyal to him.[125] To prevent this from taking place, the Congress enacted the Tenure of Office Act, which provided that federal officials who required confirmation by the Senate could not be removed from office without the concurrence of the Senate.[126] The Act permitted the suspension of a federal official while the Senate was adjourned, but if the Senate did not ratify the removal after it had reconvened, the official had to be reinstated.[127]

On February 18, 1867, the Tenure of Office Act was laid before the president for signature. When Johnson sought the advice of his cabinet, each member, including Secretary of War Stanton, expressed the view that the act was unconstitutional. Johnson vetoed the act but, once again, the Congress overrode his veto.[128]

The stage was thus set for the final act in the run-up to impeachment, the displacement of Edwin M. Stanton as Secretary of War.

### *The Removal of Secretary of War Edwin M. Stanton*

By the spring of 1867, relations between Johnson and his Secretary of War, Edwin M. Stanton, were severely strained. Stanton was one of the few hold-over cabinet secretaries from the Lincoln administration. In June, the cabinet discussed Attorney General Stanberry's legal opinions concerning the amelioration of the harshness of the military occupation of the South. In these discussions, Stanton was the sole supporter of the current regime and he was encouraged and supported in this by the Radicals. Secretary of the Navy Gideon Welles observed that "Stanton was an original advisor if not originator of these laws. He may not have drafted them, but he…devised the plan of military despotic government to rule the South."[129]

Based on Stanberry's opinion, Johnson directed the military commanders in the South to register as a voter every man who took a prescribed oath, notwithstanding his participation in the rebellion. General Philip Sheridan, the military governor of Louisiana, told Ulysses S. Grant, general in chief of the U.S. Army, that he would not carry out the president's order and Grant, replied that Sheridan should "[e]nforce your own construction of the military bill until ordered to do otherwise."[130]

The House adopted a resolution thanking Sheridan for his "able and faithful performance in his duties." Congress then proceeded to enact the Second Reconstruction Bill authorizing the military governors to remove any person holding office in the "rebel states" and other "disloyal persons." These decisions were to be subject to the review of the general of the army but not the president.[131]

Johnson vetoed the bill. In his veto message, Johnson described the Reconstruction Act as being "in palpable conflict with the plainest provisions of the Constitution and utterly destructive to the great principles of liberty and humanity for which our ancestors on both sides of the Atlantic have shed so much blood and expended so much treasure." Johnson told Congress that he would not surrender the responsibilities and authority of his office "to any number of executive officers." The House and Senate again overrode Johnson's veto.[132]

By the time Congress adjourned in July 1867, it was clear that Johnson and Stanton had become irreconcilably estranged. Johnson correctly viewed Stanton as having collaborated with the congressional Radicals to frustrate his administration.[133]

Johnson's attention again fixed on Stanton after General Philip Sheridan removed the elected governor of Texas and replaced him with the man he had defeated. Johnson had discussed replacing Sheridan but Grant had counseled against it. Johnson was convinced, as Welles had observed, that Sheridan "would never have pursued the course he has if not prompted and encouraged by others to whom he looked, from whom he received advice if not orders."[134]

Two incidents relating to the Lincoln assassination appear to have sealed Johnson's resolve to be rid of Stanton.[135] On August 5, 1867, a letter from President Johnson was delivered to Stanton stating, "Sir, Public considerations of a high character constrain me to say that your resignation as Secretary of War will be accepted."

Stanton replied immediately. Acknowledging receipt of Johnson's letter, Stanton wrote, "In reply, I have the honor to say that public considerations of a high character, which alone have induced me to continue at the head of this department, constrain me not to resign the Office of Secretary of War before the next meeting of Congress."[136]

Eight days later, Johnson asked Grant to serve as interim Secretary of War. After receiving what he believed to be Grant's assent, Johnson sent a second letter to Stanton informing him that, "By virtue of the power and authority vested in me as President by the Constitution and laws of the United States, you are hereby suspended from office as Secretary of War, and will cease to exercise any and all functions pertaining to the same. You will at once transfer to General Ulysses S. Grant, who has this day been authorized and empowered to act as Secretary of War *ad interim*, all records, books, papers, and other public property now in your custody and charge."[137]

Grant betrayed his ambivalence toward the appointment when he wrote to Stanton that "[i]n notifying you of my acceptance, I cannot let the opportunity pass without expressing to you my appreciation of the zeal, patriotism, firmness and ability with which you have ever discharged the duties of Secretary of War." Stanton informed Johnson that "inasmuch as the General commanding the armies of the United States has been appointed *ad interim*, and has notified me that he has accepted the appointment, I have no alternative but to submit under protest to a superior force."[138]

Under the Tenure of Office Act, such a suspension was to remain in effect until the Senate could take up the question of its concurrence. Congress reconvened on November 21, 1867. In his message to Congress on December 3, Johnson said that he had "deliberated much" on his continued opposition to the Act, which he deemed unconstitutional, and had concluded if such an act would "produce immediate and irreparable injury to the organic structure of government," that "the President must take the high responsibilities of office and save the life of the nation at all hazards."[139]

Johnson sent a second message to Congress on December 12 in which he explained his reasons for suspending Stanton, including Stanton's conduct in the cabinet; Stanton's complicity in the New Orleans Massacre; and Stanton's view that the Tenure of Office Act was unconstitutional. Johnson also identified Stanton as the author of Lincoln's Reconstruction policy for which Johnson claimed, "There is perhaps no act of my administration for which I have been more denounced than this."[140]

On January 13, 1868, the Senate adopted a resolution in accordance with the Tenure of Office Act that "the Senate did not concur in such suspension." Copies of the resolution were served on Johnson, Grant, and Stanton. On January 14, Grant surrendered his key to the War Department to the Assistant Adjutant General of the Army and repaired to army headquarters.[141]

After unsuccessfully offering the position to General William T. Sherman, Johnson settled on General Lorenzo Thomas, the Adjutant General, to succeed Stanton as Secretary of War. On February 21, 1868, Johnson again addressed a letter to Stanton advising him that "By virtue of the power and authority vested in me as President by the Constitution and laws of the United States, you are hereby removed from the office as Secretary of the Department of War, and your function as such will terminate upon receipt of this communication." General Thomas was appointed Secretary of War "*ad interim.*" Upon being informed of Johnson's decision by General Thomas, Stanton replied, "I do not know whether I will obey your instructions or whether I will resist them."[142]

In fact, Stanton did not surrender his office and the following day, General Thomas was arrested. After being admitted to bail, Thomas returned to the War Department where he confronted Stanton who ordered him to leave.[143]

On February 22, 1868, Johnson transmitted to the Senate his nomination of General Sherman's father-in-law, Thomas Ewing, to be Secretary of the War Department. Johnson's letter was not delivered until February 24.[144]

The response of the House to Stanton's removal was electric.[145] Two days earlier, Thaddeus Stevens had convened a meeting of the Reconstruction Committee. The report of the committee was issued at 2:20 p.m. on February 24. In a lengthy and heatedly partisan debate, the House considered a resolution, "That Andrew Johnson, President of the United States, be impeached of high crimes and misdemeanors in office." This resolution was adopted by a vote of 126 to 47. The following day Thaddeus Stevens and John Bingham informed the Senate of the House's action.[146]

A committee of impeachment was empanelled and on February 29, the committee reported ten articles of impeachment. Although the articles were initially reduced to nine, two additional articles were added during floor consideration of the committee's report.[147]

*The Impeachment and Trial*

The eleven articles comprising the bill of impeachment adopted by the House have been described as a "catchall collection."[148] In essence, Johnson was charged with four offenses: violation of the Tenure of Office Act;[149] violation of the Command of the Army Act;[150] conspiracy with General Thomas;[151] and high misdemeanors resulting from his various public statements criticizing Congress.[152]

The House appointed seven members to act as managers of the impeachment to present the case against President Johnson to the Senate. Representing the House in this capacity were: John H. Bingham, George S. Boutwell, Benjamin F. Butler, John A. Logan, Thaddeus Stevens, Thomas Williams, and James F. Wilson. At 1:05 p.m. on March 4, 1868, the House managers entered the Senate chamber and presented the articles of impeachment.[153]

President Johnson was represented before the Senate by a distinguished group of lawyers: Jeremiah S. Black, a former Secretary of State (who later withdrew due to a conflict of interest arising from other litigation); Benjamin R. Curtis, a former Associate Justice of the U.S. Supreme Court; William M. Evarts, a leading member of the New York Bar who later became Secretary of State; William S. Groebeck, a former congressman from Ohio (who took Black's place); Thomas A.R. Nelson, a former congressman from Tennessee; and Henry Stanberry, who had stepped down as Attorney General of the United States in order to represent Johnson at the trial.[154] On March 23, President Johnson submitted lengthy written answers to the charges in the articles of impeachment.[155]

The trial before the Senate commenced on March 30, 1868, and continued until May 26. General Benjamin Butler presented the opening statement for the House managers. Butler spoke for three hours.

Butler summed up the charges against Johnson as being "maladministration of the powers and duties of his office." Although Butler conceded that "the offenses or incapacities which are the groundwork for impeachment," were open "to construction," he suggested the ambiguity in the Constitution concerning impeachable conduct had been wise as "human foresight is inadequate and human intelligence fails in the task of anticipating and providing for, by positive enactment, all the infinite gradations of human wrong and sin, by which the liberties of a people and the safety of a nation may be endangered from the imbecility, corruption and unhallowed ambition of its rulers."[156]

Butler offered a definition of a high crime or misdemeanor that would warrant impeachment that appears to have been based largely on the definition put forward by Lawrence in his colloquy with Dwight.[157] Under that definition, conduct would be "in its nature or consequences subversive of some fundamental or essential principal of government, or highly prejudicial to the public interest, and may consist of a violation of the Constitution, of law, of an official duty by an act committed or omitted or, without violating a positive law, by the abuse of discretionary powers from improper motives, or for any improper purpose." Butler sought to make it clear that this definition did not contemplate only crimes. Instead, relying on English parliamentary usage, Butler argued that "any malversation in office, highly prejudicial to the public interest, or subversive of some fundamental principle of government by which the safety of a people may be in danger, is a high crime against the nation, as the term is used in parliamentary law."[158]

Following the evidentiary presentation by the House managers, Benjamin R. Curtis responded on behalf of President Johnson that removal required conviction of a criminal offense against the laws of the United

States and that in order to be considered high crimes and misdemeanors, offenses had to be "so high that they belong in this company with treason and bribery," both of which, Curtis noted, were made crimes by the laws of the United States. As Curtis also noted, "There can be no crime, there can be no misdemeanor without a law, written or unwritten, express or implied. There must be some law, otherwise there is no crime."[159]

Curtis cited Article II, Section 2 of the Constitution conferring upon the president the power to grant pardons "for offences against the United States, except in cases of impeachment." The defense interpreted this provision to mean that "causes of impeachment are, according to the express declaration of the Constitution itself, cases of offences against the United States."[160] Curtis argued that in the absence of a violation of established federal law, an impeachment for conduct not otherwise illegal would amount to an ex post facto law and bill of attainder, both of which are forbidden under the Constitution.[161]

The House managers returned to the question of what should constitute an impeachable offense in their closing arguments following the evidentiary presentation on behalf of the president. Congressman John A. Logan responded to Curtis' argument concerning the ex post facto or attainder effect of the House position by noting that the "weight of the argument is derived from the suggestion that the judgment following impeachment is in truth a punishment of crime." Logan argued, as the consequence of impeachment and conviction is only removal or disqualification from office, removal from office cannot be considered punishment.[162]

Thaddeus Stevens, the leader of the Radical Republicans in the House, contended that impeachments "apply simply to political offences—to persons holding political positions, either by appointment or election by the people," and therefore, "it is apparent that no crime containing malignant or indictable offenses higher than misdemeanors was necessary either to be alleged or proved."[163] Instead, if the president were "shown to be abusing his official trust to the injury of the people for whom he was discharging public duties, and persevered in such abuse to the injury of his constituents, the true mode of dealing with him was to impeach him for crimes or misdemeanors...and thus remove him from the office which he was abusing." Stevens dismissed the defense argument that the proof of high crimes and misdemeanors required evidence of *mens rea*, but contended instead, "Mere mistake in intention, if so persevered in after proper warning as to bring mischief upon the community, is quite sufficient to warrant the removal of the officer from the place where he is working mischief by his continuance in power."[164]

On behalf of the president, Thomas A.R. Nelson reiterated the position taken by his cocounsel, that "the word 'crimes' is to be construed in the same sense as the word 'treason'; it is to be understood as embracing felonious offences, offences punishable with death or with imprisonment in the penitentiary."[165] With respect to the ex post facto nature of the House charges, Nelson contended that "nothing is an impeachable offence under the American Constitution except that which was known as a crime or misdemeanor" and because the acts attributed to President Johnson did not constitute crimes under the "known law" at the time, Nelson questioned "whether the Congress of the United States...has a right to create a new crime, a new misdemeanor, something that was not known as a crime or as a misdemeanor at the date of the adoption of the Constitution."[166]

Finally, in his closing argument on behalf of the president, William E. Evarts addressed the definition of high crimes and misdemeanors proffered by the House managers, arguing that it was necessary "to have a crime definite under the law and Constitution, and even then it is not impeachable unless you affect it with some of the public and general and important qualities that are indicated in this definition" and thus, "you should have here what is crime against the Constitution and crime against the law, and then that it should have those public proportions that are indicated in the definition."[167]

### The Senate's Verdict

At the conclusion of the arguments by the House managers and the defense, the Senate agreed to take up consideration of the charges set forth in Article 11 first. On Saturday, May 16, without debate, the senators voted as follows: thirty-five for conviction and nineteen for acquittal.[168] The vote was one less than the two-thirds majority needed to convict Johnson, and accordingly, the Chief Justice announced that "Two-thirds not having pronounced guilty, the President is, therefore, acquitted upon this Article." The Senate thereafter adjourned.[169]

The Senate reconvened on May 26, at which time it was agreed on the motion of Senator Williams that Articles 2 and 3 would be considered. The Senate again voted without debate. Thirty-five senators voted to convict and nineteen voted to acquit and Johnson was pronounced acquitted of the charges in both articles.

At that, trial of Andrew Johnson stood "adjourned without day," ending the formal proceedings against President Johnson.[170] Thus, Johnson was denied the acquittal that he certainly would have garnered had the Senate voted on the remaining articles.

Even though no debate on the articles was reported, senators were permitted to submit their views of the case in writing within two days of the close of proceedings. Thirty senators published their opinions. Of the thirty-five senators voting to convict President Johnson, eighteen senators filed written statements and of the nineteen senators voting to acquit him, twelve senators filed statements.

Not surprisingly, the senators who had voted to acquit Johnson on the three articles would have acquitted Johnson of the other articles as well. Generally, the acquitting senators were of the view that because Stanton was a hold-over appointee of Lincoln, Stanton had not been covered by the Tenure of Office Act. Additionally, several senators concluded that the president had an inherent right under the executive powers conferred by the Constitution to remove members of his cabinet and therefore they questioned the constitutionality of the Tenure Act.[171]

It was also the decided view of these senators that the ad interim appointment of Adjutant General Thomas had not constituted an "appointment" requiring the advice and consent of the Senate under either the Constitution or Tenure Act.[172] As a consequence of this conclusion, the senators did not find the articles alleging a conspiracy between Johnson and Thomas to have been supported either in fact or in law. They also found the allegation of an attempt by President Johnson to seduce General Emory into disregarding the Command of the Army Act to have been unsubstantiated.[173]

Although a number of the acquitting senators were critical of Johnson's public comments concerning the Congress, they nevertheless agreed that Johnson had not done more than exercise "that Liberty of speech guaranteed to him by the Constitution and the laws of the country."[174] Similarly, the omnibus charges in Article 11 were criticized for their multiplicity and, as Senator Henderson remarked, the difficulty posed by the article was "to ascertain what it really charges."[175]

There were, however, senators who conceded in theory that obstruction or the refusal to execute the law could be impeachable conduct, but they found proof of such intentional conduct to be lacking.[176] Others declined to vote for removal simply on the basis of policy or political differences.[177]

As one would expect, the senators voting for conviction saw the case against President Johnson very differently. There was virtually unanimous agreement among the convicting senators that the president did not have the inherent authority under the Constitution to remove a cabinet officer. They believed that the Tenure Act was consistent with the Constitution and that the removal of Stanton was an impeachable high misdemeanor as provided in the Tenure Act. In this connection, the senators soundly rejected the contention of the defense that the removal of Stanton had been for the purpose of testing the constitutionality of the Tenure Act, and that Johnson's failure to abide by the Act should be excused by his belief in the Act's unconstitutionality.[178]

There was also unanimity in the conclusion that President Johnson had attempted to prevent execution of the Tenure Act and other Reconstruction legislation.[179] There was less unanimity regarding the articles charging conspiracy with General Thomas,[180] and the attempted violation of the Command of the Army Act.[181]

Lastly, with respect to the charges arising from Johnson's statements, a number of the convicting senators agreed with the view of the acquitting senators that Johnson's remarks, although improvident, had not risen to the gravity of impeachable conduct.[182] Other convicting senators regarded Johnson's speeches as a direct assault on Congress' authority, which posed a direct threat to constitutional government.[183]

To a great extent, the demarcation between the senators voting for conviction and those voting for acquittal was not only their varying interpretation of the facts, but it was also the lens through which those facts were viewed and their significance assessed. That lens was the individual senator's conception of what should constitute an impeachable high crime or misdemeanor. The acquitting senators embraced the legal theory put forward by the president's defense team that a high crime or high misdemeanor could only be a violation of the Constitution or of a federal statute that in seriousness and consequence was equal to the enumerated offenses of treason and bribery.[184]

The convicting senators rejected both the restriction of impeachment to violations of law and the requirement of criminal intent.[185] There was also agreement among the convicting senators that it was not the violation of law that was dispositive of impeachable conduct but rather it was the nature of the conduct and the consequences.[186] According to the convicting senators, this latitude given to the Senate in defining high crimes and misdemeanors in the Constitution was in recognition of the political nature of impeachment.[187]

### *The Aftermath*

Following his acquittal, President Johnson served out the remainder of his term with little controversy.[188] Johnson returned to Tennessee and in 1874, the legislature elected him to serve in the U.S. Senate. On March 5, 1875, Johnson received the oath of office from the Vice President, Henry Wilson, who as senator had voted for his conviction. Johnson's only speech, given two weeks later on March 22, criticized President Grant for what he described as the military occupation of Louisiana.

When the Senate adjourned on March 24, 1875, Johnson returned to Greenville. On July 29, he suffered what would prove to be a fatal stoke. Johnson died on July 31.[189]

To be sure, the political alignments of the convicting and acquitting senators played a significant part in the one-vote acquittal. However, simply viewing the "Recusant" Republicans as having saved Johnson and preserved the constitutional balance of the executive and legislative branches ignores the very substantial legal and factual issues that underlay the decision of the Senate.

It also has been suggested that there were factors independent of the impeachment case that may have influenced the Senate's verdict of acquittal. One of these factors was the uneasiness concerning Senator Benjamin Wade succeeding a convicted Johnson.[190] A second factor was that Johnson appeared to be less a threat to Congress at the time of the trial than he had been earlier in the year. Assurances had been conveyed to the conservative Republicans through Senator Grimes, whose vote for acquittal was one of the pivotal moments in the trial, that Johnson would take no action in violation of law or the Constitution,[191] and Johnson completed his term without the controversy that had characterized his presidency preceding the impeachment.[192] Indeed, it appears that as a consequence of the impeachment effort, Johnson tempered his own conduct and even the prospect of impeachment dampened presidential challenges of Congressional authority for some time thereafter.[193]

The meaning of high crimes and misdemeanors that emerges from the Johnson trial is ambiguous as well. While the criminal law theory of impeachable offenses had adherents among the acquitting senators, not all of them embraced the theory as their own. Also, the criminal law limitation can fairly be said to have been rejected by a majority of the senators.

It can also fairly be said that neither harsh nor strident criticism of Congress should constitute impeachable conduct. However, the Johnson impeachment left open the question of whether a president's refusal to enforce an act of Congress, as Johnson had in regard to the Reconstruction legislation, or a president's actions in contradiction of an act of Congress, as was Johnson's removal of Stanton in defiance of the Tenure Act, would constitute impeachable high crimes and misdemeanors. As discussed in chapter 1, such conduct by the president would be consistent with the Framers' view of high crimes and misdemeanors. In Johnson's case, the factual record of his omissions in enforcement of the civil rights legislation was equivocal and the issue of Johnson's violation of the Tenure Act was clouded by the questions of interpretation and the constitutionality of the Act itself. In contrast, were the legislation indisputably constitutional and the breach of the president's duty to see to the faithful execution of the laws clear, an impeachment could be warranted. But even in those circumstances, to be faithful to the Framers' intent, the breach would have to be of so great moment that nothing short of impeachment and removal would restore the balance of powers and the constitutional order.

3

# The Proceedings against Richard M. Nixon

It would be just over a century after the failed impeachment of President Andrew Johnson that formal impeachment proceedings were instituted against another president, Richard M. Nixon. The impetus for impeachment was not dormant during that time, however.

In 1876, William W. Belknap, President Grant's Secretary of War, was impeached by the House on charges that he had received money as a consequence of his having appointed a friend, Caleb P. Marsh, to the position of post trader at Fort Sill, Okalahoma. Although Belknap had resigned when it became clear that he would be impeached, the House, nevertheless, adopted five articles of impeachment charging Belknap with high crimes and misdemeanors. After trial by the Senate, Belknap was acquitted, there having been fewer than two-thirds of the senators voting for conviction. A number of the senators that had voted for acquittal indicated that they thought Belknap's resignation had robbed the Senate of jurisdiction.[1]

Impeachment proceedings were also brought against five federal judges during this period. In 1905, District Judge Charles Swayne was acquitted by the Senate of a variety high crimes and misdemeanors involving corruption and incompetence.[2] Judge Robert W. Archbald was convicted by the Senate in 1913 of high crimes and misdemeanors relating to self-dealing and conflict of interest.[3] In 1926, District Judge George W. English was impeached for abusive conduct, favoritism, and self-dealing but resigned before his trial by the Senate.[4] In 1933, Judge Harold Louderback was tried and acquitted by the Senate of high crimes and misdemeanors relating to alleged favoritism in the appointment of receivers in bankruptcy.[5]

Finally, in 1936, District Judge Halstead L. Ritter was convicted of high crimes and misdemeanors and removed from office by the Senate. Although he was acquitted of six of the substantive articles of impeachment lodged against him, he was nevertheless convicted of having accepted fees and having failed to pay income taxes in an article that was in essence a "catch-all" of the other articles upon which he was acquitted.[6]

Also during this time, an effort was made to impeach President Harry S. Truman as a consequence of the seizure of American steel companies during the Korean conflict.[7] Efforts were also made in 1953 and again in 1970 to impeach Supreme Court Justice William O. Douglas.[8] With respect to the charges leveled in the latter proceedings, then-Congressman Gerald R. Ford, the principal proponent of Douglas' impeachment, grandly stated that "An impeachable offense is whatever a majority of the House of Representatives considers it to be at a given moment in history."[9] Four years later, Ford was the vice president when the House instituted impeachment proceedings against President Richard M. Nixon.

In contrast to the Johnson impeachment, the proceedings against Richard M. Nixon did not progress beyond the House Judiciary Committee due to Nixon's resignation of the presidency. Those proceedings, however, revealed a strong bipartisan consensus that the domestic surveillance program (sometimes referred to as the "White House Horrors") and the obstruction of investigations into the burglary of the Democratic National Committee offices at the Watergate (the "Cover-Up") represented an abuse of the powers of the presidency constituting high crimes and misdemeanors. In reaching that consensus, the committee considered the record of those abuses beginning with the Huston Plan and intensively debated what the intent of the Framers had been in adopting high crimes and misdemeanors as grounds for impeachment and removal. Thus, the Nixon impeachment proceedings are highly instructive, not simply of what Congress considered an "impeachable offense" to be "at a given moment in history," but as a thoughtful analysis of high crimes and misdemeanors in the context of the modern presidency.

### The Domestic Surveillance Program

*The Predicate: Nixon's Ascendancy to the Presidency*

In many ways, Richard M. Nixon was an unlikely president. Nixon described himself as "an introvert in an extrovert's business"[10] and the political historian, Theodore H. White, similarly observed: "Politics, for those who chose it as a way of life, is an exercise in ego—attractive to those who had a sense of self, who enjoy the rub of their personality against others and the camaraderie of the campaign. Of this quality, Nixon had little."[11] Certainly, Richard Nixon was a complex and conflicted man.[12]

Richard Nixon was born in Yorba Linda, California on January 9, 1913. After graduating from Whittier College, Nixon studied law at Duke University and was admitted to the California Bar in 1937.[13] He practiced law in Whittier for several years and, after a brief employment with the Office of Price Administration in Washington, D.C, Nixon joined the Navy in 1942. Upon returning to California at the end of World War II, he ran a successful campaign against the Democratic incumbent, Jerry Voorhis, and was elected to Congress in 1946. Nixon's campaign centered on the charge that Voorhis was a communist—a charge Nixon later admitted was false.[14]

Fresh from his successful prosecution of Alger Hiss for giving false testimony to the House Un-American Activities Committee, Nixon reprised his anticommunist theme in his campaign for the Senate in 1950 against Helen Gahagan Douglas (whom he described as being "pink right down to her underwear"). Nixon won election to the Senate with the largest margin of any senator elected or reelected in 1950.[15]

Richard Nixon entered national politics when he was chosen as the vice-presidential candidate to run with Dwight D. Eisenhower in 1952. His nomination was due largely to his support of Eisenhower, behind the back of Earl Warren to whom Nixon and the California delegation were pledged, and his work with Henry Cabot Lodge, Eisenhower's campaign manager, on behalf of the "fair play" amendment of the convention rules, which was considered essential to Eisenhower's first ballot nomination.[16]

After winning the presidential nomination of the Republican Party in 1960, Nixon barely lost the general election to John F. Kennedy by 118,000 votes out of 6.8 million cast. Although Nixon had won in twenty-six states and Kennedy had won in twenty-three states, Kennedy had garnered 303 electoral votes to Nixon's 219 electoral votes. Despite the narrowness of the Kennedy victory, Nixon did not contest the results of the election even though there were circumstances that bespoke fraud to many.[17]

However, his defeat in 1960 and his later defeat in his campaign for Governor of California in 1962 affected his view of electoral politics. During the California gubernatorial campaign, the issue of Nixon's relationship with Howard Hughes and the loan of $205,000 by Hughes to Nixon's brother Donald that was never repaid had been revived.[18] His losses to Kennedy in 1960 and to Pat Brown in 1962 fostered in Nixon "the zeal for overreach" in future campaigns.[19]

All of these forces of Nixon's personality—his desire for secrecy; his distrust of others around him, particularly the press; his need to punish perceived enemies; his fear of defeat when electoral victory seemed assured—coalesced after Nixon's 1968 election to the presidency.

### *The Early Domestic Surveillance and the Huston Plan*

On May 9, 1969, roughly three months after Richard Nixon had taken the oath of office as the thirty-seventh president of the United States, the *New*

*York Times* published an article by William Beecher under the front page headline: "Raids in Cambodia by U.S. Unprotested." The article referred to what had been a secret bombing campaign in Cambodia that was part of a covert military campaign developed by Nixon and his national security advisor, Henry Kissinger, code-named "Menu."

Kissinger, who was with Nixon at the time in Key Biscayne, Florida, demanded that the source of the information for the Beecher article be found and "destroyed." Nixon shared Kissinger's anger at the public disclosure of classified information and suspected that the source had been one of Kissinger's closest aides, Morton Halperin.

At Nixon's direction, Kissinger contacted FBI Director J. Edgar Hoover and requested that Halperin's telephone calls be intercepted ostensibly for reasons of national security. By the evening of May 9, a wire tap had been installed by the FBI. The tap remained in place until February 1971, long after Halperin had ceased to have access to classified information.[20]

The following day, Nixon directed another Kissinger aide, Colonel Alexander Haig, to instruct the FBI to intercept the telephone calls of two other members of Kissinger's staff, Helmut Sonnenfeldt and Daniel Davidson, and of Colonel Robert Pursley, assistant to Secretary of Defense Melvin Laird. Thereafter, between May 1969 and February 1971, the telephones of at least seventeen other persons were tapped. Among those under surveillance were a consultant to the presidential campaign of Senator Edmund Muskie, a Democrat; at least three employees of the White House who were involved exclusively in domestic affairs; several journalists, including the syndicated newspaper columnist Joseph Kraft; and the president's brother, Donald Nixon.[21]

Also during this time, on June 5, 1970, President Nixon established an ad hoc committee comprised of the directors of the principal intelligence gathering agencies to study the nature and extent of threats posed by groups opposing the war in Vietnam and other dissidents. The committee issued its report on June 25, and recommended that restraints on domestic intelligence collection be relaxed. A White House staff assistant, Tom Charles Huston forwarded the committee's report to H.R. Haldeman, the president's chief of staff, with a memorandum recommending a program of "surreptitious entries" (which Huston described as "surreptitious screening"); electronic surveillance; and mail interceptions.[22] These recommendations became known as the "Huston Plan."

On July 14, 1970, Haldeman informed Huston that President Nixon had approved Huston's recommendations, including surreptitious entries. After Attorney General John Mitchell informed both Nixon and Haldeman of his opposition, Huston recalled the memorandum. The program of covert domestic surveillance went forward nonetheless.[23]

*The White House Special Investigations Unit*
*Known As "The Plumbers"*

On June 13, 1971, the *New York Times* published the first of a planned ten-part series of articles based on a 1967 study commissioned by then-Secretary of Defense Robert S. McNamara of the events resulting in the involvement of the United States in the Vietnam War. The study, entitled "History of U.S. Decision-Making Process on Vietnam Policy," comprised over 7,000 pages bound in forty-seven volumes and became known as the "Pentagon Papers."[24]

Substantially all of the study had been obtained by *New York Times* reporter Neil Sheehan from Daniel Ellsberg, a senior research associate at the M.I.T. Center for International Studies, who had been one of the authors while at the Rand Corporation.[25]

After publishing three installments, suit was filed against the *Times* by the U.S. Government to enjoin further publication. On June 18, the *Washington Post* also began publishing articles based on the Pentagon Papers. Suit was brought to enjoin publication by the *Post* as well.[26]

Daniel Ellsberg acknowledged his role in the disclosure of the Pentagon Papers two weeks after publication had begun. Nixon viewed Ellsberg as "a liberal antiwar intellectual who had leaked secrets." Nixon also saw the publication of the Pentagon Papers by the *Times* as "the product of the paper's antiwar policy rather than a consistent attachment to principle."[27]

Concern over the possibility of future embarrassing disclosures of classified information, such as the Cambodian bombing campaign, and the lack of assurance that either the FBI or the judiciary could prevent such disclosures led to the creation of the White House Special Investigations Unit that came to be known as "the Plumbers."[28] Nixon told John Ehrlichman, counsel to the president, "If we can't get anyone in this damn government to do something about the problem that may be the most serious one we have, then, by God, we'll do it ourselves."[29]

Responsibility for the Plumbers unit was given to Egil Krogh, a protégé of Ehrlichman, and to David Young, formerly an assistant to Kissinger. Their first recruits for the unit were fateful ones: G. Gordon Liddy, a former FBI agent; and E. Howard Hunt, a former CIA agent with close ties to the Cuban Nationalist Movement, who had worked for Charles W. Colson, special counsel to Nixon.[30]

At first, the Plumbers were formed to investigate the circumstances of Ellsberg's acquisition of the Pentagon Papers and their disclosure to Sheehan. Ellsberg had been indicted for misuse of classified information and in an effort to discredit Ellsburg, Nixon directed Colson to publicize disparaging information about Ellsberg and his lawyer. Colson would eventually plead guilty to obstruction of justice as a consequence of these activities.[31]

As part of this effort, in July 1971, Young requested that the CIA prepare a psychological profile of Ellsberg. Also at this time, on July 28, 1971, Hunt recommended to Colson that Ellsberg's records be obtained from his psychiatrist, Dr. Lewis Fielding, with a view toward damaging Ellsberg's public standing and credibility.[32]

Hunt and Liddy proposed breaking into Fielding's office and stealing Ellsberg's files. Krogh conveyed the Hunt/Liddy plan to Ehrlichman on August 5. The following day, Ehrlichman apprised Krogh that the president's response had been to "tell Krogh he should do whatever he considers necessary to get to the bottom of the matter—to learn what Ellsberg's motives and potential further harmful action might be." When Krogh and Young recommended that a covert operation be undertaken to examine all of the medical files still held by Ellsberg's psychiatrist concerning the two years in which Ellsberg had undergone analysis, Ehrlichman approved the recommendation with the caveat, "If done under your assurance that it is not traceable."[33]

Ehrlichman designated the burglary of Dr. Fielding's office as the "Hunt/Liddy Special Project No. 1." The cost of the operation was paid for with campaign funds obtained from Colson.[34]

The burglary was conducted on the night of September 3, 1971, which was the Friday of the long Labor Day weekend. Hunt surveilled Fielding's home while Liddy acted as the look-out at the scene. Bernard Barker, a Cuban Nationalist from Miami who had worked for Hunt when Hunt was with the CIA, led the burglary team. With Barker were Eugenio Martinez and Felipe DeDiego. Barker and Martinez would later be involved in the Watergate burglary. Although the operation was a success in the sense that the burglars were not apprehended, no records of Ellsberg's treatment were found.[35]

### The Use of Confidential Information Obtained from the Internal Revenue Service

Nixon later acknowledged that early in his presidency he had "hit the ceiling" when he learned that the Internal Revenue Service had audited his friends the Reverend Billy Graham and the actor John Wayne. He instructed members of his staff to "get the word" to the IRS that they were to "conduct field audits of those who are our opponents."[36] Huston conveyed Nixon's directive to the commissioner of Internal Revenue and on July 1, 1969, the IRS created the Special Services Staff (SSS). By September 1970, the SSS had investigated more than 1,000 institutions and 4,000 individuals.[37]

In the spring of 1970, Haldeman became aware of an IRS investigation of George C. Wallace, the governor of Alabama, and his brother Gerald Wallace. Looking forward to the reelection campaign in 1972, Clark Mollenhoff, special counsel to the president, was directed by Haldeman to obtain a copy of the confidential report of the IRS investigation. Information from the report concerning George Wallace was delivered to a newspaper columnist, Jack Anderson, and was published throughout the United States.[38]

The following spring, Ehrlichman learned that the IRS investigation of Howard Hughes' business interests, and in particular the Hughes Tool Company, had revealed payments to Lawrence O'Brien, the chairman of the Democratic National Committee. Nixon was eager for derogatory information concerning O'Brien and he told Ehrlichman and Haldeman "to ride IRS." Ehrlichman obtained information from the IRS concerning O'Brien's personal income tax returns and advised Secretary of the Treasury George Schultz that O'Brien should be interviewed. Despite an IRS policy that interviews of political candidates or persons in politically sensitive positions were not to be conducted during an election year (unless there were compelling reasons such as the running of the statute of limitations), O'Brien was interviewed by the IRS on August 17, 1972. In early September, Ehrlichman provided information regarding O'Brien's allegedly unreported income to Herbert Kalmbach and asked Kalmbach to pass on the information concerning O'Brien to Hank Greenspun, publisher of the *Las Vegas Sun* and friend of Kalmbach. Kalmbach refused to do so despite additional requests by Attorney General John Mitchell.[39]

*The Gemstone Project*

In December 1971, G. Gordon Liddy was named general counsel of the Committee to Re-Elect the President (CRP). His principal responsibility in that capacity was to implement a comprehensive intelligence gathering capability for CRP. The code name for this effort was "Gemstone."[40] The principal targets of the Gemstone Project were the Democratic National Committee and its chairman, Lawrence O'Brien.[41]

As initially presented to Attorney General Mitchell on January 27, 1972, the Liddy plan involved a variety of exotic covert activities. Liddy proposed physical assault and kidnapping of anti-Nixon demonstrators "*before* they reach the television cameras."[42] Liddy also proposed to have prostitutes on a yacht wired for video and sound recording to entrap unwary Democrats during the convention.[43] Liddy proposed that there be burglaries, along the lines of the entry into Dr. Fielding's Beverly Hills office and electronic surveillance of unidentified targets.[44]

A second meeting was held eight days later, on February 4, 1972. Liddy offered a much scaled-down plan of electronic and photographic surveillance at a cost of approximately $500,000. Mitchell suggested the Democratic National Committee (DNC) headquarters at the Watergate Office Building in Washington and at the Democratic Convention in Miami Beach as targets for the Gemstone operation. Mitchell also suggested that Gemstone include the offices Hank Greenspun, who was reported to have a file of Howard Hughes' political memoranda, which Mitchell believed could contain references to contributions by the Hughes organization to Nixon.[45]

Approval of the Gemstone project was given by Attorney General Mitchell on March 30 at a meeting in Key Biscayne. Liddy was given a budget of $250,000 to surreptitiously enter the offices of the Democratic National Committee at the Watergate. If funds became available, similar surreptitious entries were to be made at the headquarters of the various candidates for the Democratic presidential nomination in Washington and at the Democratic Convention.[46]

These actions, many of which were considered by the House Judiciary Committee as having been abuses of presidential power, were described by Attorney General Mitchell simply as the "White House Horrors."[47]

The first covert operation of the Gemstone Project was the burglary of the Democratic National Committee offices at the Watergate Office Building in Washington, D.C. To carry out the plan, Hunt asked Bernard Barker to bring a burglary team from Miami. During the early morning hours of May 28, the burglary team gained entry to the DNC offices. James McCord, a former CIA officer, installed interception devices on the telephones of Chairman O'Brien and another DNC official, Spencer Oliver. Barker and the others photographed documents.[48] Jeb Stuart Magruder, who had been the White House Communications Director and then worked at the CRP, later told the Senate Select Committee that Mitchell was not satisfied with the information being produced by the tap on O'Brien's phone. Mitchell met with Liddy and told him that materials "were not satisfactory and it [*sic*] is not worth the money that he had paid for it." Liddy told Mitchell that there had been a technical malfunction in one of the devices and that the other device had been improperly installed. Liddy assured Mitchell that he would correct the problems.[49]

The burglary team returned to the Watergate for that purpose on June 17.

*The Watergate Burglary*

On June 17, the Gemstone burglary team comprised of McCord, Bernard Barker, Frank Sturgis, Eugenio Martinez, and Virgilio Gonzales illegally entered the offices of the DNC at the Watergate. Hunt and Liddy were nearby in a room at the Watergate Hotel where they maintained communications with the burglary team and with Alfred Baldwin, a former FBI agent, who was serving as a look-out from a room at the Howard Johnson Motor Lodge across the street.[50]

The suspicions of a security guard at the Watergate Office Building, Frank Wills, were aroused when Wills discovered masking tape covering the lock on an entry door for the second time that evening, after having previously removed it.[51] Wills contacted the Washington Metropolitan Police Department, which dispatched a plainclothes unit in an unmarked car to assist him.[52]

Sergeant Paul Leeper and his men entered the office building, leaving their automobile parked in front. Despite seeing the men enter the building, Baldwin did not think anything was amiss until he saw two plainclothes officers on the terrace of the DNC offices with their weapons drawn. Baldwin radioed Hunt and Liddy and asked them, "Are our people in suits or are they dressed casually?"

When Baldwin was told that the burglary team was wearing suits, he informed Hunt and Liddy, "You have some trouble because there are some individuals around here who are dressed casually and have got their gun [*sic*] out." Moments later, the burglary team was apprehended as the men were setting up their photographic equipment. While the men were being arrested, Barker radioed Hunt, saying "They got us." Hunt, Liddy, and Baldwin each fled.[53]

After they were taken to the police station for booking, the burglars each refused to make a phone call. Nevertheless, later that evening, a lawyer, Douglas Caddy, appeared at the police station stating that he represented the men in custody. Caddy refused to disclose how he had learned that his "clients" had been arrested.[54]

The following day, Sergeant Leeper obtained a search warrant for the rooms that had been occupied by the burglary team. The ensuing search revealed a notebook with an entry for E. Howard Hunt with the notations "W.H." and "W. House."[55]

The FBI became involved in the investigation of the Watergate burglary because of the apparent violations of federal law regarding wiretaps. It was quickly determined that Hunt was associated with the White House. The FBI also learned of Hunt's association with the CIA as well as the prior employment of the Miami burglars by the CIA. As a result of these revelations, Assistant Attorney General Henry Petersen directed the FBI to ascertain from the CIA whether Hunt or the burglars were actively employed by the CIA. Petersen also directed that all information developed by the FBI in its investigation be furnished to him for transmittal to the White House.[56]

As the Senate Select Committee later observed: "The burglary was over, but the Watergate scandal had just begun."[57]

## The Cover-Up

The essence of the Watergate scandal was the cover-up—the concealment of Gemstone and the other White House Horrors, and the consequent acts of perjury and obstruction of justice. It was the cover-up rather than the Watergate burglary itself that led ultimately to the impeachment proceedings against Nixon.

### *The Initial Denials of Responsibility*

Following the arrest of the burglars at the Watergate, Liddy and Hunt immediately went to their offices and began shredding files. Colson ordered the destruction of White House directories listing Hunt.[58]

Liddy also called the CRP officials who were meeting in San Clemente. Mitchell authorized the issuance of a press release, which stated, in part that "We have just learned from news reports that a man identified as an employee of our campaign committee was one of five persons arrested at the Democratic National Committee headquarters in Washington, D.C. early Saturday morning. The person arrested is the proprietor of a private security agency who was employed by our committee months ago to assist with the installation of our security system…We want to emphasize that this man and the other people involved were not operating either in or on our behalf or with our consent." The press release indicated that the CRP was "experiencing our own security problems" and stated that: "We do not know as of this moment whether our security problems are related to the events of Saturday morning at the Democratic headquarters or not."[59]

The day after the break-in, President Nixon assigned responsibility for the White House response to Watergate to John Ehrlichman, who directed John Dean, the White House counsel, to work on it. Ehrlichman ordered Hunt's White House safe to be drilled open and the contents delivered to him.[60]

On the evening of June 19, Magruder, Frederick C. LaRue, Robert Mardian, and Dean met at Mitchell's apartment. Magruder asked what should be done with the Gemstone and other sensitive files. Mitchell remarked that "it might be a good idea if Magruder had a fire in his house." That night, Magruder burned his Gemstone files.[61]

On June 20, Haldeman, Ehrlichman, Mitchell, and Dean, all of whom knew of the CRP involvement in the burglary,[62] discussed the Watergate affair in Ehrlichman's office at the White House. Afterward, they all met with

Nixon. The Watergate burglary was discussed, and according to Haldeman's notes, it was agreed that the FBI investigation had to be contained.[63]

President Nixon held a press conference on June 22, at which he referred to earlier statements by his press secretary, Ronald Ziegler (who had described the DNC break-in as a "third-rate burglary attempt"), and by Mitchell, saying that they had "stated the facts accurately." Nixon emphasized that "As Mr. Ziegler has stated, the White House has no involvement whatever in this particular incident."[64]

On June 23, Nixon directed Haldeman and Ehrlichman to meet with the director of Central Intelligence, Richard Helms, and his deputy, Vernon Walters, to convey to them the concern of the White House that the FBI investigation of the Watergate matter could lead to disclosure of covert operations by the CIA or by the White House Special Investigations Unit—the Plumbers. Walters was asked to convey the CIA's concerns to L. Patrick Gray, who had succeeded J. Edgar Hoover as director of the FBI.[65] This conversation came to be known later as the "smoking gun" as it revealed Nixon's direct involvement in the cover-up.[66] Nixon later repeated his instruction to have the CIA limit the FBI investigation of Hunt because "He knows too damned much." Gray acceded to the request.[67]

### Containment

The House Judiciary Committee found that between late June 1972 and the election later that year in November, the president and his aides "engaged in a plan of containment and concealment which prevented disclosures that might have resulted in the indictment of high CRP and White House officials; that might have exposed Hunt and Liddy's prior illegal covert activities for the White House; and that might have put the out-come of the November election in jeopardy." To that end, White House Counsel Dean was assigned to closely monitor the FBI investigation. Dean obtained FBI reports, which he shared with CRP officials who were under investigation and with their attorneys. Ehrlichman arranged with Gray to have Dean attend investigatory interviews.[68]

Efforts were also made to prevent White House and CRP personnel from being implicated in the grand jury investigation of the Watergate affair. Dean reached agreement with Assistant Attorney General Petersen to allow key White House witnesses to have their depositions taken in lieu of their testifying before the grand jury.[69]

Various White House and CRP officials also gave false statements and testimony to investigators. When interviewed by the FBI on July 5, Mitchell denied having any information concerning the Watergate burglary. Herbert

L. Porter, an assistant in the White House Communications Office, and Magruder falsely told the FBI the funds that Liddy had received from the CRP had been for lawful intelligence gathering. Additionally, Porter and Magruder both gave false testimony to the Watergate grand jury concerning the purpose of those funds. Krogh gave false testimony concerning the activities of Liddy and Hunt before the Watergate break-in. Magruder also gave false testimony that the Mitchell-Liddy meetings in early 1972 had been to discuss Liddy's duties as CRP general counsel.[70]

The president used his press conference on August 28, 1972, to dampen calls for the appointment of an independent prosecutor. Nixon told the assembled press that "under my direction, Counsel to the President, Mr. Dean, has conducted a complete investigation of all leads which might involve any present members of the White House Staff or anybody in the Government. I can say categorically that his investigation indicates that no one in the White House Staff, no one in this administration, presently employed, was involved in this very bizarre incident." As the Judiciary Committee noted, however, "In fact, Dean had conducted no investigation."[71]

The president stated further that, "I think under these circumstances we are doing everything we can to take this incident and to investigate it and not to cover it up." With apparently unintended irony, the president noted presciently, "What really hurts in matters of this sort is not the fact they occur, because overzealous people in campaigns do things that are wrong. What really hurts is if you try to cover it up."[72]

Nixon then sought to give assurances that, "We have cooperated completely. We have indicated that we want all the facts brought out and that as far as any people who are guilty are concerned, they should be prosecuted." In contrast, the Judiciary Committee found that: "The President and his staff had not cooperated completely" with the investigating agencies and instead that the evidence showed "clearly and convincingly the President and his closest aides acted to obstruct and impede the investigations." Indeed, the Committee further found that Nixon's statements "themselves were intended to delay, impede and obstruct the investigation of the Watergate break-in; to cover-up, conceal, and protect those responsible and to conceal the existence and scope of other unlawful covert activities."[73]

The report of the Dean investigation to which Nixon had referred during his August 29 press conference was never completed.[74] Indeed, Dean later admitted that there had been no investigation and no report.[75]

According to a statement made by Nixon at a press conference on September 5, 1973, when Dean was unable to complete his report, Nixon gave the assignment to Ehrlichman to conduct a "thorough investigation."

However, Dean had informed Nixon on March 21 of Ehrlichman's involvement in the obstruction of justice and of Ehrlichman's possible exposure to criminal charges for his role in the burglary of Dr. Fielding's office. This led the Judiciary Committee to conclude that Nixon's appointment of Ehrlichman to conduct the investigation "is, in itself, evidence of the President's direction of, and complicity in, the cover-up."[76] Additionally, in spite of Nixon's earlier statement that "an investigation was conducted in the most thorough way," Ehrlichman later admitted that he had not conducted an investigation at all.[77]

### The "Hush Money" Payments

Several days after the arrest of the burglars at the Watergate, Liddy informed Mardian and LaRue that the burglars had been promised funds for their bail, support, and legal defense.[78] On June 28, $75,000 in cash was obtained from Maurice Stans, the treasurer of the CRP, and delivered surreptitiously to the burglars. Between July 7 and September 19, 1972, a total of $187,500 was delivered in this way.[79]

In November, Hunt reminded Colson that "commitments" had been made to the burglars but those commitments "had not been kept." Hunt told Colson, "We're protecting the guys who are really responsible, but...this is a two way street."[80]

Haldeman had personal control of $328,000 in proceeds of the 1972 reelection campaign. In December, at Haldeman's direction $40,000 was delivered to Hunt's attorney. In January 1973, an additional $100,000 was delivered to Hunt's attorney and $32,000 was given to the other defendants.[81]

In mid-March 1973, Hunt told Paul O'Brien, an attorney for the CRP, that he had done "seamy things" on the behalf of the White House but if he was not paid $130,000 before his sentencing, he might "reconsider his options." Apparently in response, on March 21, 1973, Nixon met with Dean in what would prove to be a fateful encounter for both men. Dean told Nixon that there was "a cancer-within-close to the Presidency that's growing." Dean explained that the problem was "compounding" and growing "geometrically" because "(1) we're being blackmailed; (2) uh, people are going to start perjuring themselves very quickly that have not had to perjure themselves to protect other people and the like." Dean added, "There is no assurance" and Nixon completed the thought saying "That it won't bust."[82]

Dean then laid out in detail what he knew of the events and actions leading up to the burglary of the DNC offices at the Watergate.[83] The

Judiciary Committee noted that during this part of their conversation "The President did not express either surprise or shock."[84]

Dean discussed the payments to Hunt and the other defendants. Dean told Nixon that Haldeman, Ehrlichman, Mitchell, and he were all implicated in the payments and that the "blackmail is continuing." Hunt, he said, was demanding $72,000 for personal expenses and $50,000 for his attorneys' fees, and had threatened to bring Ehrlichman down to his knees and put him in jail." Dean pointed out that it was likely that the blackmail would continue "when these people are in prison" and the payments "will compound the obstruction-of-justice-situation." Moreover, Dean said, "It'll cost money. It's dangerous."[85]

Nixon's response was simply "How much do you need?" When Dean told him a million dollars, Nixon replied "We could get that…you could get a million dollars. And you could get it in cash. I, I know where it could be gotten.…I mean it's not easy, but it could be done."[86]

When Haldeman joined the meeting, Nixon reiterated the need to pay Hunt. Nixon remarked that Hunt's "price is pretty high but…we should buy time on that." Nixon also instructed Haldeman and Dean to lie about the payment scheme.[87]

With respect to this exchange, the Judiciary Committee observed that Nixon "[d]id not condemn the payments or the involvement of his closest aides. He did not direct that the activity be stopped. He did not report it to the proper investigative agencies" and "he indicated familiarity with the payment scheme."[88]

Later that day, Mitchell authorized LaRue to make the payment and $75,000 in cash was delivered to Hunt's lawyer. The next day, March 22, Mitchell advised Haldeman, Ehrlichman, and Dean that Hunt was not a "problem any longer."[89]

In the Judiciary Committee's view: "This evidence clearly establishes that pursuant to the President's plan of concealment, surreptitious payments of substantial sums of money were made to the Watergate defendants for the purpose of obtaining their silence and influencing their testimony." The committee also found that when Nixon became aware that Hunt would incriminate White House and CRP personnel unless he was paid "he approved the payment to Hunt rather than taking steps to stop it from being made."[90]

*Saving the Plan*

In the meantime, on September 15, 1972, a grand jury in the District of Columbia had returned indictments against the five Watergate burglars: Bernard L. Barker; Virgilio R. Gonzales, Eugenio R. Martinez, James McCord, and Frank A. Sturgis. Also indicted were E. Howard Hunt and

G. Gordon Liddy.[91] Trial began before the Chief Judge of the District Court, John Sirica, on January 10, 1973. Hunt pleaded guilty to all of the charges on January 11. The Miami defendants—Barker, Gonzales, Martinez, and Sturgis—similarly pleaded guilty to the charges on January 15. McCord and Liddy proceeded with their trial and on January 30. After deliberating for only ninety minutes, the jury returned verdicts of guilty against both McCord and Liddy on all counts.[92] Judge Sirica scheduled the sentencing of the defendants for March 23.[93]

As the date of sentencing approached, McCord transmitted a sealed letter to Judge Sirica in which he stated that "political pressure" had been applied to the defendants "to plead guilty and remain silent," and that perjury had been committed concerning "the very structure, orientation, and impact of the government's case." As a consequence, "Others involved in the Watergate Operation were not identified during the trial." McCord requested an opportunity to speak privately with Judge Sirica following sentencing.[94] As John Dean later observed, "The dam was cracking."[95]

McCord's disclosures to Judge Sirica led to the reconvening of the grand jury to investigate the Watergate burglary and the cover-up. There was concern in the White House that Hunt would break his silence notwithstanding the "Hush Money" payments because Nixon would not fulfill Hunt's expectation of executive clemency. There were similar concerns that other key White House personnel would seek leniency from the prosecutors in exchange for their cooperation.[96]

It was at that time, the House Judiciary Committee found, that "Faced with a disintegrating situation, the President, after March 21, 1973, assumed an operational role in the detailed management of the cover-up." To that end, Nixon became even more directly involved in instructing his subordinates to give false and misleading testimony.[97]

On March 22, 1973, Nixon met with Haldeman, Ehrlichman, Mitchell, and Dean to discuss how to control the deteriorating situation. Nixon told them "I don't give a shit what happens. I want you to stonewall it, let them plead the Fifth Amendment, cover-up or anything else, if it'll save it—save the plan." Nixon also told them that they would embark on strategy of concealment and subterfuge that Erhlichman described as the "modified limited hangout."[98]

Nixon had been receiving information concerning the Justice Department's investigation from Assistant Attorney General Petersen on a confidential basis. Nixon shared that information with both Haldeman and Ehrlichman. Nixon told Haldeman that Ehrlichman should prepare Gordon Strachan, a CRP employee, to testify under the guise that Ehrlichman was conducting the investigation for the president.[99] Preparations were also made for Mitchell to be implicated in the Watergate burglary and thereby "circle the wagons around the White House."[100]

In anticipation of his appearance before the Senate Select Committee on Presidential Campaign Activities, Haldeman was provided with the audiotapes of twenty-two conversations between February and April 1973. Haldeman took detailed notes of the March 21 meeting at which the raising of the hush money was discussed. When Haldeman eventually testified before the Senate Select Committee, he recounted how Nixon had said that there would be no problem in raising a million dollars, but Haldeman added that Nixon had also said "but it would be wrong." In a statement issued later on August 22, 1973, Nixon affirmed that Haldeman's testimony concerning their March 21 conversation had been accurate.[101]

On April 30, 1973, the president made a televised address to the nation concerning Watergate. As he had in previous statements, Nixon contended that upon learning of the possible involvement of CRP personnel in the Watergate burglary he had "immediately ordered an investigation by appropriate Government authorities" and that he had "repeatedly asked those conducting the investigation whether there was any reason to believe that members of my Administration were in anyway involved. I received repeated assurances that there were not." Nixon stated that he had received "new information" that "there was a real possibility that some of these charges were true, and suggesting further that there had been an effort to conceal the facts both from the public…and from me." As a consequence, Nixon said, he had "personally assumed the responsibility for coordinating intensive new inquiries" and had "personally ordered those conducting the investigations to get all the facts and to report them directly to me." Nixon reiterated that he had ordered everyone in the government and the CRP to "cooperate fully" and that he was determined "the truth should be fully brought out—no matter who was involved."[102]

The Judiciary Committee found, however, that like the president's statement on August 29, 1972, this statement too was "false." It was the committee's conclusion that: "Both before and after March 21, 1973, the cover-up was sustained by false public statements by the President assuring that the White House or CRP were not involved, as well as, by false statements and testimony by the President's close subordinates, which the President condoned and encouraged and in some instances directed, coached and personally helped to fabricate."[103]

Contemporaneously with the grand jury's investigation of possible criminality in the Watergate affair, on February 7, 1973, the U.S. Senate unanimously adopted Resolution 60 establishing a select committee to investigate "the extent…to which illegal, improper, or unethical activities" had taken place "during the 1972 presidential campaign and election."[104]

On March 12, 1973, Nixon issued a public statement giving assurances that executive privilege would not be asserted in order to avoid disclosure of embarrassing information but, instead, executive privilege would only be invoked under "the most compelling circumstances where disclosure would harm the public interest."[105] Despite these public assurances of disclosure, beginning in April 1973, documents relevant to the Watergate affair and the various investigations were moved to a location in the Executive Office Building adjacent to the White House and the president's aides transferred their records to the president's files. Thereafter, requests by investigators for access to those records were denied on the grounds of executive privilege.[106]

*The Saturday Night Massacre and the Tapes Litigation*

On April 30, following the resignations of Haldeman, Erlichman, and Attorney General Kleindienst (who had succeeded Mitchell), Nixon nominated Elliot Richardson to succeed Kleindienst as attorney general. In announcing the Richardson nomination, Nixon stated that "I have given him complete authority to make all decisions bearing upon the prosecution of the Watergate case and related matters. I have instructed him that if he should consider it appropriate, he has the authority to name a special supervising prosecutor for matters arising out the case."[107]

On May 21, 1973, Archbald Cox, a professor at the Harvard Law School, was designated as the Special Watergate Prosecutor. Cox was to have jurisdiction not only over the investigation of the burglary of the DNC offices but also over offenses involving the 1972 presidential campaign and allegations involving the president and members of his staff. Cox was given authority to contest assertions of testimonial privileges, including executive privilege. The special prosecutor was to be subject to removal only for "extraordinary improprieties." The following day, Nixon pledged his "full support" to the special prosecutor and said that executive privilege would not be invoked with respect to any criminal conduct. Privately, Nixon told Richardson that the waiver of executive privilege extended only to testimony, not to documents.[108]

The existence of the White House taping system was publicly disclosed by Alexander Butterfield in testimony before the Senate Select Committee on July 16, 1973. Cox requested that custody of the tapes be restricted to preserve their integrity. Cox also requested the tapes of eight of the president's conversations. The president denied this request on July 23.[109]

Cox then issued a subpoena requiring the production of the tapes. When Nixon persisted in his refusal, Cox sought enforcement of the subpoena by Judge Sirica. On August 29, Judge Sirica ordered that the tapes be delivered to him for his inspection. Judge Sirica's order was upheld by the federal court of appeals on October 12.[110]

In lieu of producing the tapes as he had been ordered to do, Nixon proposed providing transcripts of the conversations that would be verified by

Senator John Stennis. Although Cox indicated that the president's proposal might be acceptable, when Nixon advised Attorney General Richardson that Cox would have to refrain from requesting additional tapes, Richardson advised him that he could not agree to the condition.[111]

On the evening of October 19, Nixon issued a public statement ordering Cox not to subpoena additional tapes or documents. Cox refused to agree to the president's directive. Nixon then ordered Richardson to fire Cox. Instead, Richardson resigned, as did his Deputy Attorney General William Ruckelshaus. Finally, the solicitor general, Robert Bork, agreed to fire Cox, which he did later that night.[112] The events of October 19 became known as the "Saturday Night Massacre."[113]

On November 1, 1973, Bork, who was acting attorney general, announced that Leon Jaworski had been named to succeed Cox as special Watergate prosecutor. On February 4, 1974, Jaworski was informed that Nixon would not comply with the outstanding requests for tapes and documents.[114]

Thereafter, on April 16, Jaworski and two of the codefendants in the case of *United States v. Mitchell, et al.*, Colson and Mardian, requested that a subpoena be issued by the District Court for the tapes and documents. Judge Sirica granted the request the following day. Nixon asserted executive privilege against producing the tapes and documents and appealed first to the court of appeals and ultimately to the U.S. Supreme Court.[115] The Supreme Court rejected Nixon's blanket assertion of executive privilege. Nixon was ordered to turn over the tapes to Judge Sirica who was to determine their relevancy.[116]

During the course of the litigation, it was disclosed that 18 ½ minutes of the president's June 20, 1972, conversation with Haldeman had been erased. This conversation had followed the meeting at which Haldeman had been briefed on Watergate by Ehrlichman, Mitchell, and Dean. It was also disclosed that the recording of another conversation on June 20 between Nixon and Colson did not exist.[117]

## The Impeachment Inquiry in the House of Representatives

Shortly after Alexander Butterfield had disclosed that presidential conversations had been tape recorded, a resolution that Richard Nixon be impeached by the House of Representatives was introduced by Congressman Robert Drinan on July 31, 1973. Other impeachment resolutions were offered following the Saturday Night Massacre in October 1973.[118]

On November 15, these resolutions were referred to the Committee on the Judiciary. Thereafter, on February 6, 1974, the House adopted Resolution 803, which directed the Committee to "investigate fully and completely whether sufficient grounds exist for the House of Representatives to exercise its constitutional power to impeach Richard M. Nixon, President of the United States of America." The Judiciary Committee was to "report to the House of Representatives such resolutions, articles of impeachment, or other recommendations as it deems proper."[119]

In the course of its investigation, the Committee issued subpoenas directed to President Nixon requiring production of tape recordings and memorializations of 147 conversations, as well as records from the files of Nixon's aides relating to the Plumbers, the Watergate burglary and the cover-up, and the meeting minutes and telephone records during five specified periods between 1971 and 1973.[120] The president refused to provide the bulk of the documents sought by the subpoena.[121]

Also in the course of its investigation, the Committee received submissions from the Watergate grand jury; the impeachment inquiry staff; James St. Clair and Charles Alan Wright, the attorneys for the president; and from the Office of Legal Counsel at the Department of Justice. The Committee also had before it 650 "statements of witnesses"; 7,200 pages of supporting documents; and the recordings of nineteen presidential conversations and dictated recollections. The Committee heard the testimony of witnesses including Alexander Butterfield, Fred LaRue, John Mitchell, John Dean, Henry Petersen, and Charles Colson. The Committee then held four days of general debate between July 24 and July 30 whether Richard Nixon should be impeached for high crimes and misdemeanors.[122]

*Report of the Impeachment Inquiry Staff*

On February 21, 1974, the Impeachment Inquiry Staff submitted to the Committee a report entitled "Constitutional Grounds for Presidential Impeachment." In that report, the staff set forth its views concerning the nature of the conduct constituting an impeachable offense.[123]

The staff suggested that historically, impeachments of both judicial and nonjudicial officers under the U.S. Constitution had involved allegations of "misconduct incompatible with the official position of the office holder" in three general categories: "(1) exceeding the constitutional bounds of the powers of the office in derogation of the powers of another branch of government; (2) behaving in a manner grossly incompatible with the proper function and purpose of the office; and (3) employing the office for an improper purpose or for personal gain."[124]

With respect to the first category, usurpation of coordinate power, the staff cited the example of Senator Blount's having conspired to compromise the neutrality of the United States and his attempt to remove the president's lawfully appointed Indian agent. The staff also cited the impeachment of Andrew Johnson, which the staff said had involved "issues going to the heart of the constitutional division of Executive and Legislative power."

With respect to the second category, conduct that is "grossly incompatible" with the office, the staff cited the intemperances of Judge Pickering and Justice Chase; the treason of Judge Humphreys; and the judicial favoritism charged against Judge English." Finally, with respect to the third category, misuse of political office, the staff cited the impeachments of Judges Peck and English as examples of alleged vindictiveness and the impeachments of Judges Swayne, Archbald, English, Louderback, and Ritter as examples of the use of public office for personal gain.[125]

In these impeachments, the staff noted, "the House has placed little emphasis on criminal conduct." Instead, the staff said, "The American impeachment cases demonstrate a common theme useful in determining whether grounds for impeachment exist—that the grounds are derived from understanding the nature, functions and duties of the office."[126]

The staff also directly addressed the issue whether "only an indictable crime can constitute impeachable conduct." The staff argued that the characteristics of the criminal law made it an inappropriate standard for presidential impeachment. First, the criminal law establishes "a general standard of conduct which all must follow" but "does not address itself to the abuses of presidential power." In contrast to a criminal case, in impeachment the president "is called to account for abusing powers which only a President possesses." Also unlike the criminal law, which is primarily prohibitory in nature, impeachment may address "a serious failure to discharge the affirmative duties imposed on the president by the Constitution" and may be based upon the president's "entire course of conduct in office."[127]

Thus, it was the staff's view that confining impeachment to "indictable offenses" could result in the erection of a standard "so restrictive as not to reach conduct that might adversely affect the system of government." That is because "[s]ome of the most grievous offenses against our constitutional form of government may not entail violations of the criminal law." Such a consequence, the staff said, would be "incompatible with the intent of the framers to provide a mechanism broad enough to maintain the integrity of constitutional government."[128] The staff concluded that "where the issue is presidential compliance with the constitutional requirements and limitations on the presidency, the crucial factor is not the intrinsic quality of behavior but the significance of its effect upon our constitutional system or the functioning of our government."[129]

### The Submission on Behalf of the President

The president's counsel took a very different view in their submission to the Committee on his behalf. They argued that "high crimes and misdemeanors" was a "more limited term" than "maladministration," for which it had been substituted in the Constitution and that high crimes and misdemeanors "inherently connote criminal offenses" that are "of such serious nature to be akin to treason and bribery." The defense also argued that use in the Constitution of terms such as "to try," "convicted," and "pardons for offenses...except...impeachment," were "all terms limited in context to criminal matters."[130]

The defense viewed the impeachment proceedings against Andrew Johnson as supporting their proposition that only indictable criminality would support presidential impeachment.[131] The defense noted that the records of the proceedings in the House reflected that the first impeachment resolution had been rejected "primarily because no specific crime was alleged to have been committed." It was also the contention of the defense that Johnson's acquittal "strongly indicated that the Senate has refused to adopt a broad view of 'other high crimes and misdemeanors' as a basis for impeaching a President." Thus, the defense argued, impeachment should lie "only for cases of the gravest kind"—that is, for "the commission of a crime named in the Constitution or a criminal offense against the laws of the United States."[132]

### The Judiciary Committee Debate

It was against this background that the Judiciary Committee took up debate on July 24, 1974. The competing interpretations of high crimes and misdemeanors were articulated during the opening statements of the members. Congressman Edward Hutchinson put forward his view that the president could only be impeached for the commission of crimes that, like treason and bribery, were "high in the sense that they are crimes directed against or having great impact upon the system of government itself." Thus, Hutchinson said, "the Constitution imposes two separate conditions for removal of a President. One, criminality, and two, serious impact of that criminality upon the Government."[133]

Congressman Harold Donohue set out the contrary view that the issue was not one of criminal conduct but of the misuse and abuse of presidential power. Thus, the Committee's inquiry was to determine whether the president "has seriously, gravely, purposefully, and persistently abused and misused the power entrusted to him by the people of the United States."[134]

The Committee considered three proposed Articles of Impeachment. The first article charged Nixon with obstructing the investigation of the Watergate burglary and concealing "other unlawful covert activities," through a course of conduct including making false statements to investigators; withholding relevant and material evidence; suborning perjury and false statements; interfering with the conduct of investigations; approving the payment of "substantial sums of money" to persons to obtain their silence or to influence their testimony; endeavoring to misuse the Central Intelligence Agency; providing information obtained from the Department of Justice to subjects of the investigation to assist them in avoiding criminal liability; making false and misleading public statements that a "thorough and complete investigation had been conducted" and that no personnel in the government or at the CRP had been involved in misconduct; and implying that persons facing criminal charges would receive clemency in exchange for their silence or false testimony.[135] After debate primarily concerning the generality of the charges, on July 27 by a vote of twenty-seven in favor (twenty-one Democrats and six Republicans) and eleven against, the Committee agreed to refer the first impeachment article to the House of Representatives.[136]

The second article charged Nixon with abusing the powers of the presidency by repeatedly violating the constitutional rights of citizens; by impairing the administration of justice and the conduct of lawful inquiries; and by contravening the laws governing Executive Branch agencies. Again, a course of conduct was specified that included unlawfully obtaining confidential information from the Internal Revenue Service and causing audits and investigations to be conducted in a "discriminatory manner"; directing the Federal Bureau of Investigation and the Secret Service to conduct unlawful electronic surveillance; authorizing the unlawful activities of the Plumbers; failing to act when he had reason to know that "close subordinates" were attempting to impede investigations of the Watergate burglary and the other unlawful activities; and by misusing his executive powers by interfering with the CIA, FBI, and the Watergate Special Prosecution Force.[137] Consideration of Article 2 engendered a spirited debate whether the abuse of power without a concomitant violation of law would support impeachment.

Charles E. Wiggins argued that to be impeachable, abusive conduct had also to constitute violations of law, in which case, he said, "we should impeach because of those violations." Otherwise, Wiggins contended, abusive conduct was no more than "an empty phrase," reflecting "our subjective views of impropriety as distinguished from the objective enunciated by society in its laws." To Wiggins, "abuse of powers" raised the spectre of attainder and risked subjecting a president to impeachment "if a Congress expresses no confidence in his conduct not because he has violated the law, but rather because that Congress declares his conduct to be abusive in terms of their subjective notions of propriety."[138]

George E. Danielson responded that the offense set forth in Article 2 was "truly a high crime and misdemeanor within the purest meaning of

those words" because the offense was "uniquely presidential" in that "[o]
nly the President can abuse the powers of the office of the President," and
because the specified conduct were "crimes or offenses against the very
structure of state, against the system of government."[139]

Representative Robert McClory replied to Wiggins' attainder argument
saying that "We are not thinking this up as an offense and then charging
the President with a violation of it." Instead, McClory characterized the
gravamen of Article 2 as being a violation of the president's oath "to see to
the faithful execution of laws." This was "quite different and distinct" from
the criminality charged in Article 1, that McClory had opposed.[140]

Lawrence J. Hogan noted that the impeachment of the Earl of Suffolk
in the fourteenth century had involved the abuse of office and that "our
Founding Fathers…used the same term, 'high crimes and misdemeanors,'
clearly intending not as a catch-all phrase with which to threaten Presidents
and confound lawyers and scholars and members of Judiciary Committees,
but as a broad, widely recognized standard of conduct." Thus, Hogan said,
"The abuse of power by those in high office, then, constituted what was
essentially the first impeachable offense, and what is still today the touch-
stone of our debate." With respect to the requirement of criminality, Hogan
noted that "the consistent abuse of power holds greater danger for the public than does a single criminal act," and therefore, Hogan considered the
charges in Article 2 to be "a much more serious offense and a far more serious charge than the one that this committee has already approved."[141]

Wayne Owens also responded to Wiggins, observing that Article 2 was
not a "grab bag of Presidential actions which the majority of the committee
thinks is unwise or bad or contrary to our national interest," but was based
upon "acts which would be clear violations of the standard of conduct for
any President, violations which are so grave and are such an abuse of the
presidential trust that the public well-being requires they be corrected."
Indeed, Owens said "each one of the abuses contained in Article II is adequate in itself to sustain impeachment." Article 2 was also consistent with
what the Framers intended "because they saw the only remedy against a
President for the unlawful enlargement of the executive power and the
encroachment upon individual liberties was through this type of stern
accountability, the only remedy."[142]

Article 2 was adopted on July 29 by a vote of twenty-eight (twenty-one
Democrats and seven Republicans) in favor and ten opposed.[143]

The third impeachment article charged the president with having "failed
without lawful cause or excuse to produce papers and things" as directed in
subpoenas issued by the Committee in the course of its investigation. By refusing to comply with the subpoenas, the Committee charged that Nixon had
"interposed the powers of the presidency against the lawful subpoenas of the

House of Representatives" and thereby had assumed "to himself functions and judgments necessary to the exercise of the sole power of impeachment vested by the Constitution in the House of Representatives." This too constituted a breach of the president's duty to see that the laws are faithfully executed.[144]

To Representative Robert W. Kastenmeier, preventing Congress from executing its constitutional duty was "a high crime in the classic sense which the Framers intended when they used that phrase in the Constitution."[145] Joshua Eilberg agreed, stating "If not by impeachment, how can the President, as a practical matter,…be disciplined or punished for non-compliance?"[146]

However, Representative M. Caldwell Butler questioned whether, standing alone, the president's "failure to cooperate in his own impeachment" should be an impeachable offense.[147] In response, Representative McClory reiterated the argument that impeachment was necessary to vindicate the Committee's subpoena power and stated that "we should tell the President, and this will be a guide for future Presidents or future impeachments, that if there is no response, or if the response is inadequate to the requests that we make, if our subpoenas are defied, why then, the Congress is going to take this kind of decisive action."[148]

On July 30, by a straight party-line vote of twenty-one in favor and seventeen opposed, the Committee adopted the third and final Article of Impeachment.[149]

*Additional Views of the Members*

Several members of the committee discussed the nature of impeachable offenses in their submissions of additional views after the debate. Congressman Danielson reiterated his conclusion that criminal conduct was not required, but rather "It is enough to support impeachment that the conduct complained of be conduct which is grossly incompatible with the offices held and which is subversive of that office and of our constitutional system of government."[150]

Ten of the Republican members of the Committee submitted what they characterized as "minority views." In their statement, the authors argued that only "serious criminal offenses," and not "errors in administration," warranted impeachment. As they explained, "There are types of misconduct by public officials—for example, ineptitutde [*sic*], or unintentional or 'technical' violations of rules or statutes, or 'maladministration'—which would not be criminal; nor could they be made criminal, consonant with the Constitution, because the element of criminal intent or *mens rea* would be lacking. Without a requirement of criminal acts or at least criminal intent, Congress would be free to impeach these officials."[151]

In his individual views, one of these minority members, Edward Hutchinson, observed that, "If the strict standards of criminal jurisprudence are not required in cases of Presidential impeachment, the issue falls away from the high plane of law and becomes political." To Hutchinson, the lack of clear standards in the absence of a requirement of criminality would grant too much discretion to use impeachment as a partisan weapon. Hutchinson warned that "In a divided government, with the Congress in control by one political party and the President of the other, impeachment becomes a threatening political tool, if one group of politicians can decide over another what is an abuse of power."[152]

## The Resignation and Pardon

Following the Supreme Court's July 24 decision that the tapes of presidential conversations had to be turned over pursuant to Judge Sirica's order, pressure grew for the president to resign rather than face impeachment and conviction in the Congress. At a pivotal meeting in the White House on August 7, 1974, Senators Barry Goldwater, John Rhodes, and Hugh Scott informed Nixon that he had the support of no more than fifteen senators. Goldwater informed Nixon that while an able lawyer might be able to mount a defense to Articles 1 and 3, Nixon would be convicted on Article 2 and, Goldwater told him, "I am leaning that way myself, Mr. President." At approximately 8:30 that evening, Nixon informed his chief of staff, Alexander Haig, that he would resign the presidency.[153]

On August 8 at 9:00 p.m., Nixon made a televised statement to the nation. He said that although he felt that it was his duty "to persevere" and to "complete the term of office" to which he had been elected, "In the past few days…it has become evident to me that I no longer have a strong enough political base in the Congress to justify continuing that effort.… Therefore, I shall resign the Presidency effective at noon tomorrow." In his only oblique reference to the Watergate and the cover-up, Nixon told the nation, "I regret deeply any injuries that may have been done in the course of the events that led to this decision. I would say only that if some of my judgments were wrong, they were made in what I believed at the time to be in the best interests of the nation."[154]

One month later, Gerald R. Ford, who had assumed the presidency upon the resignation and who had four years earlier sought the impeachment of Justice Douglas, pardoned Nixon on September 8, 1974.[155] Thus was the Watergate affair finally concluded.

Anticipation of impeachment proceedings in the House reignited scholarly discussions of whether the president could be impeached for other than indictable criminal conduct. In *Impeachment: Trials and Errors*, which was based on the statement he had submitted during consideration of the Douglas impeachment, Irving Brant argued that serious criminality was the necessary basis of impeachment and removal. The essence of Brant's argument was the same as that which had been made by the defense in the Johnson impeachment: that impeachment for other than an established criminal offense would be tantamount to an unconstitutional bill of attainder and ex post facto law.[156]

Raoul Berger, in *Impeachment: The Constitutional Problems*, took a contrary view. As noted previously, it was Berger's view that in parliamentary usage, high crimes and misdemeanors were "words of art confined to impeachments, without roots in the ordinary criminal law and which…had no relation to whether an indictment would lie in the particular circumstances." Accordingly, Berger concluded that when the Framers adopted the phrase high crimes and misdemeanors they intended to define "a category of *political* crimes against the state."[157]

A monograph published by the Committee on Federal Legislation of the Association of the Bar of the City of New York during the pendency of the Nixon proceedings also concluded that criminality was not a necessary predicate to impeachment and removal. Instead of limiting impeachment strictly to criminal offenses, the Committee argued that a president should be impeached and removed "only for conduct amounting to a gross breach of trust or serious abuse of power." The Committee further argued that high crimes and misdemeanors should be construed as conduct "which, like treason and bribery, undermine the integrity of government," regardless of "whether or not they happen to constitute offenses under the general criminal law." To the Committee, "the heart of the matter" was the determination whether "the office holder as demonstrated by his actions that he is unfit to continue in the office in question."[158]

In another work published during the pendency of the Nixon impeachment, Charles L. Black, Jr. found "the limitation of impeachable offenses to those offenses made generally criminal by statute is unwarranted—even absurd." Instead, Black argued that high crimes and misdemeanors should be understood as being of the same kind and character as treason and bribery. Thus, to Black, impeachable actions were "offenses 1) which are extremely serious, 2) which in some way corrupt or subvert the political and governmental process, and 3) which are plainly wrong in themselves to a person of honor, or to a good citizen, regardless of words on the statute books."[159]

Philip B. Kurland published *Watergate and the Constitution* several years after the conclusion of the Nixon impeachment proceedings. Kurland recognized that if interpretation of high crimes and misdemeanors were confined simply to the language of the Constitution, "a case might be made" that impeachment required evidence of crime. However, Kurland considered such a literal reading of the Constitution to be unduly strict.[160]

Kurland observed that the concern of the Framers "was over the abuse of official authority rather than concern with personal misbehavior of the office holder,"[161] and that "both at the convention that framed the Constitution and the conventions that ratified it, the essence of an impeachable offense was thought to be a breach of trust and not a violation of the criminal laws."[162] Addressing the charges lodged against President Nixon, Professor Kurland wrote that the Judiciary Committee had "proceeded to examine the evidence, not to determine whether the President had been guilty of particular violations of the criminal code, but to seek far more significant violations of the trust of his office," and had adopted articles "alleging such wrongdoings as would warrant removal from office because of that breach of faith, not because of acts that violated Title 18 of the United States Code."[163]

Nixon's resignation clearly blunted the ardor of the Congress to hold him accountable for the White House Horrors and the cover-up, including his defiance of Congress' inquiry into that conduct. The decision of the Judiciary Committee to impeach Nixon for abusive but not criminal conduct is highly significant, nevertheless. The Committee found in Nixon's conduct of the presidency the type of abuse and overreaching of presidential powers that threatened the constitutional order if left unremedied. The unjustified violation of the civil liberties of citizens, the political espionage that undermined the electoral process, and the cover-up to shield the involvement of the highest officers of government, including the president himself, in those unconstitutional acts, were high crimes and misdemeanors in the sense that the Framers intended the words to mean, regardless of whether the actions were also crimes with gross abuse of the powers of the presidency and not with the underlying criminality. Article 2 has been regarded as the essence of the case for the impeachment of a president,[164] and the charges clearly model the noncriminal breach of faith with the office that scholars as well as several of the Framers described as the true basis for impeachment.

Although the charges in Article 3 rested almost entirely on whether there was a good faith basis for the assertion of executive privilege, Nixon's steadfast refusal to produce the recordings of many of his conversations concerning the cover-up of the Watergate burglary and the White House Horrors put Nixon in a direct confrontation with Congress over the extent of Congress' authority to inquire into the conduct of his office. Nixon's intransigence in this regard resonated with his earlier refusal to apprise Congress of the covert military operations against Cambodia, and his refusal to carry out Congress' domestic policies by refusing to expend appropriated funds, both of which the Judiciary Committee considered as possible grounds for impeachment but ultimately did not pursue.[165]

In the case of Andrew Johnson, presidential defiance of Congress' authority and policies were the substance of the impeachment, while in Nixon's case his defiance was its precursor. Both impeachments underscore the risks of such defiance. To be sure, there is always a political risk, but if that defiance rises to the level of a president's derogation of Congress's legitimate authority, such that the constitutional balance of powers is threatened, then impeachment for high crimes and misdemeanors likely would follow.

# 4

# The Impeachment and Trial of William Jefferson Clinton

President William Jefferson Clinton became only the second president to be impeached, following acrimonious and highly partisan proceedings in the House. The charges of perjury and obstruction of justice that formed the basis of the impeachment arose from a lawsuit brought by Paula C. Jones alleging improper sexual conduct on Clinton's part when he was governor of Arkansas and Jones was a state employee, and Clinton's attempt to keep secret a sexual liaison he had had with a former White House intern, Monica Lewinsky, who was to be a witness in the *Jones* lawsuit. These charges differed materially from those brought against both President Johnson and President Nixon in that the misconduct attributed to Clinton, although criminal in nature, did not relate directly to his actions as president. Thus, the impeachment did not center upon an abuse of his public office or authority but rather was concerned exclusively with his character and fitness for office.

The facts underlying the charges were fairly simple, although the motivations of the principal actors were subject to multiple and contradictory interpretations. It has also been suggested that the impeachment's origins were personal animosity toward Clinton and a "scandal-soaked" and "corrosive" culture in Washington at the time.[1]

Thus, the legacy of the Clinton impeachment may be to illuminate the dangers of the impeachment remedy taken up by factions that "enlist all their animosities, partiality, influence and interest on one side or the other." For it is then, Hamilton warned, "There will always be the greatest danger that the decisions will be regulated more by the comparative strength of the parties, than by the real demonstrations of innocence or guilt."[2]

## The Starr Investigation

Among the legacies of the Watergate affair was the institutionalization of the special prosecutor by the Independent Counsel Act.[3] It was under the authority of that Act that in August 1994, Kenneth W. Starr, a former federal appellate court judge and solicitor general, was appointed to succeed Robert Fiske as the independent counsel investigating possible financial improprieties on the part of President William Jefferson Clinton and his wife Hillary in the Whitewater Land Development Corporation venture while Clinton was governor of Arkansas.[4]

Starr's investigation continued for five years. During that time, the subject matter of the investigation transmogrified to include not only the investigation of Whitewater, but an inquiry into the firing of personnel in the White House Travel Office and the misuse of FBI files relating to White House personnel. Although President Clinton would eventually be exonerated of any misconduct in these matters, Starr's investigation of the veracity of Clinton's testimony concerning his relationship with Monica Samille Lewinsky that Clinton had given in a civil lawsuit brought against Clinton by Paula Jones and later in the grand jury investigating his possible perjury, led to Starr's recommending that Clinton be impeached by the House of Representatives.

### *Paula Corbin Jones v. William Jefferson Clinton*

In 1991, Paula Rosalie Corbin was employed by the State of Arkansas in the Arkansas Industrial Development Commission. On May 8, 1991, she was working at the registration desk of a conference sponsored by the commission. She subsequently alleged that while at the registration desk, she had been approached by an Arkansas State Trooper, Danny Ferguson, who invited her to accompany him to meet the governor of Arkansas, William Jefferson Clinton.[5] Paula Jones (as she was known following her marriage) contended that shortly after entering the governor's hotel suite, Clinton had made uninvited sexual advances toward her that she rebuffed. Jones further contended that in the ensuing months, she and Clinton had one other "abhorrent" encounter in the rotunda of the state capital.[6]

On May 6, 1994, three years after her first alleged encounter with Clinton, Jones filed a civil suit in the U.S. District Court in Little Rock, Arkansas on the grounds that Clinton's conduct had deprived her of rights secured under the Constitution and the Civil Rights Act. She claimed that Clinton had conspired with Ferguson and others to deprive her of the equal protection of the laws and that his and their actions constituted an intentional infliction of emotional distress.[7] Finally, Jones claimed that she had been defamed by statements made by Clinton and others that Jones was a "liar" and was "pathetic."[8] Jones sought monetary damages in the amount of $700,000.[9]

Clinton asked the district court to dismiss the complaint on the grounds that as president he was immune from civil suit during his presidency. The district court denied the request and ordered that each side take discovery. The federal court of appeals affirmed the district court's refusal to dismiss the case but reversed the district court's decision that the trial should be stayed until Clinton left office.[10] Appeal was then taken to the U.S. Supreme Court, which on May 27, 1997, affirmed the decision of the court of appeals, allowing the suit to go forward.[11]

### *Disclosure of the Lewinsky Affair*

Beginning in early 1995, Monica Lewinsky worked as an unpaid intern in the Office of the White House Chief of Staff, Leon Panetta. At the time, Lewinsky was twenty-one years old. On November 13 of that year, Lewinsky was offered a position as a paid-staff member in the White House Office of Legislative Affairs. Two days later, Lewinsky and Clinton had the first of what Clinton would later describe as "inappropriate encounters." There would be ten such encounters between November 15, 1995, and March 29, 1997.[12]

Lewinsky discussed her relationship with Clinton with her mother, her analyst, and several of her friends. One of these friends was Linda Tripp, who had worked in the White House before transferring to the Pentagon as a Public Affairs Specialist. Lewinsky had also been transferred to the Pentagon after members of the White House staff became concerned that Lewinsky was spending too much time near the Oval Office and it was at the Pentagon that Tripp and Lewinsky met.[13]

Unbeknownst to Lewinsky, beginning in late September 1997, Tripp surreptitiously (and illegally) recorded approximately twenty-two hours of her telephone conversations with Lewinsky.[14] In November, Tripp disclosed her conversations with Lewinsky about Clinton to the attorneys representing Jones. On December 5, 1997, the attorneys identified Lewinsky as a possible witness at trial.[15]

### *Employment Assistance for Lewinsky*

In the meantime, when Lewinsky was unable to secure reassignment from the Pentagon to the White House, Lewinsky requested Clinton's help in finding employment in New York City and on or about September 30, Clinton asked members of his staff to assist Lewinsky. Not satisfied with the offer of a position at the U.S. Mission to the United Nations, Lewinsky asked Clinton whether his friend Vernon Jordan, a prominent Washington attorney, could do something for her.[16]

Lewinsky met with Jordan on November 5 to discuss other employment opportunities in New York. Jordan met with Clinton later that afternoon and on December 11, Jordan placed calls on Lewinsky's behalf to Young & Rubicam; MacAndrews & Forbes Holdings; and American Express Company.[17]

### *The Lewinsky Affidavit*

On December 15, Clinton was served with a request from the attorneys for Jones seeking documents relating to his communications with Lewinsky. During an early morning telephone conversation on December 17, Clinton informed Lewinsky that she could be called as a witness in the *Jones* case.

On December 19, Lewinsky was served with a subpoena to give testimony at a deposition in the *Jones* case. Jordan arranged for Lewinsky to be represented by an attorney, Frank Carter.[18] Jordan accompanied Lewinsky to her meeting with Carter on December 22.[19]

Lewinsky told Carter that she did not want to be drawn into the *Jones* matter and that she wanted to avoid being deposed. Carter suggested submitting an affidavit in lieu of her testimony.[20]

Carter gave Lewinsky a draft affidavit on January 6, 1998. Later that day, Lewinsky met with Jordan to review the affidavit. Lewinsky deleted a portion of the affidavit that suggested she had been alone with Clinton. Lewinsky categorically denied having had "a sexual relationship with the President." Lewinsky executed the affidavit the following day.[21]

On January 8, Lewinsky had a second interview at MacAndrews and Forbes. The vice president who interviewed her concluded that while Lewinsky was not suited to a position at MacAndrews & Forbes, he would forward her resume to Revlon, a company controlled by MacAndrews & Forbes. Later that day, Jordan called Ronald Perlman, chairman and CEO of MacAndrews & Forbes, on Lewinsky's behalf. After a further interview on January 9, Lewinsky was offered a position at Revlon. Jordan left a message for Clinton with his secretary, Betty Currie. The message was: "Mission accomplished."[22]

### *The Hearing in the District Court on January 12, 1998*

On January 12, 1998, Judge Susan Weber Wright, who was presiding over the *Jones v. Clinton* suit, held a pretrial conference to discuss, among other things, the witnesses who would be called to testify at trial. Monica Lewinsky was among the witnesses identified by Jones' counsel.

Arguing that Lewinsky should not be called to testify, the president's counsel, Robert S. Bennett, directed the judge's attention to Lewinsky's denial of a sexual relationship in her affidavit and stated that "there is absolutely no sex of any kind in any manner, shape or form, with President Clinton." The president, who was in the courtroom, remained silent during Bennett's presentation. When asked during his grand jury appearance whether he should have informed the judge "of the true state of affairs," Clinton said that he had not been paying attention.[23] When he was asked whether Bennett's statement was in fact false, Clinton famously remarked, "It depends on what the meaning of 'is' is."[24]

### Starr's Questioning of Lewinsky

Also on January 12, Linda Tripp, Lewinsky's erstwhile confidant, contacted Starr's office and told the investigators that Lewinsky was going to make false statements about her relationship with Clinton in her affidavit in the *Jones* case and that Clinton had encouraged her to do so. Tripp also told Starr's staff about the tapes of her conversations with Lewinsky. Approximately one hour later, Tripp was interviewed by Starr's investigators.[25]

The following day, Tripp met Lewinsky for lunch. Tripp was wearing a transmitting device and the FBI recorded their conversation, which lasted for approximately three hours. On January 16, the attorney general asked that Starr's authority be enlarged to include investigation of the Lewinsky matter.[26]

When Tripp again met Lewinsky for breakfast on Friday, January 15, the FBI quickly took Lewinsky into custody and escorted her to a room in the hotel in which the restaurant was located. Lewinsky was held for approximately twelve hours without being allowed to consult with her attorney despite her request to do so. During that time, Lewinsky was threatened with prosecution for a variety of federal crimes, including perjury and obstruction of justice, unless she gave testimony against Clinton and she allowed "consensual monitoring" of her conversations with Clinton, Betty Currie, and Vernon Jordan. Starr's staff also threatened to prosecute Lewinsky's mother. Lewinsky was allowed to leave the hotel at 12:23 a.m. Saturday morning with her mother, who had arrived from New York City approximately an hour earlier. Later that day, President Clinton was examined by the attorneys representing Paula Jones.[27]

### President Clinton's Deposition in the Jones Case

President Clinton was examined under oath in the *Jones* case on January 17. Judge Wright presided over the president's deposition.

Clinton was questioned extensively concerning Monica Lewinsky. Clinton testified that he had seen Lewinsky two or three times during the government shut down in the fall of 1995 but he could not recall whether they had been alone, although he stated that it was possible they had been. Clinton acknowledged receiving a few gifts from Lewinsky and giving her several gifts. Clinton denied having had a sexual relationship with Lewinsky and affirmed that the denial of a sexual relationship in Lewinsky's affidavit was "absolutely true." Clinton also said that he had been unaware of conversations between Lewinsky and Jordan concerning the *Jones* case.[28]

### *Ruling on the Admissibility of Evidence Concerning Lewinsky*

Twelve days after Clinton's deposition, on January 29, Judge Wright held a hearing on Starr's request to foreclose further discovery concerning Lewinsky that might impair Starr's investigation. Judge Wright granted Starr's request that day and held that evidence of the president's relationship with Lewinsky would not be entertained in the *Jones* case. Judge Wright stated that the Lewinsky evidence was "not essential to the core issues in this case" and that in fact, "some of this evidence might even be inadmissible as extrinsic evidence" under the Federal Rules of Evidence.[29] Judge Wright affirmed her order in a written decision on March 9.[30] On April 1, 1998, Judge Wright granted the motions for summary judgment filed by Clinton and his codefendant, Danny Ferguson, finding Jones' sexual harassment and other claims to be unsupported.[31]

### *Clinton's Testimony before the Grand Jury*

In what the Judiciary Committee majority described as "the last act of the tragedy," Clinton was examined, again under oath, by members of Starr's staff before the grand jury on August 17, 1998. In his preliminary statement, Clinton acknowledged "inappropriate intimate conduct" with Lewinsky, but denied engaging in sexual intercourse or sexual relations "as I understood that term to be defined at my January 17th deposition."[32]

Clinton testified before the grand jury for approximately five hours. Later that evening, Clinton made a televised statement concerning his grand jury testimony and his relationship with Lewinsky. With respect to his deposition testimony regarding Lewinsky, Clinton said that, "While my answers were legally accurate, I did not volunteer information." Clinton then acknowledged for the first time publicly that he had had a relationship with Lewinsky. Clinton told the nation "I did have a relationship with Miss Lewinsky that was not appropriate. In fact, it was wrong. It constituted a critical lapse in judgment and a personal failure on my part for which I am solely and completely responsible." Clinton further acknowledged that "My public comments and my silence about this matter gave a false impression," and that he had "misled people, including my wife." Nevertheless, he denied having asked "anyone to lie, to hide or destroy evidence, or to take any other unlawful action."[33]

## The Impeachment Proceedings in the House

### *The Referral by Starr*

But that, of course, was not the end of it. On September 9, 1998, apparently without notifying anyone on the Judiciary Committee, Starr delivered a report to Congress recommending impeachment.[34] The report set forth the factual "findings" of the independent counsel's investigation and was accompanied by six volumes of documents.[35] In his referral, Starr identified a total of eleven grounds for impeachment, primarily that Clinton had lied under oath in the *Jones* litigation and in the grand jury concerning his sexual relationship with Lewinsky and that he had obstructed justice in order to conceal that relationship. Starr charged that Clinton had "abused his constitutional authority" by lying to the public and to Congress.[36]

### *The Initial Response of the President*

Despite being denied an opportunity to review the Starr Report, President Clinton filed an initial response to the report on September 11 (the day of the report's public release), in which he set forth the essence of his defense to Starr's allegations of high crimes and misdemeanors.

In his response, Clinton stated that impeachment was intended "to remedy the most serious forms of public wrongdoing" and "to correct harms to the system of government itself and to protect the people from ongoing malfeasance." Thus, "Nothing less than the gravest executive wrongdoing can justify impeachment." Clinton acknowledged that his attempt to keep his affair with Lewinsky private was a "personal failure." However, because impeachment "attempts to rein in abuses of the public trust committed by public officeholders in connection with conduct in public office," public rather than private wrongdoing was to be addressed by impeachment.[37]

### *The Impeachment Inquiry Begins*

On October 5, 1998, the House Judiciary Committee met to hear the opening presentations by the Majority Chief Investigative Counsel,

David P. Shippers, and by the Minority Chief Investigative Counsel, Abbe D. Lowell. Shippers advised the Committee of the report and documents received from Starr and "some information and analysis that was furnished by the counsel for the President." Shippers told the Committee "We did not seek to procure any additional testimony from any other source."[38] Shippers then stated that there was "substantial and credible evidence," including the testimony of Lewinsky, of fifteen acts that "could constitute felonies which, in turn, may constitute grounds to proceed with the impeachment inquiry." Each of the acts related to Clinton's false statements and attempts to suborn false statements by Lewinsky and others.[39]

Minority Counsel Lowell objected to the Committee's exclusive reliance on the record provided by the Independent Counsel, whose investigation Lowell described as "one-sided." Lowell also emphasized the private consensual nature of the Clinton-Lewinsky relationship, which underlay the allegations presented by the independent counsel and the majority investigative counsel. Lowell noted that the dismissal of the *Jones* case pointed up the lack of significance of the purported misstatements. Lowell also disputed the basis and significance of the alleged obstruction of justice by Clinton.[40]

A letter signed by thirteen law professors was also entered into the record by Lowell. In their letter, the professors stated their conclusion that "The Independent Counsel's report does not make a case for presidential impeachment." The professors also stated their view that the enumerated offenses of treason and bribery are paradigmatic offenses from which the meaning of high crimes and misdemeanors can be derived, as they both involve the exercise of official executive powers, which the alleged acts by Clinton did not, and that "Short of heinous criminality, impeachment demands convincing evidence of grossly derelict exercise of official authority."[41]

On October 8, the House adopted Resolution 581, authorizing the Judiciary Committee "to investigate fully and completely whether sufficient grounds exist for the House of Representatives to exercise its constitutional power to impeach William Jefferson Clinton, President of the United States of America."[42]

On November 5, the committee issued eighty-one "Requests for Admissions of the President of the United States Related to House Resolution 581." These requests concerned Clinton's oath of office, his testimonial oath in regard to the *Jones* deposition, and his testimony before the grand jury; assistance given to Lewinsky in finding employment; Clinton's clandestine meetings with Lewinsky; Clinton's knowledge of the Lewinsky subpoena in the *Jones* litigation; Clinton's conversations with Lewinsky concerning the gifts; Clinton's knowledge of the affidavit executed by Lewinsky; Clinton's conversations with staff concerning his relationship with Lewinsky; the use of private investigators by the president's defense; allegedly false and misleading public statements; and the invocation of executive privilege by staff members.[43] Clinton responded to these requests on November 27, relying primarily on statements already in the record.[44]

The Committee held a series of hearings that were intended to illuminate the circumstances warranting the impeachment of a president and the significance of Clinton's misconduct in regard to the cover-up of the Lewinsky affair.

### The Hearing Concerning the Background and History of Impeachment

Two letters were sent to the Judiciary Committee urging that the impeachment proceedings against President Clinton not go forward. The first, dated October 28, 1998, was signed by 400 historians under the heading, "Historians in Defense of the Constitution." Although the signatories made it clear that they condoned neither Clinton's "private behavior" nor his "subsequent attempts to deceive," they stated that "the current charges against him depart from what the framers saw as grounds for impeachment." They viewed Resolution 581 as creating "a novel, all-purpose search for any offense by which to remove a President from office" and warned that such a proceeding would "leave the Presidency permanently disfigured and diminished, at the mercy as never before of the caprices of any Congress."[45]

The second letter was sent on November 6 and was signed by 432 law school professors.[46] Like the historians, the law professors also emphasized that the misconduct alleged by Starr and by Chief Investigative Counsel Shippers did not constitute high crimes and misdemeanors that would justify the impeachment and removal of Clinton.[47] The law professors observed that the crimes of treason and bribery both involve the exercise of executive powers but that "Much of the misconduct of which the President is accused does not involve the exercise of executive powers at all." Although the professors recognized that perjury and obstruction of justice could under some circumstances constitute impeachable offenses, Clinton's false statements "about sexual improprieties is not a sufficient constitutional basis to justify the trial and removal from office of the President of the United States." The law professors urged the House to exercise prosecutorial discretion and forebear from asserting its impeachment power. Such power, they said, should only be exercised "when circumstances genuinely justify the enormous price the nation will pay in governance and stature if its president is put through a long, public, voyeuristic trial."[48]

Many of these themes were debated in hearings held on November 9, 1998, by the Judiciary Committee's Subcommittee on the Constitution concerning the background and history of impeachment. While the proceedings were aptly described by one of the witnesses who testified as "mind numbing,"[49] there was a broad discussion of the conflicting interpretations of high crimes and misdemeanors by the nineteen witnesses who testified. Their testimony reflected the larger debate in the Congress, where there was little consensus concerning the appropriate grounds for presidential impeachment.

Although there was general agreement among the witnesses that proof of indictable criminality was not a requirement for impeachment, there was sharp disagreement over the significance of the misconduct that had been attributed to Clinton. These disagreements centered on whether Clinton should be impeached because his conduct demonstrated a lack of integrity and fitness to serve as president or because he had violated his oath of office to "take care that the laws were faithfully executed." There was also sharp disagreement whether private wrongdoing was an adequate basis for removal from office or whether such wrongdoing had to arise from the performance of official duties and whether, in any event, Clinton's alleged misconduct rose to the level of seriousness intended by the Framers as grounds for impeachment.

### Fitness for Office

Four members of a panel of professors argued that conduct reflecting on the president's fitness for office could warrant impeachment. John C. Harrison of the University of Virginia stated that "serious misconduct that compromises the officer's integrity or fitness for office" would support impeachment "whether or not the conduct itself involves abuse of office or injures the government."[50] Richard D. Parker of Harvard University similarly testified that "impeachable conduct" is that which damages the president's capacity to lead and thus, "gravely impairs his fitness for office."[51] John O. McGinnis of Yeshiva University agreed that impeachment could reach "all serous and objective misconduct that undermines an official's fitness for further service in office" regardless of whether such misconduct arose in the performance of public duties because" "the real purpose" of impeachment is "removing an official who is unfit for office."[52] Thus, to Stephen B. Presser of Northwestern University, "when it becomes clear that the President has committed acts which raise grave doubts about his honesty, his virtue, or his honor, impeachment is available as a remedy."[53]

This view of impeachable conduct was disputed by Laurence H. Tribe of Harvard University and Susan Low Bloch of Georgetown University. Tribe warned that a fitness-based standard would result in a standard that was too broad and vague, which would leave the president as the "creature of Congress" that Madison had warned against.[54] Bloch also argued that a standard based on fitness for office was "much too broad and amorphous" and that "transgressions which some believe might make him unfit for office are to be judged not by Congress but by the electorate."[55]

### Oath to Take Care that the Laws are Faithfully Executed

Presser, Parker, and McGinnis further argued that conduct constituting a breach of the president's oath to "take care that the laws are faithfully executed" would also be grounds for impeachment. They were joined in this position by Griffin B. Bell, a former federal appellate judge and attorney general of the United States, who concluded that, "A President cannot faithfully execute the laws if he himself is breaking them."[56] Conformity with the oath of office was also central to Presser's analysis because to Presser, violation of the president's oath of office put into question whether he was "the kind of man of virtue, honor and integrity that his constitutional office demands." Presser noted that George Washington had emphasized in his farewell address that "if oaths ever lost their sacred sense of obligation…it would shake the foundation of the fabric of government itself."[57] McGinnis similarly observed that "fidelity to one's oath is also critical to retain the public trust and confidence of a republican leader because it demonstrates that despite his high position, he is as much subject to the social contract as any other citizen, even the least of the citizens."[58] Parker suggested that if the president were found to have violated the oath of office, it was the responsibility of the House "to impose some discipline upon the President."[59]

Tribe and Bloch disputed these contentions as well. Tribe observed that were the "Take Care" argument to be adopted, it would make it easier to impeach presidents than any other federal officer, including the vice president, because presidents would be "in the unique position of being subject to impeachment and removal whenever it becomes possible to pin a federal offense—any federal offense—on them."[60] Bloch too saw the risk that the Take Care argument "makes every single potential crime that a president might commit an impeachable offense," which simply "goes too far."[61]

### Public or Private Conduct

The witnesses differed sharply over whether private conduct could support impeachment or whether conduct relating to the execution of official duty was required. The impeachments of Judges Harry E. Claiborne,[62] Alcee L. Hastings,[63] and Walter L. Nixon,[64] were cited as precedent for impeachment based on private conduct. Citing the impeachment of Judge Claiborne on tax-related charges, Harrison argued that private conduct not involving an abuse of private office could be grounds for impeachment when the misconduct "bears on fitness for office" and "calls into question…integrity and truthfulness."[65] McGinnis agreed, noting that the unfitness of a judge is "far less damaging to the republic than the unfitness of its Chief Magistrate."[66]

To Judge Bell, however, the "good behavior" provision of judicial appointments suggested a "loose" impeachment standard for judges because they are subject to removal for misbehavior.[67] Cass R. Sunstein of the University of Chicago similarly noted that because judges enjoy life tenure, unlike presidents who are accountable to the electorate, "Congress has always treated federal judges very differently."[68] One of the ways in which judges are treated differently, as Block observed, is that judges may be convicted of crimes while in office and thus, there could be "the spectacle of judges convicted of crimes, sitting in jail, while collecting a paycheck as a federal judge," as Judge Claiborne had. Bloch further observed that removing a judge was "not at all comparable to the wrenching effect of removing the President," and therefore, "Enduring such a wrenching effect is not necessary unless the misconduct undermines the constitutional scheme."[69]

Michael J. Gerhardt of the College of William & Mary testified that the historical record showed that the Framers intended impeachment to redress "great or dangerous offenses causing some serious injury to the republic and/or reaching special trust held by virtue of the office held," which the Framers regarded as being political crimes. These political crimes were not the equivalent of indictable crimes but were "serious abuses of political power or serious breaches of the public trust, which might also, but not necessarily be punishable in the courts," and were limited to "the kinds of misconduct that can only be committed by some public officials by virtue of public offices or special trust that they hold."[70] Sunstein agreed that impeachment was intended to address "a narrow category of large-scale abuses of authority that came from the exercise of distinctly presidential powers," that is, "egregious misconduct that amounts to an abusive misuse of the authority of his office."[71]

Matthew Holden of the University of Virginia observed, as Justice Curtis had in the trial of Andrew Johnson, that the misconduct had to be "of a status equal to treason and bribery."[72] Tribe also viewed use of "other" in connection with crimes and misdemeanors as a "dead give away" that the misconduct must "bear some strong resemblance" to treason and bribery and thus, "must refer to major offenses against our very system of government, or serious abuses of the governmental power with which a public official has been entrusted…or grave wrongs in pursuit of governmental power."[73] Bloch too found in the use of "other" and the enumeration of treason and bribery as the "quintessential impeachable offenses" that "impeachable wrongs are those that undermine the state or our constitutional system,"[74] or as Arthur M. Schlesenger of the City University of New York described them, "grave and momentous offenses against the Constitution."[75]

## The Balance of Powers

Several witnesses put impeachable conduct in the larger context of the balance of powers. Jack N. Rakove of Stanford University cited the Framers' concern with the untested presidency and noted that the Framers were "thinking primarily, indeed exclusively, about failure to perform the duties of office or a misuse of its powers, in ways that manifestly endangered the public good." Rakove acknowledged the possibility that a "reprehensible private act" might rise to the level of high misdemeanor, but the Framers "were preoccupied with the public performance of institutions and office holders, not the regulation of all the human vices."[76]

Father Robert F. Drinan of Georgetown University, who as a congressman had been a member of the Judiciary Committee during the Nixon proceedings, also viewed impeachment in the framework of the balance of powers. Drinan told the Committee that "it seems clear…that impeachment was placed in the Constitution as a final safety net in case somehow the separation of powers did not work and that a near tyrant in the executive branch could not be stopped by any means short of removal."[77] To Drinan, the impeachment power was to be reserved "only for a dire situation for which no other political remedy exists" in which there has been a "reprehensible exercise of official authority by the President."[78]

## Clinton's Conduct

Several witnesses addressed the specific allegations made by Starr. Sunstein told the Committee that in his view, while a "false statement about illicit consensual sexual relationship, is not excusable or acceptable…it is not a high crime or misdemeanor under the Constitution" and that "it trivializes the Constitution to say that any false statement under oath, regardless of its subject matter, provides a proper basis for impeachment."[79] Daniel H. Pollit of the University of North Carolina said that as impeachment is to be grounded on "conduct totally incompatible with the constitutional obligations of the presidential office," in his view, "it is doubtful that perjury in a civil suit reaches the onerous requirements of an impeachable offense."[80] Sunstein noted that a false statement under oath would be grounds for impeachment, "if and only if the false statement involved conduct that by itself raises serious questions about the abuse of office."[81]

Thus, Rakove observed, "Whatever insult the president's conduct may have delivered to the legal system—and the consequences of that insult remain both speculative and doubtful—must be weighed against the palpable stretching of the boundaries of impeachable offenses that this inquiry risks entailing." In Rakove's view, the alleged misconduct "lies at the far boundaries of what might be considered impeachable" because the allegations involved "essentially private and non-official conduct."[82]

The Reports of the Impeachment Staff on the<br>Grounds for Impeachment

On November 5, just prior to the hearing on the background and history of impeachment, the Majority Impeachment Staff issued its report on the constitutional grounds for impeachment.[83] On December 16, the Minority Staff issued its report.[84] The competing views of the Majority and Minority Staffs reflected the fundamental differences among the members of the Judiciary Committee itself.

The ostensible purpose of the Majority Staff report was to provide the Judiciary Committee with an updated version of the report that had been prepared for the Committee by the Impeachment Staff in 1974.[85]

The Majority Staff eschewed an intention to define the offenses that would subject a federal official to impeachment by the House, in favor of a case-by-case approach.[86] Following that approach, the Majority Staff presented its interpretation of the Claiborne, (Walter) Nixon, and Hastings impeachments. The Majority Staff endorsed the conclusion that the same constitutional standards should apply to both judicial and other civil officers, including the president.[87]

The Majority Staff also referred to the impeachment proceedings against President Nixon. The staff recognized that "it is impossible to know how the House of Representatives and the Senate would have viewed the articles of impeachment." However, the staff observed that "the first article emphasized the obstruction of justice by President Nixon and the second article emphasized his abuse of power."[88]

The Majority Staff drew four conclusions, or "guiding principles," concerning impeachable conduct. Those conclusions were: "First, in most instances of impeachment since 1974, making false and misleading statements under oath has been the most common compelling basis for impeachment—whether it is before a jury, a grand jury, or on a tax return; Second, the constitutional standard for impeachable offenses is the same for federal judges as it is for presidents and all other civil officers; Third, impeachable offenses can involve both personal and professional misconduct; Fourth, impeachable offenses do not have to be federal or state crimes."[89]

Not surprisingly, the Minority Staff was quite critical of the Majority Staff report, whose conclusions were characterized as being "misleading if not outright false." The Minority Staff presented a lengthy discussion of its view of the intent of the Framers, the Watergate staff report, the Johnson and Nixon proceedings and the "views of the scholars," all to the effect that "a president should only be impeached for conduct which constitutes an abuse or subversion of the powers of the executive office." In keeping with this view of impeachable conduct, the Minority Staff interpreted the high crimes and misdemeanors standard as meaning conduct that is "in the nature of large scale abuses of public office—similar to treason and bribery." The Minority Staff read the proceedings of the constitutional convention as establishing that "the Framers intended impeachment to be a very limited remedy, reserved for the most egregious misconduct subversive of government."[90]

The Minority Staff also took exception to the Majority Staff's representation of the Watergate staff report. The Minority Staff noted that while there was agreement that "violation of the criminal laws is not a prerequisite for impeachment," the Watergate staff had concluded that criminal conduct did not necessarily warrant impeachment but rather that "the misconduct is so grave as to threaten our constitutional form of government or the president's duties there under[.]" With respect to the Johnson and Nixon impeachments, the Minority Staff argued that those proceedings also demonstrated that in order for offenses to be impeachable, "they must arise out of a president's public, not private conduct."[91]

The Minority Staff differed with the Majority Staff as to the relevance of judicial impeachment to the impeachment of the president. It was the opinion of the Minority Staff that "[a] review of the historical record and consideration of the different responsibilities and roles of presidents and judges under the Constitution make it clear that the positions are and should be subject to differing impeachment considerations." The Minority Staff concluded, "for Congress to reverse the choice of the electorate and remove the nation's leader raises concerns of a wholly different magnitude than are at issue in judicial proceedings."[92]

*The Hearing Concerning the Consequences of*
*Perjury and Related Crimes*

Several witnesses at the Committee's earlier hearing on the background and history of impeachment testified that perjury would constitute high crimes and misdemeanors under English common law[93] and within the meaning of the Constitution.[94] Subsequently, a hearing was held by the

Judiciary Committee on December 1, 1998, directed at whether perjury and obstruction of justice as alleged against President Clinton would rise to the level of high crimes and misdemeanors warranting impeachment.[95]

A variety of witnesses testified. Two women, Pam Parsons and Dr. Barbara Battalino, testified concerning their convictions for perjury and obstruction of justice as a consequence of their having given false testimony in civil trials concerning illicit sexual relations.[96] Two retired military officers, Rear Admiral Leon A. Edny and Lieutenant General Thomas P. Carney, testified concerning the importance of honesty and integrity in the code of ethics of the armed forces.[97] Three federal judges spoke to the legal significance of perjury to the functioning of the judicial system.[98]

Law Professors Alan M. Dershowitz and Jeffrey Rosen of George Washington University expressed skepticism whether "an ordinary citizen" would be prosecuted under the same circumstances as those in Clinton's case. Rosen joined with Professor Stephen A. Saltzburg of George Washington University and former Attorney General Elliot L. Richardson in urging the committee to consider censure rather than impeachment. Rosen noted that regardless of Congress's action, Clinton would face civil and criminal sanction after leaving office.[99]

### *The Presentation on Behalf of the President*

The factual basis for the Committee's deliberations was the record prepared by the independent counsel, summarized in the *Starr Report*. Starr appeared before the Committee on November 19.[100] The president was also allowed to make a presentation to the Committee on December 8 and 9.[101] The president's defense reprised several themes that had been developed by witnesses in the earlier hearings. The first panel of witnesses addressed the nature of impeachment and whether the alleged misconduct was sufficiently grave to support impeachment. Two panels of witnesses who had been members of Congress and investigators in the Watergate matter drew comparisons between the Nixon and Clinton proceedings. The last panel, comprised of former federal prosecutors, responded to several witnesses in the hearing on the consequences of perjury and gave their views of the prosecutorial merit of the case against Clinton. In all, sixteen witnesses testified on behalf of the president.

With respect to the nature and grounds of impeachment, former Attorney General Nicholas Katzenbach urged the Committee to be mindful that impeachment was intended as a means of "removing a person from office whose conduct is so egregious as to justify reversing the process by which he was appointed or elected," and when viewed in that light,

Katzenbach told the Committee, "I cannot see any constitutional basis for impeachment." Sean Wilenz of Princeton University distinguished between a "political" procedure and a "politicized one," and cautioned the Committee against allowing the proceedings to become partisan. Samuel H. Beer of Harvard University likened the House proceedings to a vote of "no confidence" in the British Parliament and urged the Committee to consider whether "the national interests require the removal from office of the President." Beer noted that "the American people have twice answered that question by electing him to the American presidency."[102]

The two Watergate-related panels generally made unfavorable comparisons between the Nixon and Clinton proceedings. Former Congresswoman Elizabeth Holzman cautioned the Committee not to vote for impeachment "unless there is a strong likelihood of conviction in the Senate." Congressman Wayne Owens stressed both the bipartisanism of the Nixon proceedings and the gravity of the abuses of presidential power that had been at issue.[103] James Hamilton, the former deputy chief counsel of the Judiciary Committee, also pointed out that the purpose of impeachment was not to subject the president to impeachment, but rather "to protect the state and society against great and dangerous offenses that might reoccur if he is allowed to remain in office." Hamilton added that the allegations against Clinton "do not indicate that he is a danger to the nation."[104]

The panel of former federal prosecutors opined that "a responsible federal prosecutor" would not pursue the case laid out in the Starr report. As Ronald Noble, a former deputy attorney general, explained, a federal prosecution would not be brought under Department of Justice guidelines because the testimony was given in a civil suit and concerned lawful sexual activities between consenting adults; the testimony was irrelevant to the issue in the suit, and was immaterial, and ultimately inadmissible in the case; there was a settlement by the party who knew of the alleged false testimony; and there was evidence that the lawsuit had been funded by a political opponent of the president.[105]

The hearing concluded with the comments of the Chief White House Counsel, Charles F.C. Ruff. Ruff had served as the U.S. attorney for the District of Columbia, as well as the last Watergate special prosecutor. As other witnesses on behalf of the president had done, Ruff primarily addressed the inadequacies in and the lack of prosecutive merit of Starr's case. However, with respect to the issue of impeachable conduct, Ruff observed that while the opinions expressed to the Committee had not been unanimous, "any fair-minded observer must conclude that the weight of the historical and scholarly evidence leads to the conclusion that in order to have committed an impeachable offense, the President must have acted to subvert our system of government." Thus, Ruff told the Committee, "the core principle governing your deliberation should be that the only conduct that merits the drastic remedy of impeachment is that which subverts our system of government or renders the President unfit or unable to govern."[106]

### *The Deliberations in the House of Representatives*

After hearing presentations by Majority Counsel Shippers and Minority Counsel Lowell on December 10,[107] the Committee on the Judiciary took up consideration of articles of impeachment. Clinton was charged with various instances of perjury in his testimony in the *Jones* litigation and in the grand jury concerning his relationship with Lewinsky (Article 1). Clinton was also charged with perjury in regard to answers he had provided to written questions in the *Jones* case concerning other extramarital sexual relations (Article 2). Clinton was further charged with obstruction of justice in connection with his having encouraged Lewinsky to execute a false affidavit and to give false testimony; with his having endeavored to prevent disclosure of gifts exchanged with Lewinsky; with his having allowed his attorney to make false or misleading statements in the *Jones* case; and by making false or misleading statements to potential witnesses in the *Jones* case (Article 3). Lastly, Clinton was charged with abuse of his official powers by refusing to respond to written questions propounded by the Committee (Article 4).[108] The votes in favor of and in opposition to these articles reflected the political party affiliations of the committee members.[109] The articles were referred to the House by the Judiciary Committee on December 16.

The House debated the articles of impeachment on December 18 and 19. On December 19, the House adopted two articles of impeachment, the former Article 1 (perjury) and the former Article 3 (obstruction of justice). Once again, the votes of the House generally reflected the party affiliations of the members.[110]

### The Trial in the Senate

On January 7, 1999, the House managers appeared before the Senate and the trial of President Clinton was convened.[111] On January 8, the Senate summoned President Clinton to appear and answer the charges levied against him by the House.[112]

Clinton submitted his answer to the articles of impeachment on January 11, 1999. In his answer to Article 1, Clinton denied giving false testimony before the grand jury concerning his relationship with Lewinsky, or concerning the statements made to Judge Wright by his attorney and denied that he had attempted to influence the testimony of any witness. In answer to Article 2, Clinton denied encouraging Lewinsky to submit a false affidavit and noted that Lewinsky had testified that no one had asked her to lie or had promised her employment in exchange for her silence. Clinton denied obstructing justice by encouraging Lewinsky to conceal the gifts he had given her and denied that he had sought to prevent her from testifying by helping her find employment in New York City. Clinton also denied having attempted to influence the testimony of Betty Currie, or that he had obstructed justice when he misled his family, friends, and staff concerning his relationship with Lewinsky. Clinton objected to both Articles 1 and 2 as being vague and charging multiple offenses in each article.[113] The House managers responded by denying each factual assertion by Clinton and by opposing each affirmative defense in the president's answer.[114] The issues thus joined, the Senate proceeded to consider the articles of impeachment.

### The Presentation by the House

The Senate heard the factual presentations of the House managers on January 14 and 15. On January 16, House managers Stephen E. Buyer, Charles T. Canady, and Lindsey O. Graham presented the case for why the misconduct charged in the articles of impeachment warranted Clinton's removal. Manager Buyer stated the position of the House that "The core of the President's constitutional responsibilities is his duty to 'take care that the laws be faithfully executed.' And because perjury and obstruction of justice strike at the rule of law itself, it is difficult to imagine crimes that more clearly and directly violate the core Presidential constitutional duty."[115] Manager Graham opined that it is a "high crime" when "an important person hurts somebody of low means…It doesn't have to be a crime. It is just when you start using your office and you are acting in a way that hurts people, you have committed a high crime."[116] Manager Canady asserted that restricting impeachment to instances of the abuse of presidential power was "contrary to common sense" because who could "seriously argue that our Constitution requires that a President guilty of crimes such as murder, sexual assault or tax fraud remain in his office undisturbed?" Canady argued that as perjury and obstruction of justice interfere with "the proper exercise of governmental power," whether a president misuses the power vested in him or interferes with the exercise of power by other branches of government, "the result is the same: the due functioning of our system of government is in some respect hindered or defeated." In sum, Canady opined that viewed in the light of both British and American historical precedents, the purpose to be served by impeachment was "to provide a remedy for corrupt and lawless acts of public officials."[117]

Henry J. Hyde (chairman of the House Judiciary Committee) concluded the presentation of the House. Hyde emphasized that the case presented by the House was not "about sexual misconduct, infidelity or adultery," which, Hyde said, were "private acts and none of our business." Instead, Hyde contended, what was before the Senate was "willful, premeditated, deliberate corruption of the nation's system of justice, through perjury and obstruction of justice," which were "public acts." Hyde eschewed any "mean-spirited" motive on the part of the House but claimed that the case was about the "rule of law."[118]

## The Presentation by the President

On January 19, Chief White House Counsel Ruff opened the presentation of the president's defense. Before addressing the constitutional principles that would guide the Senate's deliberations, Ruff briefly reviewed "the events that have brought us here today." Ruff criticized the "central premise" of the House case that perjury should be impeachable "no matter the forum or the circumstances in which it is committed." Ruff argued in this connection that perjury "about some official act may indeed be a constitutionally acceptable basis for impeachment" but that perjury "about a purely private matter should, at the very least, lead this body to question whether…the drastic remedy of removal from office is the proper response."[119]

Ruff also challenged the second major premise of the House's case that because federal judges had been removed on the basis of perjury, the president must be removed as well if he too committed perjury. Ruff pointed out that "whether weighing the constitutional or governmental implications of removal or asking whether the accused can be expected to perform his duties, the Senate has always recognized the test will be different depending on the office the accused holds." Thus, in making the ultimate determination "whether the conduct charged against President Clinton would, in its nature, be inconsistent with a decision to allow him to continue to perform the duties of his office," the Senate had to consider whether "removal is required despite the institutional trauma it may cause" and whether removal from office was necessary when, unlike judges, the president's term of office is finite and is subject to popular election.[120]

Ruff concluded his presentation with a close analysis of the defects and deficiencies of each of the impeachment articles.[121] Greg Craig, special counsel to the president, and Cheryl Mills, deputy White House counsel, continued the president's presentation on January 20. Special Counsel Craig addressed the facts underlying the allegations of perjury before the grand jury set forth in Article 1.[122] Deputy White House Counsel Mills spoke to the allegations in Article 2 of obstruction of justice in regard to gifts that Lewinsky had asked Currie to hold for her and in regard to a conversation between the president and Currie following the President's deposition in the *Jones* lawsuit.[123] The president's personal lawyer, David Kendall, completed the president's presentation concerning the articles of impeachment by addressing the remaining allegations of obstruction of justice in Article 2.[124] Finally, Dale Bumpers, who had served both as governor of Arkansas and as its senator, spoke to his former senatorial colleagues of the political and personal considerations of the impeachment, and the need for "proportionality."[125]

### *Questions by the Senate*

During the two days of questioning by the Senate of the managers and counsel, there was relatively little colloquy concerning the nature of impeachable conduct. In answer to a question propounded by Senator Robert C. Byrd asking how the president had violated or abused the public's trust, White House counsel Ruff stated that "When we speak of the kind of political…offenses against the man in his public role, we speak of offenses which this body must ultimately judge as being so violative of his public responsibilities that our system cannot abide his continuing in office." Thus, Ruff said, the issue for the Senate was whether the constitutional system was "so endangered that we must not only turn the President over to the same rule of law that any other citizen would be put under, after he leaves office, but must we cut short his term and overthrow the will of the nation?" The House managers argued to the contrary that while the president should not be impeached for a "mistake in judgment" or a "momentary lapse," a president should be impeached and removed "if he engages in a conscious and deliberate and settled choice to violate the laws of the land."[126]

In response to a question from Senator Robert G. Torricelli and Senator John D. Rockefeller whether a president could be impeached for nonofficial conduct, Ruff responded that private conduct could not be "so egregious that the people simply could not contemplate the notion of a president's remaining in office." Thus, he said, "the focus of attention must be…on the public character of the man and of his acts."[127]

The following day, Manager Graham made several startling concessions on behalf of the House. Replying to a question from Senators Peter

G. Fitzgerald, Orrin G. Hatch, Gordon Smith, and Strom Thurmond, concerning the proportionality argument made by former Senator Bumpers, Graham conceded that the standard for the impeachment of federal judges was different from the standard for impeachment of a president (thereby distinguishing the precedents of Judges Claiborne, Nixon, and Hastings upon which the House had previously relied). Graham also conceded that even were the Senate to conclude that Clinton's conduct amounted to a high crime or misdemeanor, the Senate also had to consider "the impact on society" of a decision to remove the president. Finally, in response to a question posed by Senators Herb Kohl and John Edwards, Graham further conceded that even if the Senate found that Clinton had engaged in the conduct alleged in the articles of impeachment, "reasonable people" could disagree whether the conduct constituted high crimes or misdemeanors warranting removal.[128]

White House Counsel Ruff seized on these concessions in his reply to a question put forward by Senators Mike DeWine, Rick Santorum, and Peter Fitzgerald whether the allegations if provided would constitute impeachable offenses. Ruff told the Senate that "not only can reasonable people differ on the facts, but reasonable people may differ on the outcome." That being the case, Ruff said, "if, indeed, reasonable people can differ, doesn't that mean by the very statement of that proposition that this body cannot meet its constitutional heavy mandate," which was to determine whether or not "the Senate can legitimately determine that [the president] ought to be removed from office."[129]

In lieu of calling witnesses, the Senate allowed video-taped depositions to be taken of Monica Lewinsky, Vernon Jordan, and Sidney Blumenthal, an assistant to the president.[130] After hearing the final presentations of the House managers and the counsel for the president on February 6[131] and February 8,[132] the Senate met in closed session on February 10[133] and February 11[134] to deliberate over the articles of impeachment.


*The Deliberations in the Senate*


The comments of the senators following their deliberations, as well as their written statements submitted for the record, reflected a broad disparity of views not only as to Clinton's factual guilt or innocence of the charges set forth in the articles of impeachment, but also as to the essential nature of the conduct that would warrant Clinton's removal. As Senator Russell Feingold observed, "The historical and legal authorities on the question of what constitutes 'other high crimes or misdemeanors' are varied and not wholly consistent."[135] Indeed, of the eight senators whose statements took the view that perjury and obstruction of justice were high crimes and misdemeanors, four voted to acquit Clinton.[136]

A number of senators voting to convict Clinton focused on the sanctity of the testimonial oath. As Senator James N. Inhofe said, Clinton, "had a moral obligation, as a citizen, to comply with ordinary and proper legal procedure and to faithfully abide by the standard oath 'to tell the truth, the whole truth, and nothing but the truth.'"[137] Agreeing with Senator Inhofe's sentiment, Senator Charles Hagel also viewed the question in moral terms, that "there can be no shading of right and wrong."[138] Other senators saw Clinton's acts as a betrayal of his office,[139] while several senators focused on the implications of Clinton's conduct for the "rule of law."[140]

In contrast, other senators argued, as did Senator Arlen Specter, that removal was not simply a question of factual guilt or innocence of the charges but required consideration of the national interest. According to Senator Specter, "Whether to impeach and convict transcends the facts and law to what is in the national interest at a specific time in the nation's history on the totality of circumstances." Such circumstances to Senator Specter included "clear and present danger to the integrity and stability of the national government," or conduct that was "so vile and reprehensible as to establish unfitness for office" or whether the electorate had "lost confidence in the President to the extent that he cannot govern."[141] In this regard, it was said that removal required proof of serious or "high" offenses,[142] such as "serious breaches of the Constitutional order which threaten the country in a direct and immediate manner" or "conduct that involves the President in the impermissible exercise of the powers of his office to upset the Constitutional Order."[143] Thus, as Senator Olympia J. Snowe observed, high crimes and misdemeanors under the Constitution, "speak to offenses that go to the heart of matters of governance, social authority, and institutional power—offenses that, in Hamilton's words, 'relate to injuries done immediately to society itself.'"[144] Both Senator Snowe and Senator Joseph R. Biden viewed removal as warranted only when necessary to protect the people and the Constitutional order from immediate danger. Thus, Senator Biden observed that in view of the "undemocratic nature" of the impeachment process and "the great dangers inherent in the too ready exercise of that power," impeachment and removal should be "reserved for breaches of the public trust by a president who so violates his official duties, misuses his official powers or places our system of government at such risk that our constitutional government is put in immediate danger by his continuing to serve out the term to which the people of the United States elected him."[145]

On February 12, 1999, the Senate convened in open session to announce the verdict. With respect to Article 1, charging Clinton with perjury before the grand jury, forty-five senators voted "guilty" and fifty-five senators voted "not guilty" and accordingly, President Clinton was acquitted of Article 1. As to Article 2, which charged Clinton with obstruction of justice, the Senate divided evenly, fifty senators voting "guilty" and fifty senators voting "not guilty," and thus, Clinton was acquitted of Article 2 as well. Thereafter, the Court of Impeachment was adjourned.[146]

Even in retrospect, it is difficult to separate the constitutional controversy surrounding whether there were adequate grounds for the impeachment and removal of President Clinton from the strongly partisan conflict that drove the impeachment effort forward, and perhaps they should not be. Commentators have suggested that the motive of the impeachment movement in the House was to satisfy the conservative base of the Republican Party in anticipation of the 1998 mid-term congressional elections.[147] Despite the strongest mid-term election showing of an incumbent president's party since 1934,[148] the Republican House leadership moved the impeachment forward expeditiously so that a bill of impeachment could be returned before the expiration of the 105th Congress.[149] This has led to the view that the impeachment was more a political stratagem than a vindication of the rule of law.[150]

In all events, the impeachment reflected a personal animosity toward Clinton reminiscent of that of the Radical Republicans toward Andrew Johnson. This animosity was startlingly personal.[151] But Clinton was also seen, particularly by "cultural conservatives," as a symbol of the moral ambiguity of American culture since the 1960s. As Judge Richard A. Posner observed, "it is not what Clinton says or does, but what he is, that is the provocation."[152] It was this personal dimension of the impeachment that caused Senator Byron L. Dorgan to caution his colleagues during the Senate deliberations, "Let us not aim at Bill Clinton and hit the Constitution."[153]

However, it would be a mistake, or at least an oversimplification, to examine the Clinton impeachment only through the lens of partisanship. Indeed, the failed effort to remove Clinton advanced the jurisprudence of American constitutional impeachment, in spite of itself.

First, the Clinton impeachment finally put to rest the question of whether criminality standing alone would justify impeachment and removal of the president. The failure of the impeachment charges based on Clinton's conduct outside of his official duties also resolved the corollary issue of whether a single standard for impeachment and removal was applicable to the president and to all other civil officers, particularly judges. While to be sure, Clinton's criminal culpability for perjury and obstruction of justice was not established to the satisfaction of even a majority of the Senate (only forty-five senators found Clinton "guilty" of perjury and fifty senators voted to convict Clinton of obstruction of justice), there was evidence from which a reasonable person could have found that Clinton had engaged in the acts charged in the articles of impeachment. Thus, half of the Senate concluded either that Clinton was not guilty of the crimes alleged or that the alleged crimes did not warrant impeachment and removal.

A fair reading of the record strongly suggests that the vote of the Senate was not confined to a determination of whether the House Managers had carried their burden of proof. Instead, both the weight of scholarly testimony and the deliberations in the Senate were to the effect that though some crimes may rise to the level of high crimes and misdemeanors, all crimes—even very serious, indictable crimes—do not necessarily do so. In that respect, the arguments of the impeachment advocates to establish an identity between criminality and high crimes and misdemeanors plainly failed and were rejected.

The Clinton proceedings also lend additional weight to the view that impeachable conduct, whether criminal or not, must either rise from, or relate to, or, at the very least have a direct substantial effect on, the execution of the public responsibilities of the president. In this regard as well, the proponents of the impeachment never fully overcame the argument that the gravamen of their case was the shielding from public scrutiny of an illicit but consensual sexual liaison. There was no suggestion that Clinton's misbehavior arose from the performance of his public office and notwithstanding the dire and often florid rhetoric to the contrary, there was virtually no evidence that Clinton's personal moral failings had had any effect on his ability to lead the country, domestically or internationally.

In this respect, the Clinton case also dispelled the theory that any conduct inconsistent with the president's duty to see to the faithful execution of the laws would support impeachment. Again to the contrary, the Clinton impeachment demonstrated that to be a fit subject of impeachment, the president's conduct must amount to a plain breach of constitutional duties or otherwise be so inimical to those duties as to be the equivalent of such a breach.

Finally, the Clinton proceedings demonstrated that there must be substantial and wide-spread, bipartisan support, certainly beyond a simple majority, for the immediate removal of the president from office before the impeachment power is invoked. Clinton's personal conduct had been extensively (if not exhaustively) ventilated during his first term in office and during his campaign for reelection. Yet, he was returned to office and even in the face of disclosure of his relationship with Monica Lewinsky and of his attempts at concealment, Clinton's approval ratings in public opinion polls were very high. Thus, it appears that the public was able to distinguish between Clinton's personal moral failings, of which the public did not approve,[154] and Clinton's performance of his public duties, of which the public generally approved, and accordingly, the public did not favor impeachment.[155]

Although the Republican majority in the House assured Clinton's impeachment, it was clear from the outset that there would not be sufficient votes in the Senate to remove him. The fact that the House proceeded with the impeachment despite the virtual certainty of acquittal also gave powerful support to the perception that the action of the House and its Republican leadership had as its object a purpose other than the discharge of the grave and momentous obligation to protect the Constitution and the Union from the usurpations of a corrupt or dangerous president.

Thus, the consequences of the Clinton impeachment stand in stark contrast to the impeachment proceedings against Presidents Johnson and Nixon. As several of the witnesses in the House proceedings observed, the charges against Clinton lacked the constitutional gravity that the Framers intended by high crimes and misdemeanors. By invoking the awesome power of impeachment in so sordid a way, the House brought dishonor upon itself and Congress, just as Clinton had brought dishonor upon himself and his presidency.

5

# Conclusion

When the delegates to the constitutional convention met in Philadelphia over the summer of 1787, the government they envisioned to replace the failed confederacy was one of enlarged but limited powers. Among the innovations to effectuate that vision was the creation of an Executive Magistracy endowed with broad powers to see to the faithful execution of the laws enacted by the bicameral congress. These powers would be centered in one individual, the newly created President of the United States.

The Executive Department was to enjoy a dignity equal to that of the Legislative and the Framers were at some pain to ensure that the president would not be subservient to or a creature of Congress. However, the fear that a concentration of power in the Executive could lead to a monarchy, albeit an elected one, dominated the constitutional debate. To meet the threat that would be posed to the separation of powers by a president who transgressed the political bounds of the office, the Framers recalled the long established English parliamentary practice of impeachment and removal.

In fashioning the impeachment process to their own purposes, the Framers relied upon not only their knowledge of English parliamentary usage but they also drew on the experience of the colonies and later the states where impeachment of executive and judicial officers had become an established practice. Similarly, in formulating the grounds for impeachment, the specification of treason, bribery, and "other high crimes and misdemeanors" was derived from their knowledge of English practice, their own new world experience, and their aspirations for the government they were creating.

Thus, when George Mason proposed high crimes and misdemeanors as an alternative to maladministration, he spoke in the shorthand of English parliamentary usage that had been brought to the minds of the delegates by the proceedings then ongoing in Parliament against Hastings. There was no debate as to the meaning of high crimes and misdemeanors because the Framers under-stood that Parliament had redressed as high crimes and misdemeanors official misconduct and perceived abuses of official power that were not within the contemplation of the common law, such as those asserted against Hastings, and therefore were considered to be beyond the jurisdiction of the courts.

However, by the time the issue of impeachment was resolved by the con-vention, the English practice of attainder (and implicitly the bills of pains and penalties) had been prohibited, thereby depriving Congress of Parliament's jurisdiction to adjudicate acts of individuals and to declare those acts to be criminal. Consistent with this, the consequences of impeachment and conviction were limited to removal and disqualification from public office. Thus, high crimes and misdemeanors as used by the Framers should be seen as having descriptive meaning informed by the shared sense among the Framers of what was to be accomplished by impeachment.

Nevertheless, the lack of specificity in the Constitution, or illumina-tion in the convention debates, has given rise to contentious dispute over the intended meaning of high crimes and misdemeanors, virtually from the earliest impeachment of the hapless Judge Pickering, which remains vibrant. At the heart of this debate are two principal issues: whether high crimes and misdemeanors require evidence of criminality and whether high crimes and misdemeanors relate solely to official misconduct or whether private misconduct is included as well.

## The Criminality of Impeachable Conduct is Irrelevant

While there is language in the constitutional debates suggesting that impeachment was to address "great offenses,"[1] there is virtually no evi-dence in the records of the debates that the grounds for impeachment, and specifically high crimes and misdemeanors, were to be restricted to violations of the criminal law and neither the textual argument[2] nor the claim of ex post facto law or attainder[3] is to the contrary. Indeed, had the Framers intended that crime be the basis of impeachment, they would have said so plainly and unequivocally, as they did with respect to the extradition of persons "charged in any State with Treason, Felony or other Crime,"[4] and in respect of the immunity of members of Congress from arrest, "in all cases, except Treason, Felony, and Breach of Peace."[5] In contrast, the comments of the Framers were practically unanimous that impeachment was intended to address misdemeanor in the perfor-mance of the president's office, whether maladministration;[6] malpractice and neglect of duty;[7] misfeasance;[8] perfidy;[9] or abuse of power;[10] as well as treason, bribery or corruption[11] that would constitute "high crimes and misdemeanors against the United States."[12]

It was also the view of the contemporaneous learned commentaries in the early part of the nineteenth century that high crimes and misdemeanors were not crimes in the ordinary sense. Rather, such offenses, as William Rawle said, "can only have reference to public character and official duty."[13] Alexander Hamilton described impeachable conduct as "those offences which proceed from the misconduct of public men, or…from the abuse or violation of some public trust…which may with particular propriety be denominated political,"[14] and James Wilson wrote that impeachments were "confined to political characters, to political crimes and misdemeanors."[15]

Joseph Story also agreed with Hamilton and Wilson that impeachment applied to "offences, which are committed by public men in violation of their public trust and duties."[16] Story agreed as well with Rawle's view that impeachment was not intended for ordinary crimes. Story wrote that "It will not be sufficient to say, that in the cases, where any offence is punished by any statute of the United States, it may, and ought to be deemed an impeachable offence."[17] Accordingly, Story observed that "Murder, burglary, robbery, and indeed all offences not immediately connected with office, except the two expressly mentioned [treason and bribery] are left to the ordinary course of judicial proceeding,"[18] because impeachment "is not so much designed to punish an offender, as to serve the state against gross official misdemeanors."[19]

However, equating impeachable high crimes and misdemeanors to violations of the criminal law is seductive. Requiring evidence of criminal conduct as a predicate to impeachment holds the promise of both certainty and objectivity. Generally speaking, there is greater clarity in the law of crimes concerning the conduct that is forbidden because of the liberty interests that are implicated. There is also extensive decisional law concerning the assessment of intent and personal responsibility for the proscribed conduct. Proof of a felony also carries with it the assurance that the alleged impeachable conduct is, indeed, serious and is contrary to accepted norms of social behavior (and would be regarded as such by the general population). Also, because everyone is presumed to have knowledge of the law (whether or not they do),[20] an impeachment grounded on a violation of the established criminal law is less likely to be (or to be perceived as being) an arbitrary, ex post facto determination of wrongdoing.

Moreover, engrafting a criminal law standard on presidential impeachment would provide greater assurance of fairness. The elements of an offense that must be proven are well established. Also, should the Senate determine to follow them, there are well-established rules concerning the evidence of an offense that can be considered and how the probitiveness of the evidence is to be weighed against other fairness considerations.

To the contrary, however, as several scholarly commentators have pointed out, there are crimes that rationally should not be considered impeachable conduct,[21] just as there are derelictions in office that should give rise to impeachment but that are neither criminal nor illegal.[22] That analysis lead Charles Black to conclude that limiting impeachment to violations of the criminal laws was "unwarranted" and "absurd."[23]

In fact, equating impeachable conduct to criminality is quite beside the point. Impeachment is a political process aimed at redressing political wrongs done by the president, such as abusing the powers of office, overreaching constitutional authority, and breaching the public trust. On the other hand, it is the prerogative of the courts to vindicate society's interest in peace and good order as represented in the criminal law. Each proceeding operates independently of the other in accordance with the societal interest each uniquely serves. That conduct warranting impeachment and removal of the president may also be criminal is a matter of chance coincidence but is not a constitutional requirement.

### High Crimes and Misdemeanors Relate Solely to Official Misconduct and Not to Private Misbehavior

Just as there is no substantial evidence that the Framers considered criminality to be a prerequisite of impeachment, there is nothing to suggest that the Framers, or anyone else, even considered private misconduct that did not affect the performance of public duties to be a basis of impeachment.[24] It should be recalled, for example, that Jefferson's vice president, Aaron Burr, served out his term without even the threat of impeachment despite having been indicted for the murder of Alexander Hamilton in 1804.[25]

The impeachment and removal of federal judges for misconduct off the bench is not to the contrary. Impeachment has been primarily a proceeding for the removal of federal judges and Congress has fashioned a standard for impeachment focused on fitness to continue in office rather than a strict requirement of high crimes and misdemeanors as is the case in presidential impeachment. Such a standard is consistent with the views expressed by Mason and Hamilton and derives from the life tenure of judicial appointments "during good behavior."[26] The removal of the eight judges upon conviction by the Senate accord with this view.[27] This broader standard for the removal of judges also reflects the different societal interests at stake.[28]

Observed through the lens of almost a century and a half of history, the Johnson impeachment may be viewed (as it was by some members of Congress at the time) as arising from Johnson's willful violation of federal law and refusal to enforce laws duly enacted by the Congress. However, those voting to acquit Johnson, including the Recusant Republicans, recognized that impeachment was not to be a referendum on policy or a vote of "no confidence" in an unpopular president, and so the Johnson impeachment is viewed today.[29]

In contrast, the articles of impeachment adopted by the Judiciary Committee charged Nixon with a pattern of misconduct, some of it criminal and some of it not, that thoroughly implicated Nixon's performance of his office as president.[30] Of equal significance, the Judiciary Committee considered, but rejected, two additional articles as to which the Committee believed the nexus to abuse of presidential power was too attenuated.

The first of these articles related to Nixon's having willfully attempted to evade the payment of income taxes for the years 1969 to 1972. Had the proceeding involved a federal judge rather than the president, impeachment would clearly have been sustained, as it had been in the Claiborne matter. In Nixon's case, however, the conduct was deemed to be personal and therefore not properly redressable by impeachment.

The second rejected article of impeachment involved Nixon's concealment of the bombing of Cambodia under the Menu Campaign. Although Nixon's actions were seen as a derogation of Congress' power to declare war, the Judiciary Committee recognized that the president was also invested with broad war powers. Thus, the Committee questioned whether the violation of the separation of powers and the usurpation of Congress' authority could be made out with sufficient clarity to support Nixon's removal on that basis.

The Clinton impeachment stood on a very different footing, however. Although the contrary has been argued,[31] in light of the record, it is difficult to conclude that the Clinton impeachment was other than partisan in its inception and in its result. Indeed, it was clear from the outset of the proceedings in the House that if the Democratic members remained opposed, the impeachment would fail in the Senate regardless of whether the Republican senators uniformly voted to convict Clinton, which they did not. The strong showing by the Democratic party in the mid-term elections coupled with Clinton's high job-approval ratings during the entire proceeding clearly suggest that the public did not support impeachment either.

Moreover, as is clear from the articles of impeachment themselves, the Clinton impeachment failed on constitutional grounds as well. Stripped of the sometimes sanctimonious prose, the essence of the misconduct underlying the impeachment was a moral failing on Clinton's part that was neither personally nor politically expedient to confess. Clinton's conduct was reprehensible and, as reflected in public opinion polls at the time, the electorate regarded his conduct as such. But Clinton's omissions, half-truths, and apparent lies about his personal sexual conduct simply are not the stuff of high crimes and misdemeanors within the contemplation of the Framers.

Nevertheless, the Clinton impeachment represents an even greater threat than the Johnson impeachment to presidential independence and the separation of coequal powers. Even though the eventual outcome of the Senate trial may not have been in doubt, during the six months that the impeachment was pending, the Framers' conception of a president who was independent of Congress hung in the balance.

The presidency and the Republic itself were put in this quandary not because Clinton was alleged to have overreached his office, as Johnson was, or that he had abused the powers of his office, as Nixon was, but because he would not admit to engaging in a consensual extramarital affair and had tried to prevent its public disclosure.

The Clinton impeachment has been criticized as lacking "constitutional gravity."[32] Regardless of how one views the merits of the proceedings against Clinton, it is unquestionably correct that when the House undertakes the removal of a president, the charges of high crimes and misdemeanors must be both substantial and weighty.[33] Hamilton described impeachment as "the national inquest into the conduct of public men,"[34] and so it must be.

It is not an overstatement to view the effect of impeachment as being second in gravity only to assassination. Impeachment of the president raises grave questions concerning the legitimacy of government, both with respect to actions and decisions of the president who now stands charged with high crimes and misdemeanors, and prospectively until the issue of the president's continuation in office is resolved.

In the meantime, the ability of the Executive Branch to govern effectively is compromised. In the conduct of foreign policy, the credibility of the president to speak on behalf of the nation is impaired, for what statesman would place much store by the commitments of a president whose integrity has been challenged by his or her own government and whose tenure in office may be cut short. Similarly, the adverse effect of impeachment on the president's ability to implement domestic policy is also severe. Indeed, one wonders how an impeached president (or even a president facing the realistic threat of impeachment) can continue to carry on the nation's business with a House of Representatives determined to indict and prosecute, and a Senate that will ultimately sit in judgment and possibly convict.

For those reasons, impeachment is not a course to be lightly or unadvisedly followed, and the gravity of the official misconduct giving rise to impeachment must be commensurate with the risks posed to the nation. In short, impeachment should be reserved for "great offences"[35] and "large-scale abuses that involve the authority that comes from occupying a particular office."[36]

Certainly, reasonable people have disagreed in good faith whether specific instances of presidential misconduct rose to the level of high crimes and misdemeanors. Having fashioned impeachment as a political rather than a judicial process, the Framers no doubt anticipated that such disagreements would occur. But it is clear that, as contemplated by the Framers, an impeachable high crime and misdemeanor must be a breach of faith with the Constitution that is so egregious and so exigent that rather than allowing the electorate to do so in an election, the president must be ejected from office immediately by the Congress, in order to vindicate the Constitution and preserve the Republic.

When viewed together, the debates in the constitutional and ratifying conventions, the contemporaneous writings of scholars and commentators, and the subsequent usage of Congress have infused Mason's impeachment shorthand with weight and content. Although the meaning of high crimes and misdemeanors continues to elude precise definition, history teaches that when contemplating the impeachment of the president for high crimes and misdemeanors, that content and the underlying aspiration of the Framers for an independent but accountable president must be respected.

# Appendix I: In the matter of – William Blount

## Articles

Exhibited by the House of Representatives of the United States, in the name of themselves, and of all the people of the United States, against WILLIAM BLOUNT, in maintenance of their impeachment against him for high crimes and misdemeanours.

## Article 1

That, whereas the United States, in the month of February, March, April, May and June, in the year of our Lord , one thousand seven hundred and ninety-seven, and for many years then past, were at peace with his Catholic Majesty the King of Spain; And whereas, during the months aforesaid, his said Catholic Majesty and the King of Great Britain were at war with each other,—yet, the said William Blount, on or about the months aforesaid, then being a Senator of the United States, and well knowing the premises, but disregarding the duties and obligations of his high station, and designing and intending to disturb the peace and tranquility of the United States, and to violate and infringe the neutrality thereof, did conspire and contrive to create, promote, and set on foot, within the jurisdiction and territory of the United States, and to conduct and carry on, from thence, a military hostile expedition against the territories and dominions of his said Catholic Majesty in the Floridas and Louisiana, or a part thereof, for the purpose of wresting the same from his Catholic Majesty, and of conquering the same for the King of Great Britain, with whom his said Catholic Majesty was then at war, as aforesaid, contrary to the duty of his trust and station as a Senator of the United States in violation of the obligations of neutrality, and against the laws of the United States, and the peace and interests thereof.

## Article 2

That, whereas on the twenty-seventh day of October, in the year of our Lord one thousand seven hundred and ninety-five, a treaty of friendship, limits and navigation had been made and concluded between the United States and his Catholic Majesty, by the fifth article thereof it is stipulated and agreed, "that the two high contracting parties shall, by all the means in their power, maintain peace and harmony among the several Indian nations who inhabit the country adjacent to the lines and rivers, which, by the preceding articles, form the boundaries of the two Floridas. And the better to obtain this effect, both parties oblige themselves expressly to restrain by force all hostilities on the part of the Indian nation living within their boundary: so that Spain will not suffer her Indians to attack the citizens of the United States, nor the Indians inhabiting their territory; nor will the United States permit these last-mentioned Indians to commence hostilities against the subject of his Catholic Majesty, or his Indians, in any manner whatever." Yet the said William Blount, on or about the months of February, March, April, May and June, in the year of our Lord one thousand seven hundred and ninety-seven, then being a Senator of the United States, and well knowing the premises, and that the United States were then at peace with his said Catholic Majesty, and that his Catholic Majesty was at war with the King of Great Britain, but disregarding the duties of his high station, and the stipulations of the said treaty, and the obligations of neutrality, did conspire and contrive to excite the Creek and Cherokee nations of Indians, then inhabiting within the territorial boundary of the United States, to commence hostilities against the subjects and possessions of his Catholic Majesty, in the Floridas and Louisiana, for the purpose of reducing the same to the dominion of the King of Great Britain, with whom his Catholic Majesty was then at war, as aforesaid, contrary to the duty of his trust and station as a Senator of the United States, in violation of the said treaty of friendship, limits and navigation, and of the obligations of neutrality, and against the laws of the United States, and the peace and interests thereof.

## Article 3

That, whereas by the ordinances and acts of Congress for regulating trade and intercourse with the Indian tribes, and for preserving peace on the frontiers, it has been made lawful for the President of the United States, in order to secure the continuance of the friendship of the said Indian tribes, to appoint such persons, from time to time, as temporary agents, to reside among the Indians as he shall think fit: And whereas, in pursuance of the said authority, the President of the United States, on or about the eighth day of September, in the year of our Lord one thousand seven hundred and ninety-six, did appoint Benjamin Hawkins, to be principal temporary agent for Indian affairs, within the Indian nations south of the river Ohio, and north of the territorial line of the United States: And whereas, the said Benjamin Hawkins accepted the said appointment, and on the twenty-first day of April, in the year of our Lord one thousand seven hundred and ninety-seven, and for a long time before and afterwards, did exercise the functions, powers and duties attached to the same, yet the said William Blount, on or about the said twenty-first day of April, in the year of our Lord one thousand seven hundred and ninety-seven, then being a Senator of the United States, and well knowing the premises, did, in the prosecution of his criminal designs and of his conspiracies aforesaid, and the more effectually to accomplish his intention of exciting the Creek and Cherokee nations of Indians, to commence hostilities against the subject of his Catholic Majesty, further conspire and contrive to alienate and diverse the confidence of the said Indian tribes or nations from the said Benjamin Hawkins, the principal territory agent aforesaid, and to diminish, impair, and destroy the influence of the said Benjamin Hawkins with the said Indian tribes, and their friendly intercourse and understanding with him, contrary to the duty of his trust and station as a Senator of the United States: and against the ordinances and laws of the United States, and the peace and interests thereof.

## Article 4

That, whereas by the ordinances and acts of Congress aforesaid, it is made lawful for the President of the Unites States to establish trading houses at such places and posts on the western and southern frontiers, or in the Indian country, as he shall judge most convenient for the purposes of carrying on a liberal trade with the several Indian nations within the limits of the United States, and to appoint an agent at each trading house established as aforesaid with such clerks and assistances as may be necessary for the execution of the said acts: And whereas, by a treaty made and concluded on the second day of July, in the year of our Lord one thousand seven hundred and ninety-one between the United States and the Cherokee nation of Indians, inhabiting within the limits of the United States, it is stipulated and agreed that "the United States will send such and so many persons to reside in said nation as they may judge proper, not exceeding four, who shall qualify themselves to act as interpreters." And whereas, the President of the United States, as well in pursuance of the authorities in this article mentioned, as of the acts of Congress referred to in the third article, did appoint James Carey to be interpreter for the United States to the said Cherokee nation of Indians, and assistant at the public trading-house established at the Tellico Block-house, in the State of Tennessee: And whereas, the said James Carey did accept the said appointments, and on the twenty-first day of April, in the year of our Lord one thousand seven hundred and ninety-seven, and for a long time before and afterwards, did exercise the functions and duties attached to the same; yet the said William Blount, on or about the said twenty-first day of April, in the year last aforesaid, then being a Senator of the United States, and well knowing of the premises, did, in prosecution of his criminal designs, and in furtherance of his conspiracies aforesaid, conspire and contrive to seduce the said James Carey from the duty and trust of his said appointments, and to engage the said James Carey to assist in the promotion and execution of his said criminal intentions and conspiracies aforesaid; contrary to the duty and trust and station as a Senator of the United States, and against the laws and treaties of the United States, and against the laws and treaties of the United States, and the peace and interests thereof.

## Article 5

That, whereas certain tribes or nations of Indians inhabit within the territorial limits of the United States, between whom, or many of them, and the settlements of the United States, certain boundary lines have, by successive treaties, been stipulated and agreed upon, to separate the lands and possessions of the said Indians, from the lands and the possessions of the United States and the citizens thereof: And whereas, particularly by the treaty in the last article mentioned to have been made with the Cherokee nation, on the second day of July, in the year of our Lord one thousand seven hundred and ninety-one, the boundary line between the United States and the said Cherokee nation, was agreed and defined; and it was further stipulated that the same should be ascertained and marked plainly by three persons appointed on the part of the United States, and three Cherokees on the part of their nation: And whereas, by another treaty made with the said Cherokee nation on the twenty-sixth day of June, in the year of our Lord one thousand seven hundred and ninety-one, was confirmed and established, and it was mutually agreed that the said boundary line should be actually ascertained and marked in the manner prescribed by the said last mentioned treaty: And whereas, in pursuance of the said treaties, commissioners were duly nominated and appointed on the part of the United States, to ascertain and mark the said boundary line; yet the said William Blount, on or about the twenty-first day of April, in the year of our Lord on thousand seven hundred and ninety-seven, then being Senator of the United States, and well knowing the premises; in further prosecution of his said criminal designs and of his conspiracies aforesaid, and the more effectually to accomplish his intention of exciting the said Indians to commence hostilities against the subjects of his Catholic Majesty, did further conspire and contrive to diminish and impair the confidence of the said Cherokee nation in the government of the United States, and to create and foment discontents and disaffection among the said Indians, towards the government of the United States, in relation to the ascertainment and marking of the said boundary line: contrary to the duty of his trust and station as a Senator of the United States, and against the peace and interests thereof.

And the House of Representatives, by protestation, saving to themselves the liberty of exhibiting, at any time hereafter, any further articles, or other accusation or impeachment, against the said William Blount, and also of replying to his answers which he shall make unto the said articles, or any of them, and of offering proof to all and every the aforesaid articles, and to all and every other articles, impeachment, or accusation, which shall be exhibited by them, as the case shall require, do demand that the said William Blount may be put to answer the said crimes and misdemeanours, and that such proceedings, examinations, trials, and judgments may be thereupon had and given as are agreeable to law and justice.

# Appendix II: In the matter of – John Pickering

**Article 1**

That whereas George Wentworth, surveyor of the district of New Hampshire, did, in the port of Portsmouth, in the said district, on waters that are navigable from the sea by vessels of more than ten tons burthen, on the fifteenth day of October, in the year of one thousand eight hundred and two, seize the ship called the Eliza, of about two hundred and eighty-five tons burthen, whereof William Ladd was later master, together with her furniture, tackle, and apparel, alleging that there had been unladen from on board of said ship, contrary to law, sundry goods, wares, and merchandise, of foreign growth and manufacture, of the value of four hundred dollars and upwards, and did likewise seize on land within said district, on the seventh day of October, in the year one thousand eight hundred and two, two cables of the value of two hundred and fifty dollars, part of the said goods, which were alleged to have been unladen from on board the said ship as aforesaid, contrary to law: and whereas Thomas Chadbourne, a deputy marshal of the said district of New Hampshire, did, on the sixteenth day of October, in the year one thousand eight hundred and two, by virtue of an order of the said John Pickering, judge of the district court of the said district of New Hampshire, arrest and detain in custody, for trial, before the said John Pickering, judge of the said district court, the said ship called the Eliza, with her furniture, tackle, and apparel, and also the two cables aforesaid; and whereas, by an act of Congress passed on the second day of March, in the year one thousand seven hundred and eighty-nine, it is among other things provided that "upon the prayer of any claimant to the court, that any ship or vessel, goods, wares, or merchandise, so seized and prosecuted, or any part thereof, should be delivered to such claimant to the court, that any ship or vessel, goods, wares, or merchandise, so seized and prosecuted, or any part thereof, should be delivered to such claimant, it shall be lawful for the court to appoint three proper persons to appraise such ship or vessel, goods, wares, or merchandise, who shall be sworn in open court for the faithful discharge of their duty; and such appraisement shall be made at the expense of the party on whose prayer it is granted; and on the return of such appraisement, if the claimant shall, with one or more sureties, to be approved by the court, execute a bond in the usual form to the United States, for the payment of a sum equal to the sum of which the ship or vessel, goods, wares, or merchandise, so prayed to be delivered and appraised, and moreover produce a certificate from the collector of the district wherein such trial is had, and of the naval officer thereof, if any there be, that the duties on the goods, wares, and merchandise, or tonnage duty on the ship or vessel, so claimed, have been paid or secured, in like manner as if the goods, wares, or merchandise, ship or vessel, had been legally entered, the court shall, by rule, order such ship or vessel, goods, wares, or merchandise, to be delivered to the said claimant"; yet the said John Pickering , judge of the said district court of the said district of New Hampshire, the said act of Congress not regarding, but with intent to evade the same, did order the ship called Eliza, with her furniture, tackle, and apparel, and the said two cables, to be delivered to a certain Eliphalett Ladd, who claimed the same, without his, the said Eliphalett Ladd's, producing any certificate from the collection and naval officer of the said district that the tonnage duty on the said ship, or the duties on the said cables, had been paid or secured, contrary to his trust and duty as judge of the said district court, against the laws of the United States, and to the manifest injury of their revenue.

## Article 2

That whereas, at a special district court of the United States begun and held at Portsmouth, on the eleventh day of November, in the year one thousand eight hundred and two, by Johnson Pickering, judge of said court, the United States, by Joseph Whipple, their collector of said district, having libeled, propounded, and given the said judge to understand and informed that the said ship Eliza, with her furniture, tackle, and apparel, had been seized as aforesaid because there had been unladen therefrom, contrary to law, two cables and one hundred pieces of check, of the value of four hundred dollars and upwards, and having prayed in their said libel that the said ship, with her furniture, tackle, and apparel, might, by the said court, be adjudged to be forfeited to the United States and be disposed of according to law, and a certain Eliphalett Ladd, by his proctor and attorneys, having come into the said court and having claimed the said ship Eliza, with her with her tackle, furniture, and apparel, and having denied that the said two cables and the said one hundred pieces of check had been unladen from the said ship, with her furniture, tackle, and apparel, might be restored to him, the said Eliphalett Ladd, the said John Pickering, judge of the said district court, did proceed to the hearing and trial of the cause thus depending between the United States on the one part, claiming that said ship Eliza, with her furniture, tackle, and apparel, as forfeited bylaw, and the said Eliphalett Ladd, on the other part, claiming the said ship Eliza, with her furniture, tackle, and apparel,, in his own proper right; and whereas John S. Sherburne, attorney for the United States in and for the district of New Hampshire, did appear in the said district court, as his special duty it was by law, to prosecute the said cause in behalf of the United States, and did produce sundry witnesses to prove the facts charged by the United States in their libel, filed by their collector as aforesaid in the said court, and to show that the said ship Eliza, with her tackle, furniture, and apparel, was justly forfeited to the United States, and did pray the said court that the said witnesses might be sworn in behalf of the United States, yet the said John Pickering, being then judge of the said district court, and then in court sitting, with intent to defeat the just claims of the United States, did refuse to hear the testimony of the said witnesses so, as aforesaid, produced in behalf of the United States, and without hearing the said testimony so adduced in behalf of the United States in the trial of the said cause did order and decree the said ship Eliza, with her furniture, tackle, and apparel, to be restored to the said Eliphalett Ladd, in violation of the laws of the United States and to the manifest injury of their revenue.

## Article 3

That whereas it is provided by an act of Congress, passed on the twenty-fourth day of September, in the year one thousand seven hundred and eighty-nine, "that from all final decrees in a district court in causes of admiralty and maritime jurisdiction, where the manner in dispute exceeds the sum or value of three hundred dollars, exclusive of costs, an appeal shall be allowed to the next circuit court to be held in such district;" and whereas, on the twelfth day of November, in the year one thousand eight hundred and two, at the trial of the aforesaid cause, between the United States, on the one part, claiming the said ship Eliza, with her furniture, tackle, and apparel, as forfeited, for the causes aforesaid, and the said Eliphalett Ladd, on the other part, claiming the said ship Eliza, with her furniture, tackle, and apparel, in his own proper right, the said John Pickering, judge of the said district court of the district of New Hampshire, did decree that the said ship Eliza, with her tackle, furniture, and apparel, should be restored to the said Eliphalett Ladd, the claimant: and the said district of New Hampshire, and prosecuting the said cause for and on the part of the United States, on the said twelfth day of November, in the year one thousand eight hundred and two, in the name and behalf of the United States, claim an appeal from the said decree of the district court to the next circuit court to be held in the said district of New Hampshire, and did pray the said district court to allow the said appeal, in conformity to the provisions of the act of Congress last aforesaid, yet he said John Pickering judge of the said district court, disregarding the authority of the laws, and wickedly meaning and intending to injure the revenues of the United States, and thereby to impair their public credit, did absolutely and positively refuse to allow the said appeal, as prayed for and claimed by the said John S. Sherburne in behalf of the United States, contrary to his trust and duty as judge of the said district court, against the laws of the United States, to the great injury of the public revenue, and in violation of the solemn oath which he had taken to administer equal and impartial justice.

## Article 4

That whereas, for the due, faithful, and impartial administration of justice, temperance and sobriety are essential qualities in the character of a judge, yet the said John Pickering, being a man of loose morals and intemperate habits, on the eleventh and twelfth days of November, in the year one thousand eight hundred and two, being then judge of the district court in and for the district of New Hampshire, did appear upon the bench of the said court for the purposes of administering justice in a state of total intoxication, produced by the free and intemperate use of inebriating liquors, and did then and there frequently, in a most prophane and indecent manner, invoke the name of the Supreme Being, to the evil example of all the good citizens of the United States; and was then and there guilty of other high misdemeanors, disgraceful to his own character as a judge and degrading to the honor and dignity of the United States. And the House of Representatives, by protestation, saving to themselves the liberty of exhibiting at anytime hereafter any further articles, or other accusation or impeachment against the said John Pickering, and also of replying to his answers which he shall make to the said articles, or any of them, offering proof to all and every the aforesaid articles and to all and every other articles, impeachment, or accusation which shall be exhibited by them, as the case shall require, do demand that he said John Pickering may be put to answer the said high crimes and misdemeanors, and that such proceedings, examinations, trials, and judgments may be thereupon had and given as may be agreeable to law and justice.

# Appendix III: In the matter of – Samuel Chase

### Article 1

That, unmindful of the solemn duties of his office, and contrary to the
sacred obligation by which he stood bound to discharge them "faithfully
and impartially and without respect to persons," the said Samuel Chase,
on the trial of John Fries, charged with treason before the circuit court of
the United States held for the district of Pennsylvania, during the months
of April and May, one thousand eight hundred, whereat the said Samuel
Chase presided, did, in his judicial capacity, conduct himself in a manner
highly arbitrary, oppressive and unjust. viz:

1. In delivering an opinion in writing on the question of law, on
   the construction of which the defence of the accused materially
   depended, tending to prejudice the minds of the jury against the
   case of the said John Fries, the prisoner, before counsel had been
   heard in this defence.
2. In restricting the counsel for the said Fries from recurring to such
   English authorities as they believed apposite, or from citing certain statutes of the United States which they deemed illustrative of
   the position upon which they intended to rest the defence of their
   client.
3. In debarring the prisoner from his constitutional privilege of
   addressing the jury (through his counsel) on the law, as well as on the
   fact, which was to determine his guilt or innocence, and at the same
   time endeavoring to wrest the question of law, as well as the question
   of fact, involved in the verdict which they were required to give.

In consequence of which irregular conduct of the said Samuel Chase, as
dangerous to our liberties as it is novel to our laws and usages, the same
John Fries was deprived of the right secured to him by the eighth article
amendatory of the Constitution, and was condemned to death without

having been heard, by counsel, in his defence, to the disgrace of the character of the American bench, in manifest violation of law and justice, and in open contempt of the rights of juries, on which, ultimately, rest the liberty and safety of the American people.

## Article 2

That, prompted by a similar spirit of persecution and injustice, at a circuit court of the United States, held at Richmond. In the month of May, one thousand eight hundred, for the district of Virginia, whereat the said Samuel Chase presided, and before which a certain James Thompson Callender was arraigned for libel on John Adams, then President of the United States, the said Samuel Chase, with intent to oppress and procure the conviction of the said Callender, did overrule the objection of John Basset, one of the jury, who wished to be excused from serving on the said trial because he had made up his mind as the publication from which the words charged to be libellons in indictment were extracted, and the said Basset was accordingly sworn, and did serve on the said jury, by whose verdict the prisoner was subsequently convicted.

## Article 3

That, with intent to oppress and procure the conviction of the prisoner, the evidence of John Taylor, a material witness on behalf of the aforesaid Callender, was not permitted by the said Samuel Chase to be given in, on pretence that the said witness could not prove the truth of the whole of one of the charges contained in the indictment, although the said charge embraced more than one fact.

## Article 4

That the conduct of the said Samuel Chase was marked, during the whole course of the said trial, by manifest injustice, partiality, and intemperance, viz:

1. In compelling the prisoner's counsel to reduce to writing and submit to the inspection of the court for their admission or rejection all questions which the said counsel meant to propound to the above-named John Taylor, the witness.
2. In refusing to postpone the trial, although an affidavit was regularly filed, stating the absence of material witnesses on behalf of the accused,

and although it was manifest that, with the utmost diligence, the attendance of such witnesses could not have been procured at that term.

3. In the use of unusual, rude, and contemptuous expressions towards the prisoner's counsel, and in falsely insinuating that they wished to excite the public fears and indignation, and to produce that insubordination to law to which the conduct of the judge did, at the same time, manifestly tend.

4. In repeated and vexatious interruptions of said counsel on the part of the said judge, which at length induced them to abandon their cause, and their client, who was thereupon convicted and condemned to fine and imprisonment.

5. In an indecent solicitude, manifested by the said Samuel Chase, for the conviction of the accused, unbecoming even a public prosecutor, but highly disgraceful to the character of a judge, as it was subversive of justice.

## Article 5

And whereas it is provided by the act of Congress, passed on the 24th day of September, 1780, entitled "An act to establish the judicial courts of the United States," that for any crime or offence against the United States the offender may be arrested, imprisoned, or bailed agreeably to the usual mode of process in the state where such offender may be found: and whereas it is provided by the laws of Virginia that, upon presentment by any grand jury of an offence not capital, the court shall order the clerk to issue a summons against the person or persons offending to appear and answer such presentment at the next court: yet the said Samuel Chase did, at the court aforesaid, award a capias against the body of the said James Thompson Callender, indicted for an offence not capital, whereupon the said Callender was arrested and committed to close custody, contrary to law in that case made and provided.

## Article 6

And whereas it is provided by the thirty-fourth section of the aforesaid act entitled "An act to establish the judicial courts of the United States," that the laws of the several States, except where the Constitution, treaties, or statutes of the United States shall otherwise require or provide, shall be regarded as the cases where they apply; and whereas by the laws of Virginia it is provided that in cases not capital the offender shall not be held to answer any presentment of a grand jury until the court next succeeding that during which such presentment shall have been made, yet the said Samuel Chase, with intent to oppress and procure the conviction of the said James Thompson Callender, did, at the court aforesaid, rule and adjudge the said Callender to trial during the term at which he, the said Callender, was presented and indicted, contrary to law in that case made and provided.

## Article 7

That, at a circuit court of the United States for the district of Delaware, held at New Castle, in the month of June, one thousand eight hundred, whereat the said Samuel Chase presided, the said Samuel Chase, disregarding the duties of his office, did descend from the dignity of a judge and stoop to the level of an informer by refusing to discharge the grand jury, although entreated by several of the said jury so to do: and after the said grand jury had regularly declared, through their foreman, that they had found no bills of indictment, nor had any presentments to make by observing to the said grand jury that he, the same Samuel Chase understood "that a highly seditious temper had manifested itself in the State of Delaware among a certain class of people, particularly in New Castle County, and more especially in the town of Wilmington, where lived a most seditious printer, unrestrained by any principle of virtue and regardless of special order; that the name of the printer was"—but checking himself, as if sensible of the indecorum which he was committing, added "that it might be assuming too much to mention the name of this person, but it becomes your duty, gentlemen, to inquire diligently into this matter," or words to that effect; and that, with intention to procure the prosecution of the printer in question, the said Samuel Chase did, moreover, authoritatively enjoin on the district attorney of the United States the necessity of procuring a file of the papers to which alluded (and which were understood to be those published under the title of "Mirror of the Times and General Advertiser"), and by a strict examination of them to find some passage which might furnish the groundwork of a prosecution against the printer of the said paper, thereby degrading his high judicial functions and tending to impair the public confidence in and respect for the tribunals of justice, so essential to the general welfare.

## Article 8

And whereas mutual respect and confidence between the Government of the United States and those of the individual States and between the people and those governments, respectively, are highly conducive to that public harmony without which there can be no public happiness, yet the said Samuel Chase, disregarding the duties and dignity of his judicial character, did, at a circuit court for the district of Maryland, held at Baltimore in the month of May, one thousand eight hundred and three, pervert his official right and duty to address the grand jury then and there assembled on the matters coming within the providence of the grand jury, for the purpose of delivering to the said grand jury an intemperate and inflammatory political harangue, with intent to excite the fears and resentment of the said grand jury and of the good people of Maryland against their State government and constitution, a conduct highly censurable in any, but peculiarly indecent and unbecoming in a judge of the Supreme Court of the United States; and, moreover, that the said Samuel Chase then and there, under pretence of exercising his judicial right to address the said grand jury as aforesaid, did, in a manner highly unwarrantable, endeavor to excite the odium of the said grand jury and of the good people of Maryland against the Government of the United States by delivering opinions which, even if the judicial authority were competent to their expression on a suitable occasion and in a proper manner, were at the time and as delivered by him highly indecent, extrajudicial, and tending to prosecute the high judicial character with which he was invested to the low purpose of an electioneering partizan.

# Appendix IV: In the matter of – Andrew Johnson

**Article 1**

That said Andrew Johnson, President of the United States, on the twenty-first day of February, in the year of our Lord one thousand eight hundred and sixty-eight, at Washington, in the District of Columbia, unmindful of the high duties of his office, of his oath of office, and of the requirement of the Constitution that he should take care that the laws be faithfully executed, did unlawfully and in violation of the Constitution and laws of the United States, issue an order in writing for the removal of Edwin M. Stanton from the office of Secretary for the Department of War, said Edwin M. Stanton having been theretofore duly appointed and commissioned, by and with the advice and consent of the Senate of the United States, as such Secretary, and said Andrew Johnson, President of the United States, on the twelfth day of August, in the year of our Lord one thousand eight hundred and sixty-seven, and during the recess of said Senate, having suspended by his order Edwin M. Stanton from said office, and within twenty days after the first day of the next meeting of said Senate, that is to say, on the twelfth day of December in the year last aforesaid having reported to said Senate such suspension with the evidence and reasons for his action in the case and the name of the person designated to perform the duties of such office temporarily until the next meeting of the Senate, and said Senate thereafterwards, on the thirteenth day of January, in the year of our Lord one thousand eight hundred and sixty-eight, having duly considered the evidence and reasons reported by said Andrew Johnson for said suspension, and having refused to concur in said suspension, whereby and by force of the provisions of an act entitled "An act regulating the tenure of certain civil offices," passed March second, eighteen hundred and sixty-seven, said Edwin Mr. Stanton did forthwith resume the functions of his office, whereof the said Andrew Johnson had then and there due notice, and said Edwin M. Stanton, by reason of the premises, on said twenty-first day of February, being lawfully entitled to hold said office of Secretary for the Department of War, which said order for the removal of said Edwin M. Stanton is in substance as follows, that is to say:

> "EXECUTIVE MANSION,
> "*Washington, D.C., February 21, 1868.*

"SIR: By virtue of the power and authority vested in me as President by the Constitution and laws of the United States you are hereby removed from office as Secretary for the Department of War, and your functions as such will terminate upon the receipt of this communication.

"You will transfer to Brevet Major General Lorenzo Thomas, Adjutant General of the army, who has this day been authorized and empowered to act as Secretary of War *ad interim*, all records, books, papers, and other public property now in your custody and charge.

"Respectfully yours,

> "ANDREW JOHNSON.

"To the Hon. EDWIN M. STANTON, *Washington, D.C.*"

Which order was unlawfully issued with intent then and there to violate the act entitled "An act regulating the tenure of certain civil offices," passed March second, eighteen hundred and sixty-seven, and with the further intent, contrary to the provisions of said act, in violation thereof, and contrary to the provisions of the Constitution of the United States, and without the advice and consent of the Senate of the United States, the said Senate then and there being in session, to remove said Edwin M. Stanton from office of Secretary for the Department of War, the said Edwin M. Stanton being then and there Secretary for the Department of War, and being then and there in the due and lawful execution and discharge of the duties of said office, whereby said Andrew Johnson, President of the United States, did then and there commit and was guilty of a high misdemeanor in office.

## Article 2

That on the said twenty-first day of February, in the year of our Lord one thousand eight hundred and sixty-eight, at Washington, in the District of Columbia, said Andrew Johnson, President of the United States, unmindful of the high duties of his office, of his oath of office, and in violation of the Constitution of the United States, and contrary to the provisions of an act entitled "An act regulating the tenure of certain civil offices," passed March second, eighteen hundred and sixty-seven, without the advice and consent of the Senate of the United States, said Senate then and there being in session, and without authority of law, did, with intent to violate the Constitution of the United States, and the act aforesaid, issue and deliver to one Lorenzo Thomas a letter of authority in substance as follows: that is to say:

"EXECUTIVE MANSION,
*"Washington, D.C., February 21, 1868.*

"SIR: The Hon. Edwin M. Stanton, having been this day removed from office as Secretary for the Department of War, you are hereby authorized and empowered to act as Secretary of War *ad interim*, and will immediately enter upon the discharge of the duties pertaining to that office.

"Mr. Stanton has been instructed to transfer to you all the records, books, papers, and other public property now in his custody and charge.

"Respectfully yours,

"ANDREW JOHNSON.

"To Brevet Major GENERAL LORENZO THOMAS
*"Adjutant General U.S. Army, Washington, D.C."*

Then and there being no vacancy in said office of Secretary of the Department of War, whereby said Andrew Johnson, President of the United States, did then and there commit and was guilty of a high misdemeanor in office.

## Article 3

That said Andrew Johnson, President of the United States, on the twenty-first day of February, in the year of our Lord one thousand eight hundred and sixty-eight, at Washington, in the District of Columbia, did commit and was guilty of a high misdemeanor in office in this, that, without authority of law, while the Senate of the United States was then and there in session, he did appoint one Lorenzo Thomas to be Secretary for the Department of War *ad interim*, without the advice and consent of the Senate, and with intent to violate the Constitution of the United States, no vacancy having happened in said office of Secretary for the Department of War during the recess of the Senate, and no vacancy existing in said office at the time, and which said appointment, so made by said Andrew Johnson, of said Lorenzo Thomas, is in substance as follows, that is to say:

"EXECUTIVE MANSION,
*"Washington, D.C., February 21, 1868.*

"SIR: The Hon. Edwin M. Stanton, having been this day removed from office as Secretary for the Department of War, you are hereby authorized and empowered to act as Secretary of War *ad interim*, and will immediately enter upon the discharge of the duties pertaining to that office.

"Mr. Stanton has been instructed to transfer to you all the records, books, papers, and other public property now in his custody and charge.
"Respectfully yours,

"ANDREW JOHNSON.

"To Brevet Major GENERAL LORENZO THOMAS
*"Adjutant General U.S. Army, Washington, D.C."*

Then and there being no vacancy in said office of Secretary of the Department of War, whereby said Andrew Johnson, President of the United States, did then and there commit and was guilty of a high misdemeanor in office.

## Article 4

That said Andrew Johnson, President of the United States, unmindful of the high duties of his office and of his oath of office, in violation of the Constitution and laws of the United States, on the twenty-first day of February, in the year of our Lord one thousand eight hundred and sixty-eight, at Washington, in the District of Columbia, did unlawfully conspire with Lorenzo Thomas, and with other persons to the House of Representatives unknown, with intent, by intimidation and threats, unlawfully to hinder and prevent Edwin M. Stanton, then and there the Secretary for the Department of War, duly appointed under the laws of the United States from holding said office of Secretary for the Department of War, contrary to and in violation of the Constitution of the United States, and of the provisions of an act entitled "An act to define and punish certain conspiracies," approved July thirty-first, eighteen hundred and sixty-one, whereby said Andrew Johnson, President of the United States, did then and there commit and was guilty of a high crime in office.

## Article 5

That said Andrew Johnson, President of the United States, unmindful of the high duties of his office and of his oath of office, on the twenty-first day of February, in the year of our Lord one thousand eight hundred and sixty-eight, and on divers other days and times in said year, before the second day of March, in the year of our Lord one thousand eight hundred and sixty-eight, at Washington, in the District of Columbia, did unlawfully conspire with one Lorenzo Thomas, and with other persons to the House of Representatives unknown, to prevent and hinder the execution of an act entitled "An act regulating the tenure of certain civil offices," passed March second, eighteen hundred and sixty-seven, and in pursuance of said conspiracy, did unlawfully attempt to prevent Edwin M. Stanton, then and there being Secretary for the Department of War, duly appointed and commissioned under the laws of the United States, from holding said office, whereby the said Andrew Johnson, President of the United states, did then and there commit and was guilty of a high misdemeanor in office.

## Article 6

That said Andrew Johnson, President of the United States, unmindful of the high duties of his office and of his oath of office, on the twenty-first day of February, in the year of our Lord one thousand eight hundred and sixty-eight, at Washington, in the District of Columbia, did unlawfully conspire with one Lorenzo Thomas by force to seize, take, and possess the property of the United States in the Department of War, and then and there in the custody and charge of Edwin M. Stanton, Secretary for said department, contrary to the provisions of an act entitled "An act to define and punish certain conspiracies," approved July thirty-one, eighteen hundred and sixty-one, and with intent to violate and disregard an act entitled "An act regulating the tenure of certain civil offices," passed March second, eighteen hundred and sixty-seven, whereby said Andrew Johnson, President of the United States, did then and there commit a high crime in office.

## Article 7

That said Andrew Johnson, President of the United States, unmindful of the high duties of his office and of his oath of office, on the twenty-first day of February, in the year of our Lord on thousand eight hundred and sixty-eight, at Washington, in the District of Columbia, did unlawfully conspire with one Lorenzo Thomas with intent unlawfully to seize, take, and possess the property of the United States in the Department of War, in the custody and charge of Edwin M. Stanton, Secretary for said department, with intent to violate and disregard the act entitled, "An act regulating the tenure of certain civil offices," passed, March second, eighteen hundred and sixty-seven, whereby said Andrew Johnson, President of the United States, did then and there commit a high misdemeanor in office.

## Article 8

That said Andrew Johnson, President of the United States, unmindful of the high duties of his office and of his oath of office, with intent unlawfully control the disbursements of the moneys appropriated for the military service and for the Department of War, on the twenty-first day of February, in the year of our Lord one thousand eight hundred and sixty-eight, at Washington, in the District of Columbia, did unlawfully and contrary to the provisions of an act entitled "An act regulating the tenure of certain civil offices," passed March second, eighteen hundred and sixty-seven, and in violation of the Constitution of the United States, and without the advice and consent of the Senate of the United States, and while the Senate was then and there in session, there being no vacancy in the office of Secretary for the Department of War, and with intent to violate and disregard the act aforesaid, then and there issue and deliver to one Lorenzo Thomas a letter of authority in writing, in substance as follows, that is to say:

"EXECUTIVE MANSION,
"*Washington, D.C., February 21, 1868.*

"SIR: The Hon. Edwin M. Stanton, having been this day removed from office as Secretary for the Department of War, you are hereby authorized and empowered to act as Secretary of War *ad interim*, and will immediately enter upon the discharge of the duties pertaining to that office.

"Mr. Stanton has been instructed to transfer to you all the records, books, papers, and other public property now in his custody and charge.

"Respectfully yours,

"ANDREW JOHNSON.

"To Brevet Major GENERAL LORENZO THOMAS
"*Adjutant General U.S. Army, Washington, D.C.*"

Whereby said Andrew Johnson, President of the United States, did then and there commit and was guilty of a high misdemeanor in office.

### Article 9

That said Andrew Johnson, President of the United States, on the twenty-second day of February, in the year of our Lord one thousand eight hundred and sixty-eight, at Washington, in the District of Columbia, in disregard of the Constitution, and the laws of the United States duly enacted, as commander-in-chief of the army of the United States, did bring before himself then and there William H. Emory, a major general by brevet in the army of the United States, actually in command of the department of Washington and the military forces thereof, and did then and there, as such commander-in-chief, declare to and instruct said Emory that part of a law of the United States, passed March second, eighteen hundred and sixty-seven, entitled "An act making appropriations for the support of the army for the year ending June thirtieth, eighteen hundred and sixty-eight, and for other purposes," especially the second section thereof, which provides, among other things, that "all orders and instructions relating to military operations, issued by the President or Secretary of War, shall be issued through the General of the army, and, in case of his inability, through the next rank," was unconstitutional, and in contravention of the commission of said Emory, and which said provision of law had been theretofore duly and legally promulgated by General Orders for the government and direction of the army of the United States, as the said Andrew Johnson then and there well knew, with intent thereby to induce said Emory, in his official capacity as commander of the department of Washington, to violate the provisions of said act, and to take and receive, act upon, and obey such orders as he, the said Andrew Johnson might make and give, and should not be issued through the General of the army of the United States, according to the provisions of the said act, and with the further intent thereby to enable him, the said Andrew Johnson, to prevent the execution of the act entitled "An act regulating the tenure of certain civil offices," passed March second, eighteen hundred and sixty-seven, and to unlawfully prevent Edwin M. Stanton, then being Secretary for the Department of War, from holding said office and discharging the duties thereof, whereby said Andrew Johnson, President of the United States, did then and there commit and was guilty of a high misdemeanor in office.

And the House of Representatives, by protestation, saving to themselves the liberty of exhibiting at any time hereafter any further articles, or other accusation of impeachment against the said Andrew Johnson, President of the United States, and also of replying to his answers which he shall make unto the articles herein preferred against him, and of offering proof to the same, and every part thereof, and to all and every other article, accusation, or impeachment which shall be exhibited by them, as the case shall require, DO DEMAND that the said Andrew Johnson may be put to answer the high crime and misdemeanors in office herein charged against him, and that such proceedings, examinations, trials, and judgments may be thereupon had and given as may be agreeable to law and justice.

## Article 10

That said Andrew Johnson, President of the United States, unmindful of the high duties of his office, and the dignity and proprieties thereof, and of the harmony and courtesies which ought to exist and be maintained between the executive and legislative branches of the government of the

Unites States, designing and intending to set aside the rightful authority and powers of Congress, did attempt to bring into disgrace, ridicule,
hatred, contempt, and reproach the Congress of the United States, and
the several branches thereof, to impair and destroy the regard and respect
of all good people of the Unites States for the Congress and legislative
powers thereof, (which all officers of the government ought inviolably to
preserve and maintain,) and to excite the odium and resentment of all the
good people of the United States against Congress and the laws by it duly
and constitutionally enacted; and in pursuance of his said design and
intent, openly and publicly, and before divers assemblages of the citizens
of the United States, convened in divers parts thereof to meet and receive
said Andrew Johnson as the Chief Magistrate of the United States, did, on
the eighteenth day of August, in the year of our Lord one thousand eight
hundred and sixty-six, and on divers and other days and times, as well
before as afterward, make and deliver, with a loud voice, certain intemperate, inflammatory, and scandalous harangues, and did therein utter
loud threats and bitter menaces, as well against Congress as the laws of
the United States duly enacted thereby, amid the cries, jeers, and laugh-
ter of the multitudes then assembled and in hearing, which are set forth
in the several specifications hereinafter written, in substance and effect,
that is to say:

*Specification first.*—In this, that at Washington, in the District of
Columbia, in the Execution Mansion, to a committee of citizens who
called upon the President of the United States, speaking of and concerning
the Congress of the United States, said Andrew Johnson, President of the
United States, heretofore, to wit, on the eighteenth day of August, in the
year of our Lord one thousand eight hundred and sixty-six, did, in a loud
voice, declare, in substance and effect, among other things, that is to say:

"So far as the executive department of the government is concerned,
the effort has been made to restore the Union, to heal the breach, to pour
oil into the wounds which were consequent upon the struggle, and (to
speak in common phrase) to prepare, as the learned and wise physician
would, a plaster healing in character and co-extensive with the wound. We
thought, and we think, that we had partially succeeded; but, as the work
progresses, as reconstruction seemed to be taking place, and the country
was becoming reunited, found a disturbing and marring element opposing
us. In alluding to that element I shall go no further than your convention,
and the distinguished gentleman who has delivered to me the report of its
proceedings. I shall make no reference to it that I do not believe the time
and occasion justify.

"We have witnessed in one department of government every endeavor
to prevent the restoration of peace, harmony and union. We have seen

hanging upon the verge of the government, as it were, a body called, or which assumes to be, the Congress of the United States, while, in fact, it is a Congress of only a part of the States. We have seen this Congress pretend to be for the Union, when its every step and act tended to perpetuate disunion and make a disruption of the States inevitable. * * * We have seen Congress gradually encroach, step by step, upon constitutional rights, and violate, day after day and month after month, fundamental principles of the government. We have seen a Congress in a minority assume to exercise power which, allowed to be consummated, would result in despotism or monarchy itself."

*Specification second.*—In this, that at Cleveland, in the State of Ohio, heretofore, to wit, on the third day of September, in the year of our Lord one thousand eight hundred and sixty-six, before a public assemblage of citizens and others, said Andrew Johnson, President of the United States, speaking of and concerning the Congress of the United States, did, in a loud voice, declare, in substance and effect, among other things, that is to say:

"I will tell you what I did do. I called upon your Congress that is trying to break up the government."

* * *

"In conclusion, besides that, Congress had taken much pains to poison their constituents against him. But what had Congress done? Have they done anything to restore the Union of these States? No; on the contrary, they had done everything to prevent it; and because he stood now where he did when the rebellion commenced, he had been denounced as a traitor. Who had run great risks or made greater sacrifices than himself? But Congress, factious and domineering, had undertaken to poison the minds of American people?

*Specification third.*—In this, that at St. Louis, in the State of Missouri, heretofore, to wit, on the third day of September, in the year of our Lord one thousand eight hundred and sixty-six, before a public assemblage of citizens and others, said Andrew Johnson, President of the United States, speaking of and concerning the Congress of the United States, did, in a loud voice, declare, in substance and effect, among other things, that is to say:

"Go on. Perhaps if you had a word or two on the subject of New Orleans you might understand more about it than you do. And if you will go back—if you will go back and ascertain the cause of the riot at New Orleans, perhaps you will not be so prompt in calling out 'New Orleans." If you will take up the riot at New Orleans, and trace it back to its source or its immediate cause, you will find out who is responsible for the blood that was shed there. If you will take up the riot at New Orleans and trace it back to the radical Congress, you will find that the riot at New Orleans was substantially planned. If you will take up the proceedings in their caucuses you will understand that they there knew that a convention was to be called which was extinct by its power having expired; that it was said that the intention was that a new government was to be organized, and on the organization of that government the intention was to enfranchise one portion of the population, called the colored population, who had just been emancipated, and at the same time disfranchise white men. When you design to talk about New Orleans you ought to understand what you are talking about. When you read the speeches that were made, and take up the facts on the Friday and Saturday before that convention sat, you will find there that speeches were made incendiary in their character, exciting in that portion of the population, the black population, to arm themselves and prepared for the shedding of blood. You will also find that the convention did assemble in violation of law, and the intention of that convention was to supercede the reorganized authorities in the State government of Louisiana, which had been recognized by the government of the United States; and every man engaged in that rebellion in that convention, with the intention of superceding and uptuning the civil government which had been recognized by the government of the United States, I say that he was a traitor to the Constitution of the United States, and hence you find that another rebellion was commenced, *having its origin in the radical Congress.*

✲ ✲ ✲

"So much for the New Orleans riot. And there was the cause and the origin of the blood that was shed, and every drop of blood that was shed is upon their skirts, and they are responsible for it. I could test this thing a little closer, but will not do it here to-night. But when you talk about the causes and consequences that resulted from proceedings of that kind, perhaps, as I have been introduced here, and you have provoked questions of this kind, though it does not provoke me, I will tell you a few wholesome things that have been done by this radical Congress in connection with New Orleans and the extension of the elective franchise.

"I know that I have been traduced and abused. I know it has come in advance of me here as elsewhere, that I have attempted to exercise an arbitrary power in resisting laws that were intended to be forced upon the government; that I had exercised that power; that I had abandoned the party that elected me, and that I was a traitor, because I exercised the veto power in attempting, and did arrest for a time, a bill that was called a 'Freedman's Bureau' bill; yes, that I was a traitor. And I have been traduced, I have been slandered, I have been maligned, I have been called Judas Iscariot, and all that. Now, my countrymen, here to-night, it is very easy to indulge in epithets; it is easy to call a man Judas and cry out traitor; but when he is called upon to give arguments and facts he is very often found wanting. Judas Iscariot-Judas. There was a Judas, and he was one of the twelve apostles. Oh! yes, the twelve apostles had a Christ. The twelve apostles had a Christ, and he never could have had a Judas unless he had had twelve apostles. If I have played the Judas, who has been my Christ that I have played the Judas with? Was it Thad. Stevens? Was it Wendall Phillips? Was it Charles Sumner? These are the men that stop and compare themselves with the Saviour; and everybody that differs with them in opinion, and to try to stay and arrest their diabolical and nefarious policy, is to be denounced as a Judas." * * *

"Well, let me say to you, if you will stand by me in this action, if you will stand by me in trying to give the people a fair chance—soldiers and citizens—to participate in these offices, God being willing, I will kick them out. I will kick them out just as fast as I can.

"Let me say to you, in concluding, that what I have said I intended to say. I was not provoked into this, and I care not for their menaces, the taunts, and the jeers. I care not for threats. I do not intend to be bullied by my enemies nor overawed by my friends. But, God willing, with your help I will veto their measures when any of them come to me."

Which said utterances, declarations, threats, and harangues, highly censurable in any, are peculiarly indecent and unbecoming in the Chief Magistrate of the United States, by means whereof said Andrew Johnson has brought the high office of the President of the United States into contempt, ridicule, and disgrace, to the great scandal of all good citizens, whereby said Andrew Johnson, President of the United States, did commit, and was then and there guilty of a high misdemeanor in office.

## Article 11

That said Andrew Johnson, President of the United States, unmindful of the high duties of his office, and of his oath of office, and in disregard of the Constitution and laws of the United States, did, heretofore, to wit, on the eighteenth day of August A.D. eighteen hundred and sixty-six, at the city of Washington, and the District of Columbia, by public speech, declare and affirm, in substance, that the thirty-ninth Congress of the United States was not a Congress of the United States authorized by the Constitution to exercise legislative power under the same, but, on the contrary, was a Congress of only part of the States, thereby denying, and intending to deny, that the legislation of said Congress was valid or obligatory upon him, the said Andrew Johnson, except in so far as he saw fit to approve the same, and also thereby denying, and intending to deny, the power of the said thirty-ninth Congress to propose amendments to the Constitution of the United States; and, in pursuance of said declaration, the said Andrew Johnson, President of the United States, afterwards, to wit, on the twenty-first day of February, A.D. eighteen hundred and sixty-eight, at the city of Washington, in the District of Columbia, did, unlawfully, and in disregard of the requirements of the Constitution, that he should, take care that the laws be faithfully executed, attempt to prevent the execution of an act entitled "An act regulating the tenure of certain civil offices," passed March second, eighteen hundred and sixty-seven, by unlawfully devising and contriving, and attempting to devise and contrive means by which he should prevent Edwin M. Stanton from forthwith assuming the functions of the office of Secretary for the Department of War notwithstanding the refusal of the Senate to concur in the suspension theretofore made by said Andrew Johnson of said Edwin M. Stanton from the said office of Secretary for the Department of War; and also, by further unlawfully devising and contriving, and attempting to devise and contrive means, then and there, to prevent the execution of an act entitled "An act making appropriations for the support of the army for the fiscal year ending June thirtieth, eighteen hundred and sixty-eight, and for other purposes," approved March second, eighteen hundred and sixty-seven; and, also to prevent the execution of an act entitled "An act to provide for the more efficient government of the rebel States," passed March second, eighteen hundred and sixty-seven, whereby the said Andrew Johnson, President of the United States, did, then, to wit, on the twenty-first day of February, A.D. eighteen hundred and sixty-eight at the city of Washington, commit, and was guilty of, a high misdemeanor in office.

# Appendix V: In the matter of – Richard M. Nixon

### Article 1

In his conduct of the office of the President of the United States, Richard M. Nixon, in violation of his constitutional oath faithfully to execute the office of President of the United States and, to the best of his ability, preserve, protect, and defend the Constitution of the United States, and in violation of his constitutional duty to take care that laws be faithfully executed, has prevented, obstructed, and impeded the administration of justice, in that:

On June 17, 1972, and prior thereto, agents of the Committee for Re-election of the President committed unlawful entry of the headquarters of the Democratic National Committee in Washington, District of Columbia, for the purpose of securing political intelligence. Subsequent thereto, Richard M. Nixon, using the powers of his high office, engaged personally through his subordinates and agents, in a course of conduct or plan designed to delay, impede, and obstruct the investigation of such unlawful entry; to cover up, conceal and protect those responsible; and to conceal the existence and scope of other unlawful covert activities.

The means used to implement this course of conduct or plan included one or more of the following:

(1) making or causing to be made false or misleading statements to lawfully authorized investigative officers and employees of the United States;

(2) withholding relevant and material evidence or information from lawfully authorized investigative officers and employees of the United States;

(3) approving, condoning, acquiescing in, and counseling witnesses with respect to the giving of false or misleading statements to lawfully authorized investigative officers and employees of the United States and false or misleading testimony in duly instituted judicial and congressional proceedings;

(4) interfering or endeavoring to interfere with the conduct of investigations by the Department of Justice of the United States, the Federal Bureau of Investigation, the Office of Watergate Special Prosecution Force, and Congressional Committees;

(5) approving, condoning, and acquiescing in, the surreptitious payment of substantial sums of money for the purposes of obtaining the silence or influencing the testimony of witnesses, potential witnesses or individuals who participated in such unlawful entry and other illegal activities;

(6) endeavoring to misuse the Central Intelligence Agency, an agency of the United States; disseminating information received from officers of the Department of Justice of the United States to subjects of investigations conducted by lawfully authorized investigative officers and employees of the United States, for the purpose of aiding and assisting such subjects in their attempts to avoid criminal liability;

(7) making false or misleading public statements for the purpose of deceiving the people of the United States into believing that a thorough and complete investigation and had been conducted with respect to allegations of misconduct on the part of personnel of the executive branch of the United States and personnel of the Committee for the Re-election of the President, and that there was no involvement of such personnel in such misconduct; or

(8) endeavoring to cause prospective defendants, and individuals duly tried and convicted, to expect favored treatment and consideration in return for their silence or false testimony, or rewarding individuals for their silence or false testimony.

In all of this, Richard M. Nixon has acted in a manner contrary to his trust as President and subversive of constitutional government, to the great prejudice of the cause of law and justice and to the manifest injury of the people of the United States.

Wherefore Richard M. Nixon, by such conduct, warrants impeachment and trial, and removal from office.

## Article 2

Using the powers of the office of President of the United States, Richard M. Nixon, in violation of his constitutional oath faithfully to execute the office of President of the United States and, to the best of his ability, preserve, protect, and defend the Constitution of the United States, and in disregard of his constitutional duty to take care that the laws be faithfully executed, has repeatedly engaged in conduct violating the constitutional rights of citizens, impairing the due and proper administration of justice and the conduct of lawful inquiries, or contravening the laws governing agencies of the executive branch and the purposes of these agencies.

This conduct has included one or more of the following:

(1) He has, acting personally and through his subordinates and agents, endeavored to obtain from the Internal Revenue Service, in violation of the constitutional rights of citizens, confidential information contained in income tax returns for purposes not authorized by law, and to cause, in violation of the constitutional rights of citizens, income tax audits or other income tax investigations to be initiated or conducted in a discriminatory manner.

(2) He misused the Federal Bureau of Investigation, the Secret Service, and other executive personnel, in violation or disregard of the constitutional rights of citizens, by directing or authorizing such agencies or personnel to conduct or continue electronic surveillance or other investigations for purposes unrelated to national security, the enforcement of laws, or any other lawful function of his office; he did direct, authorize, or permit the use of information obtained thereby for purposes unrelated to national security, the enforcement of laws, or any other lawful function of his office; and he did direct the concealment of certain records made by the Federal Bureau of Investigation of electronic surveillance.

(3) He has, acting personally and through his subordinates and agents, in violation or disregard of the constitutional rights of citizens, authorized and permitted to be maintained a secret investigative unit within the office of the President, financed in part with money derived from campaign contributions, which unlawfully utilized the resources of the Central Intelligence Agency, engaged in covert and unlawful activities, and attempted to prejudice the constitutional right of an accused to a fair trial.

(4) He has failed to take care that the laws were faithfully executed by failing to act when he knew or had reason to know that his close subordinates endeavored to impede and frustrate lawful inquiries by duly constituted executive, judicial, and legislative entities concerning the unlawful entry into the headquarters of the Democratic National Committee, and the cover-up thereof, and concerning other unlawful activities, including those relating to the confirmation of Richard Kleindienst as Attorney General of the United States, the electronic surveillance of private citizens, the break-in into the offices of Dr. Lewis Fielding, and the campaign financing practices of the Committee to Re-elect the President.

(5)  In disregard of the rule of law, he knowingly misused the executive power by interfering with agencies of the executive branch, including the Federal Bureau of Investigation, the Criminal Division, and the Office of Watergate Special Prosecution Force, of the Department of Justice, and the Central Intelligence Agency, in violation of his duty to take care that the laws be faithfully executed.

In all of this, Richard M. Nixon has acted in a manner contrary to his trust as President and subversive of constitutional government, to the great prejudice of the cause of law and justice and to manifest injury of the people of the United States.

Wherefore Richard M. Nixon, by such conduct, warrants impeachment and trial, and removal from office.

## Article 3

In his conduct of the office of the President of the United States, Richard M. Nixon, contrary to his oath faithfully to execute the office of President of the United States and, to the best of his ability, preserve, protect, and defend the Constitution of the United States, and in violation of his constitutional duty to take care that the laws be faithfully executed, has failed without lawful cause or excuse to produce papers and things as directed by duly authorized subpoenas issued by the Committee on the Judiciary of the House of Representatives on April 11, 1974, May 15, 1974, May 30, 1974, and June 24, 1974, and willfully disobeyed such subpoenas. The subpoenaed papers and things were deemed necessary by the Committee in order to resolve by direct evidence fundamental, factual questions relating to Presidential direction, knowledge, or approval of actions demonstrated by other evidence to be substantial grounds for impeachment of the President. In refusing to produce these papers and things, Richard M. Nixon, substituting his judgment as to what materials were necessary for the inquiry, interposed the powers of the Presidency against the lawful subpoenas of the House of Representatives, thereby assuming to himself functions and judgments as necessary to the exercise of the sole power of impeachment vested by the Constitution in the House of Representatives.

In all of this, Richard M. Nixon has acted in a manner contrary to his trust as President and subversive of constitutional government, to the great prejudice of the cause of law and justice, and to the manifest injury of the people of the United States.

Wherefore Richard M. Nixon, by such conduct, warrants impeachment and trial, and removal from office.

# Appendix VI: In the matter of – William Jefferson Clinton

**Article 1**

In his conduct while President of the United States, William Jefferson Clinton, in violation of his constitutional oath faithfully to execute the office of President of the United States and, to the best of his ability, preserve, protect, and defend the Constitution of the United States, and in violation of his constitutional duty to take care that the laws be faithfully executed, has willfully corrupted and manipulated the judicial process of the United States for his personal gain and exoneration, impeding the administration of justice in that:

On August 17, 1998, William Jefferson Clinton swore to tell the truth, the whole truth, and nothing but the truth before a Federal grand jury of the United States. Contrary to that oath, William Jefferson Clinton willfully provided perjurious, false and misleading testimony to the grand jury concerning on or more of the following: (1) the nature and details of his relationship with a subordinate Government employee; (2) prior perjurious, false and misleading testimony he gave in a Federal civil rights action brought against him; (3) prior false and misleading statements he allowed his attorney to make to a Federal judge in that civil rights action; and (4) his corrupt efforts to influence the testimony of witnesses and to impede the discovery of evidence in that civil rights action.

In doing this, William Jefferson Clinton has undermined the integrity of his office, has brought disrepute on the Presidency, has betrayed his trust as President, and has acted in a manner subversive of the rule of law and justice, to the manifest injury of the people of the United States.

Wherefore, William Jefferson Clinton, by such conduct, warrants impeachment and trial, and removal from office and disqualification to hold and enjoy any office of honor, trust, or profit under the United States.

## Article 2

In his conduct while President of the United States, William Jefferson Clinton, in violation of his constitutional oath faithfully to execute the office of the President of the United States and, to the best of his ability, preserve, protect, and defend the Constitution of the United States, and in violation of his constitutional duty to take care that the laws be faithfully executed, has prevented, obstructed, and impeded the administration of justice, and has to that end engaged personally, and through his subordinates and agents, in a course of conduct or scheme designed to delay, impede, cover up, and conceal the existence of evidence and testimony related to a Federal civil rights action brought against him in a duly instituted judicial proceeding.

The means used to implement this course of conduct or scheme included one or more of the following acts:

(1) On or about December 17, 1997, William Jefferson Clinton corruptly encouraged a witness in a Federal civil rights action brought against him to execute a sworn affidavit in that proceeding that he knew to be perjurious, false or misleading.

(2) On or about December 17, 1997, William Jefferson Clinton corruptly encouraged a witness in a Federal civil rights action brought against him to give perjurious, false and misleading testimony if and when called to testify personally in that proceeding.

(3) On or about December 28, 1997, William Jefferson Clinton corruptly engaged in, encouraged, or supported a scheme to conceal evidence that had been subpoenaed in a Federal civil rights action brought against him.

(4) Beginning on or about December 7, 1997, and continuing through and including January 14, 1998, William Jefferson Clinton intensified and succeeded in an effort to secure job assistance to a witness in a Federal civil rights action brought against him in order to corruptly prevent the truthful testimony of that witness in that proceeding at a time when the truthful testimony of that witness would have been harmful to him.

(5) On January 17, 1998, at his deposition in a Federal civil rights action brought against him, William Jefferson Clinton corruptly allowed his attorney to make false and misleading statements to a Federal judge characterizing an affidavit, in order to prevent questioning deemed relevant by the judge. Such false and misleading statements were subsequently acknowledged by his attorney in a communication to that judge.

(6)  On or about January 18 and January 20–21, 1998, William Jefferson Clinton related a false and misleading account of events relevant to a Federal civil rights action brought against him to a potential witness in that proceeding , in order to corruptly influence the testimony of that witness.

(7)  On or about January 21, 23, and 26, 1998, William Jefferson Clinton made false and misleading statements to potential witnesses in a Federal grand jury proceeding in order to corruptly influence the testimony of those witnesses. The false and misleading statements made by William Jefferson Clinton were repeated by the witnesses to the grand jury, causing the grand jury to receive false and misleading information.

In all of this, William Jefferson Clinton has undermined the integrity of his office, has brought disrepute on the Presidency, has betrayed his trust as President, and has acted in a manner subversive of the rule of law and justice, to the manifest injury of the people of the United States.

Wherefore, William Jefferson Clinton, by such conduct, warrants impeachment and trial, and removal from office and disqualification to hold and enjoy any office of honor, trust, or profit under the United States.

# Notes

## 1  Original Meaning

1. U.S. Constitution, Article II, Section 4.
2. Proceedings of Commissioners to Remedy Defects of the Federal Government (September 11, 1786), reprinted in Arthur Taylor Prescott, *Drafting the Federal Constitution* (Baton Rouge: Louisiana State UP, 1941) 3–11.
3. Although the day fixed for meeting had been Monday, May 14, James Madison recorded in his notes that "a small number only had assembled. Seven states were not convened until Friday, May 25th." James Madison, *Notes of Debates in the Federal Convention of 1787* (New York: Norton, 1987) 23 ("Notes").
4. Madison had been the first delegate from outside Pennsylvania to come to Philadelphia, arriving on May 5. George Mason, the last of the Virginia delegates arrived on May 17. The delegation immediately began meeting for several hours a day. Jack N. Rakove, *Original Meanings: Politics and Ideas in the Making of the Constitution* (New York: Knopf, 1996) 59. Indeed, as Rakove has noted, Madison came to Philadelphia with his own plan for the new government. Jack N. Rakove, *James Madison and the Creation of the American Republic*, 2d ed. (London: Longman, 2002) 49.
5. Madison, *Notes*, 30–33.
6. Rakove, *Original Meanings*, 59.
7. William Pierce, a delegate from Georgia, wrote that "Mr. Randolph…came forward with the postulate, or first principles, on which the convention acted, and he supported them with a force of eloquence and reasoning that did him great honor." Prescott, *Drafting the Federal Constitution*, 33.
8. Raoul Berger observed that "in the impeachment debate, the convention was almost exclusively concerned with the President." Berger, *Impeachment: The Constitutional Problems* (Cambridge, MA: Harvard UP, 1973) 100.
9. This hostility toward the exercise of royal power in the colonies was translated into a conception of separation of powers that would later find form in the Constitution. Harvey C. Mansfield, "Separation of Powers in the American Constitution," Bradford P. Wilson and Peter W. Schramm, eds., *Separation of Powers and Good Government* (Lanham: Rowman & Littlefield, 1994) 9. Joseph M. Besette and Gary J. Schmitt also noted the effect of the colonial experience on the convention's conception of the presidency. Joseph M. Besette and Gary J. Schmitt, "Executive Power and the American Founding," Wilson and Schramm, eds., *Separation of Powers and Good Government*, 51–52.

10. Max Farrand noted that over the course of the convention the conception of the president had evolved from an office dependent on the Congress to "an independent figure of importance." Thus, Farrand wrote, "It was a new officer whom they were creating and he loomed all the larger in their eyes that from the very limitations of their experience they were compelled to think of him in terms of monarchy, the only form of national executive power they knew." Max Farrand, *The Framing of the Constitution of the United States* (New Haven: Yale UP, 1972) 161–162. Akhil Reed Amar similarly observed that "Nothing quite like this new office had ever existed." Akhil Reed Amar, *America's Constitution: A Biography* (New York: Random House, 2005) 131.

    The fear of centralized power in the president was reflected in the convention debates. Although favoring a "vigorous executive," Charles Pinckney warned that conferring congressional powers such as peace and war on the president "would render the executive a monarchy, of the worst kind, to wit an elective one." Edmund Randolph similarly described the president as "The foetus of monarchy." Madison, *Notes*, 45–47. George Mason (who would later propose high crimes and misdemeanors as grounds for removing the president) warned that "If strong and extensive Powers are vested in the Executive, and that Executive consists of only one Person, the Government will of course degenerate…into a monarchy." Robert A. Rutland, ed., *The Papers of George Mason* (Chapel Hill: North Carolina UP, 1970) vol. 3: 897. Thus, David K. Nichols observed that "the purpose of the constitutional provisions regarding the presidency was to prevent the president from becoming a tyrant." David K. Nichols, "Congressional Dominance and the Emergence of the Modern Presidency," Wilson and Schramm, eds., *Separation of Powers and Good Government*, 121–122.

11. Carol Berkin, *A Brilliant Solution: Inventing the American Constitution* (New York: Harcourt, 2002) 152.

12. Madison, *Notes*, 32.

13. Ibid., 49.

14. Madison's comments were recorded in an aide memoire of William Pierce of Georgia. Max Farrand, ed., *The Records of the Federal Convention* (New Haven: Yale UP, 1966) vol. 1: 74. Madison did not record these comments in his *Notes*.

15. Madison, *Notes*, 116.

16. Dickinson explained that he "did not like the plan of impeaching the great officers of state" but it was necessary "to place the power of removing somewhere." Roger Sherman also recommended that the president be subject to removal by Congress "at pleasure." Madison opposed making the president "the mere creature of the legislature," because to do so would be "a violation of the fundamental principles of good government." Both Madison and James Wilson opposed removal of the president by the state legislatures. The Dickenson motion was rejected. Ibid., 55–58.

17. Ibid., 120.

18. Ibid.

19. Ibid., 139.

20. Ibid., 150–151. In the meantime, the delegates had continued to be concerned with the independence of the president. Opposing the proposal that the president be appointed by Congress, Gouverneur Morris argued that "If the Executive be chosen by the National Legislature, he will not be independent of it; and if not independent, usurpation and tyranny on the part of the legislature will be the consequence." Ibid., 308. Madison likewise saw the threat of tyranny in dependence of the president on the Congress. Madison noted that "The Executive could not be independent of the Legislature if dependent on the pleasure of that branch for reappointment," and observed that "a dependence of the Executive on the Legislature, would render it the Executor as well as the maker of laws; and then according to the observation of Montesquieu, tyrannical laws may be made that they may be executed in tyrannical manner." Ibid., 311. The proposal that the president serve during good behavior, similar to judges, had implications for impeachment. Madison argued that such an indeterminate term would depend on "the practicality of instituting a tribunal for impeachment as certain and as adequate in the one case as in the other." Skeptical, Mason stated that "It would be impossible to define the misbehavior in such a manner as to subject it to popular trial; and perhaps still more impossible to compel so high an offender holding his office by such tenure to submit a trial." Ibid., 312. Mason's comment on the impossibility of defining "misbehavior" strongly suggests Mason did not have criminality in mind for the grounds of impeachment since if he had, Mason could simply have referred to settled law. Later, Morris argued that impeachment was a "dangerous part of the plan" because even the threat of impeachment would hold the president "in such dependence that he will be no check on the legislature." Ibid., 323–324.
21. Ibid., 331.
22. Ibid. Mason was not necessarily referring to violations of the criminal laws as "great crimes." Addressing the Virginia Ratification Convention on June 14, 1788, Mason expressed skepticism that senators would convict themselves of bribery if they were impeached. Rutland, *The Papers of George Mason*, vol. 3: 1076–1077.
23. Madison, *Notes*, 332.
24. Ibid.
25. Ibid.
26. Madison also argued that removal of the executive by means of impeachment was necessary because in contrast to the legislature or "any other public body holding public offices of limited duration," the powers of the executive would be exercised by a single individual and therefore, "loss of capacity or corruption was more within the compass of probable events." To Madison, either this loss of capacity or corruption "might be fatal to the republic." Ibid., 332–333.
27. Ibid., 333–334.
28. Ibid., 334.
29. Ibid., 335.
30. Ibid.

31. Ibid., 372, 383.
32. Ibid., 379.
33. Ibid., 393.
34. Debate on the impeachment provision had been postponed on August 27 at the request of Gouverneur Morris. Ibid., 535. The impeachment provision along with the other provisions that had been postponed was referred to the "Committee of Eleven," comprised of a member of each delegation. Ibid., 569.

    On September 4, the Committee of Eleven issued a partial report to the convention of "additions and alterations" to the proposed constitution. In that report, the committee proposed that the president be removed "on impeachment by the House of Representatives, and conviction by the Senate, for Treason or bribery." Ibid., 575. The committee's report was taken up by the convention on September 8.
35. A reference to the impeachment of Warren Hastings, governor general of India, then pending in the Commons.
36. Madison, *Notes*, 605.
37. Ibid.
38. Ibid. A short time later, the clause was amended by substituting "United States" for "State." Ibid., 606. However, without explanation in the record, when the Committee on Style and Arrangement submitted the draft of the Constitution in final form on September 12, the clause "against the Untied States" had been dropped and the provision as adopted by the convention stated that "the president, vice president and all civil officers of the United States, shall be removed from office on impeachment for, and conviction of treason, bribery or other high crimes and misdemeanors." Ibid., 624.
39. For example, in the debate concerning extradition under Article XV of the draft prepared by the Committee of Detail, which provided for the return of persons charged with "treason, felony or high misdemeanor" (Ibid., 394), Madison recorded that "the words 'high misdemeanor,' were struck out, and the words 'other crime' inserted in order to comprehend all proper cases: it being doubtful whether 'high misdemeanor' had not a technical meaning too limited." Ibid., 545.
40. Peter Charles Hoffer and N.E.H. Hull, *Impeachment in America, 1635–1805* (New Haven: Yale UP, 1984) 46–47.
41. Hoffer and Hull, *Impeachment in America*, 47.
42. Bernard Bailyn, *The Ordeal of Thomas Hutchinson* (Cambridge, MA: Harvard UP, 1974) 202; John Adams, *Papers of John Adams*, ed. Robert J. Taylor, vol. 1 (Cambridge, MA: Harvard UP, 1977) 252 (ed. note).
43. Those opposing payment of colonial officials from the civic list viewed the practice as a threat to their autonomy over their local officials. John Quincy Adams, *Life of John Adams* printed in John Adams, *The Works of John Adams*, ed. Charles Francis Adams (Boston: Little, 1856) vol. 1: 116–117.
44. A committee of the assembly immediately denounced Hutchison's royal salary as "a dangerous innovation which renders him a governor not dependent on the people, as the charter has prescribed…It destroys that mutual check

and dependence which each branch of the legislature ought to have upon the others, and the balance of power which is essential to all free governments." Bailyn noted that when it was learned a short time later that the judges would also receive salaries from the crown, "indignation, fear, and rage roared like a sheet of flame across the troubled community." Bailyn, *The Ordeal of Thomas Hutchinson*, 203, 205.

45. Adams, *Papers of John Adams*, vol. 1: 252–253 (ed. note); Bailyn, *The Ordeal of Thomas Huntchinson*, 206. As described by Bailyn, "the Boston Proceedings found a wide and fervent audience throughout Massachusetts." Ibid., 206, 207.

46. Adams, *Papers of John Adams*, vol. 1: 310 (ed. note); also Bailyn, *The Ordeal of Thomas Hutchinson*, 207, 209.

47. The essence of Brattle's argument concerning judicial compensation and the independence of the judiciary was that judges held a life estate in their commissions because they served "during good behavior" and therefore the source of their compensation was irrelevant. In this regard, Brattle contended that "The Governor and Counsel cannot legally or constitutionally remove a justice of the Superior Court…unless there is a fair hearing and trial, and then judgment that he had behaved ill." Adams contended that "No such tenure had ever actually existed in Massachusetts or elsewhere," and cited a variety of precedents, including Lord Coke's *Institutes of the Lawes of England* (1628), to the effect that judges held their offices at the King's pleasure. Adams argued that the Massachusetts charter granted to the General Court the authority to create the courts and define their responsibilities. Adams, *Papers of John Adams*, vol. 1: 268–306.

48. Bailyn, *The Ordeal of Thomas Hutchinson*, 207.

49. Massachusetts Historical Society, Journals of the House of Representatives of Massachusetts 1773–1774 (Boston, 1981) 117.

50. Adams, *Papers of John Adams*, vol. 2: 8. When the General Court went into session in January 1774, statements from the judges were accepted.

51. Bailyn, *The Ordeal of Thomas Hutchinson*, 265–266. Adams made a similar observation in his autobiography. John Adams, *Diary and Autobiography of John Adams*, ed. L.H. Butterfield, vol. 3 (Cambridge, MA: Harvard UP, 1961) 298.

52. Although by his own account, Adams' suggestion of impeaching the judges was initially received by Winthrop's guests as novel (see *Diary*, 300 and letter to William Tudor, *Works of John Adams*, vol. 10: 237, 238), in fact another prominent lawyer, Josiah Quincy, had raised the prospect of impeachment in an article published by the *Boston Gazette and Country Journal* on January 4, 1768. In that article, Quincy inveighed against the "usurpation of public authority" by British officials who had "obtained, by a veneral *Amassment of Power*, such unlimited sway, in the State, as to be able with impunity, *to Condemn the Innocent as a Judge and destroy the Constitution as a Statesman.*" *Boston Gazette and Country Journal*, January 4, 1768, 1 (emphasis original). Quincy noted in "happy contrast," however, that the "wise and venerable ancestors" of the Americans who had been "conscious of the predominate vices of mankind," had been "eminently careful in guarding every avenue where it would be probable the ambitious and intrepid Enemy would labor

to enter, by strategies and force, in order to destroy that nobel fabrick...the *British Constitution.*" Under that constitution, "no subject, however great and powerful, is beyond the reach of a strict examination into his conduct, or out of danger of a scourage for his crimes." The vehicle for this "strict examination" and "scourage," Quincy explained, was impeachment of a commoner or peer by the Commons and trial before the Lords. Quincy discussed the procedure for impeachment citing various British authorities and impeachment proceedings. *Boston Gazette and Country Journal,* 1.

53. John Adams, letter to William Tudor, January 24, 1817, Adams, *Works of John Adams,* vol. 10: 236.

54. Adams, *Diary (The Works of John Adams,* vol. 2), 329–330.

55. Adams, *Diary (The Works of John Adams,* vol. 2), 330.

56. *Journals of the House of Representatives of Massachusetts 1773–1774,* 146–147.

57. Adams, *Diary (The Works of John Adams,* vol. 2), 331; letter to William Tudor, *The Works of John Adams,* vol. 10: 239.

58. Adams, *Papers of John Adams,* vol. 2: 11,13.

59. Ibid., 13–14.

60. Ibid., 14.

61. Ibid., 16. The House added that, in any event, his compensation was "always fully equal to the Merit of his Services" because "as it is well known...he was appointed to said Office without previous Education and regular Study in the law." Ibid., 17.

62. Ibid., 17. This description of Oliver's high crimes and misdemeanors closely parallels the language used in the impeachments of, for example, Lord Kimbolton, Denzil Hollis, Sir Arthur Hazelrig, John Pym, John Hampden, and William Strode for high treason, where it was charged that "they have traitorously endeavoured to subvert the fundamental laws and government of this kingdom, to deprive the king of his regal power, and to place in the subjects an arbitrary and tyrannical power, over the lives, liberties and estates of his majesty's liege subjects" and "they have traitorously endeavoured, by many foul aspersions upon his majesty and his government, to alienate the affections of his people, and to make his majesty odious to them." Thomas Bayly Howell, *A Complete Collection of State Trials and Proceedings for High Treason and Other Crimes and Misdemeanors from the Earliest Period to the Year 1783* (London: R. Bagshaw, 1809) vol. 4: 83 ("State Trials"); and William Cobbett, *The Parliamentary History of England from the Earliest Period to the Year 1803* (London: T.C. Hansard, 1808) vol. 2: 1005 ("Parliamentary History of England"). Similar language can be found in the impeachment of Edward, Earl of Clarendon, the Lord High Chancellor of England, for "high Treason and other high Crimes and Misdemeanors" in 1663. Howell, *State Trials,* vol. 6: 291; and Cobbett, *Parliamentary History of England,* vol. 4: 157; and in the impeachment of Thomas, Earl of Danby, the Lord High Treasurer of England, in 1678 also for "high Treason and other high Crimes and Misdemeanors." Howell, *State Trials,* vol. 2: 600; and Cobbett, *Parliamentary History of England,* vol. 4: 693.

63. Adams, *The Papers of John Adams*, vol. 2: 10 (ed. note).
64. Adams, *Diary* (*The Works of John Adams*, vol. 2), 332. Adams, *The Life of John Adams* (*The Works of John Adams*, vol. 1), 139. Adams also referred to this rebellion of the jurors in his letter to William Tudor in 1817. Adams, *The Works of John Adams*, vol. 10: 240–241.
65. Adams, *Diary* (*The Works of John Adams*, vol. 2), 330 and Letter to William Tudor, Adams, *The Works of John Adams*, vol. 10: 238.
66. Mason, *The Papers of George Mason*, vol. 1: 303 (ed. note).
67. Ibid., 308.
68. Hoffer and Hull, *Impeachment in America*, 10. For example, both Hale's *Pleas of the Crown* and Blackstone's *Commentaries* were in John Adam's library. H. Trevor Colbourn, *The Lamp of Experience: Whig History and the Intellectual Origins of the American Revolution* (Indianapolis: Liberty Fund, 1998) Appendix A.
69. Sir Matthew Hale, *Pleas of the Crown: A Methodical Summary*, vol. 1 (London: Professional Books, 1972) 150.
70. Blackstone, *Commentaries*, vol. 4: 256.
71. Ibid., 256–258.
72. Blackstone described maladministration as including embezzlement of public funds and "contempts of the executive magistrate, as demonstrate themselves by some arrogant and undutiful behavior towards the king and government." These were contempts: against the King's prerogative (such as: "preferring the interests of a foreign potentate to those of our own," or "doing or receiving anything that may create an undue influence in favor of such extrinsic power, as by taking a pension from any foreign prince without consent of the King," or disobeying the lawful commands of the King); against the King's person and government (such as: speaking or writing against the King or government, wishing the King ill, circulating scandalous stories against the King, or "doing any thing that may tend to lessen him in the esteem of his subjects, may weaken his government, or may raise jealousies between him and his people"); against the King's title (such as: denying the King's right to the crown, stating that the common law "ought not to direct the right of the crown of England," or refusing to take oaths required by statute for public office); and against the King's palaces or courts of justice (such as: striking the King's person, drawing a sword or assaulting a judge in Westminster Hall or the Assises, aiding a prisoner to escape, or injuring those who are "immediately under the protection of a court," including adversaries, lawyers, jurors, or dissuading a witness from testifying). Ibid., 121–126.
73. Ibid., 121.
74. Ibid., 258.
75. Richard Wooddeson, *A Systematical View of the Laws of England; As Treated of in a Course of Vinerian Lectures, Read at Oxford, During a Series of Years, Commencing in Michaelmas Term, 1777,* vol. 2 (Dublin: E. Lynch, 1792) 601–602 ("A Systematical View of the Laws of England").
76. Blackstone, *Commentaries*, vol. 4: 258.

77. Ibid., 258.
78. Wooddeson, *A Systematical View of the Laws of England*, vol. 2: 596–597.
79. Blackstone, *Commentaries*, vol. 4: 308.
80. Sir Matthew Hale, *The History of the Common Law of England*, ed. Charles M. Gray (Chicago: Chicago UP, 1971) 35. W.S. Holdsworth also commented on the distinction between accusation by appeal and by impeachment in his treatise. Holdsworth wrote that appeal and impeachment were "historically very far apart." W.S. Holdsworth, *A History of English Law*, vol. 1 (London: Methuen, 1903) 381. Blackstone also distinguished between attainder and impeachment. Blackstone wrote that the "acts of parliament to attaint particular persons of treason or felony, or to inflict pains and penalties, beyond or contrary to the common law, to serve a special purpose" were "to all intents and purposes new laws, made pro re nata, and by no means an execution of such as are already in being." On the other hand, Blackstone viewed "an impeachment before the lords by the commons of Great Britain, in parliament," as "a prosecution of the already known and established law…being a presentment to the most high and supreme court of criminal jurisdiction by the most solemn grand inquest of the whole kingdom." Blackstone, *Commentaries*, vol. 4: 256. Wooddeson agreed. Wooddeson, *A Systematical View of the Laws of England*, vol. 2: 611.
81. To Holdsworth, it was "only natural that the Commons, when they discovered that royal officials or others had broken the law, and that the government of the state was therefore badly conducted, should make a complaint to the House of Lords, which took the form of an accusation against the delinquents; and that the Lords should entertain and deal with it." Thus, it was Holdsworth's view that "the practice of impeachment arose partly from the alliance of the two Houses to secure the sanctity of the law as against royal officials or favourites, and partly from the wide and indefinite jurisdiction which the House of Lords exercised at the time." Holdsworth, *A History of English Law*, vol. 1: 380–381. Wooddeson shared this view of impeachment as carrying the law "into effectual execution where it might be obstructed by too powerful delinquents, or not easily discerned in the ordinary course of jurisdiction, by reason of the peculiar quality of the alleged crimes." Wooddeson, *A Systematical View of the Laws of England*, vol. 2: 611.
82. Sir James Fitzjames Stephen, *A History of the Criminal Law of England*, vol. 1 (London: Macmillan, 1883) 146. Also at this time, "during the rule of Henry III," Hubert deBurgh, the Lord Chief Justice and "one of the King's favorites," was tried before Parliament. According to Sir Edward Coke, deBurgh had gained the King's favor by counseling the King to cancel the *Magna Carta* and the *Carte de Forestra*. Subsequently, deBurgh "fell into the King's heavy indignation" and he was convicted by Parliament for his actions. Sir Edward Coke, *The Golden Passage in the Great Charter of England Called Magna Carta* (London: E. and C. Dilly, 1775) 5–6. This parliamentary trial appears to have taken place in the aftermath of the civil war between the crown and the barons in 1264–1265. The reference to Parliament is probably to assemblies of nobles summoned by the King to discuss "the business of the King

and his kingdom." Goldwin Smith, *A Constitutional and Legal History of England* (New York: Scribner, 1955) 146–148.

83. Stephen, *A History of the Criminal Law of England*, vol. 1 (New York: Scribner, 1955) 146–147.

84. Ibid., 147–148. T.F.T. Plucknett disputed Berkeley's contentions. T.F.T. Plucknett, *Studies in English History* (London: Hambledon, 1983) 545–546.

85. Stephen, *A History of the Criminal Law of England*, vol. 1: 148. Hallam similarly observed that the charges against Latimer were "The earliest instance of parliamentary impeachment, or of a solemn accusation of any individual by the commons at the bar of the lords." Henry Hallam, *The Constitutional History of England: From the Accession of Henry VII to the Death of George II*, 7th ed., vol. 1 (London: John Murray, 1854) 357. Stephen, *A History of the Criminal Law of England*, vol. 1: 147–148.

86. John Hatsell, *Precedents of Proceedings in the House of Commons*, vol. 4 (London: Hansard and Sons, 1818) 56–57.

87. Ibid., 69.

88. Ibid., 69–72.

89. Thomas Salmon, *Critical Review of the State Trials and Impeachments for High Treasons*, vol. 1 (London: J. and J. Hazard, 1737) 1 ("Critical Review of the State Trials"). Hatsell, *Precedents of Proceedings in the House of Commons*, vol. 4: 57. According to M.V. Clarke, by the time that Commons lodged its charge against de la Pole, "impeachments had become a recognized part of parliamentary practice and a recognized form of the expression of hostility to royal officials and servants." M.V. Clarke, "The Origin of Impeachment," Herbert Edward Salter, ed., *Oxford Essays in Medieval History* (Oxford: Clarendon Press, 1934, Freeport: Books for Libraries Press, 1968) 165.

90. Salmon, *Critical Review of the State Trials*, vol. 1, 1; Hatsell, *Precedents of Proceedings in the House of Commons*, vol. 4: 57.

91. Salmon, *Critical Review of the State Trials*, vol. 1: 1. He was later impeached and convicted of treason in 1388 and he was executed. Ibid. These charges were brought before Parliament by "appeal" of the Duke of Gloucester, who was the uncle of Richard II, and other "lords appellant." Stephen described the "substance of the charges" against de la Pole as having been "that they have led Richard II to misgovern in various ways, and in particular that they had induced him to resist or evade an act passed in 1386 which particularly put the Royal Power in commission, and that they had procured an opinion from five judges and a sarjeant-at-law that the commission so issued was void, and that those who procured it were liable to be punished as traitors." Ibid., 152.

92. M.V. Clarke attributed the reemergence of impeachment to Sir Edward Coke. Clarke, "The Origin of Impeachment," 185.

93. Stephen, *A History of the Criminal Law of England*, vol. 1: 158. Hatsell made this observation as well. Hatsell, *Precedents of Proceedings in the House of Commons*, vol. 4: 72. Hallam noted that impeachment "had fallen into disuse…partly from the preference the Tudor princes had given to bills of attainder or of pains and penalties, when they wished to turn the arm of

parliament against an obnoxious subject." Hallam, *The Constitutional History of England*, vol. 1: 357. Holdsworth also noted that "the practice of impeachment fell into abeyance (like the other branches of the judicature of the Parliament) between 1459 and 1621. The place of impeachments was taken by acts of attainder." Holdsworth, *A History of English Law*, vol. 1: 190. George Burton Adams similarly in his *Constitutional History of England* observed that impeachment had "fallen into abeyance" because "during the whole or nearly two centuries parliament had not attempted seriously to oppose the sovereign." George Burton Adams, *Constitutional History of England* (New York: Holt, 1926) 280–281. Sir David Lindsay Keir has suggested that removal of ministers during the Tudor period was more the result of the loss of royal favor than of judicial process. Sir David Lindsay Keir, *The Constitutional History of Modern Britain* (London: Adam & Charles Black, 1966) 39.

94. David L. Smith, *A History of the Modern British Isles 1603–1707* (Oxford: Blackwell, 1998) 59.

95. Howell, *State Trials*, vol. 2: 1120, 1132. Hallam, *The Constitutional History of England*, vol. 1: 357.

96. Sir Francis Bacon, the Lord Chancellor, also was impeached on charges of corruption for having accepted bribes to influence litigation and to obtain offices in government. Howell, *State Trials*, vol. 1: 73. Bacon was convicted and as a consequence was fined £ 40,000 and deprived of public office. Smith, *A History of the Modern British Isles*, 59. Keir, *The Constitutional History of Modern Britain*, 193.

97. Howell, *State Trials*, vol. 2: 1135–1136; Cobbett, *Parliamentary History of England*, vol. 1: 1232.

98. J.R. Tanner, *English Constitutional Conflicts of the Seventeenth Century* (Cambridge: Cambridge UP, 1966) 47–50.

99. Tanner, *English Constitutional Conflicts of the Seventeenth Century*, 50. As M.V. Clarke observed, "Impeachment was, in fact, a direct challenge to the royal prerogative, but, by discreet simulation of the 'ancient law of the land,' a bridge was thrown up between normal usage and revolution…It had grown naturally into the 'Law of Parliament.'" Clarke, "The Origin of Impeachment," 189.

100. Hallam, *The Constitutional History of England*, vol. 1: 358.

101. Howell, *State Trials*, vol. 2: 1184; Cobbett, *Parliamentary History of England*, vol. 1: 1411.

102. Howell, *State Trials*, vol. 2: 1184; Cobbett, *Parliamentary History of England*, vol. 1: 1411.

103. Howell, *State Trials*, vol. 2: 1184; Cobbett, *Parliamentary History of England*, vol. 1: 1411.

104. There was, however, the tortured proceedings against the Duke of Buckingham in 1626, reflecting the Commons' displeasure with the policy regarding Spain and France. In 1626, the Earl of Bristol, an opponent of Buckingham, was accused by Charles I of high treason relating to his duplicity in the negotiation of a treaty with Spain. His defense to the charge

included accusations concerning Buckingham's own actions in Spain. Buckingham, in turn, was impeached by Commons on charges that he had conspired to encourage Charles to convert to the Roman Church as a consequence of his marriage to Henrietta Maria, sister of Philip, King of Spain. Buckingham was also impeached for "Misdemeanors, Misprisions, Offences and Crimes" in regard to his service as lord high admiral, including allegations that he had procured the position corruptly and had misused his office for personal gain. Howell, *State Trials*, vol. 2: 1268; Cobbett, *Parliamentary History of England*, vol. 1: 1411.

105. Howell, *State Trials*, vol. 3: 1283.

106. Ibid.

107. Tanner, *English Constitutional Conflicts of the Seventeenth Century*, 75.

108. Howell, *State Trials*, vol. 3: 1283.

109. Ibid.

110. Cobbett, *Parliamentary History of England*, vol. 2: 526–527.

111. Tanner, *English Constitutional Conflicts of the Seventeenth Century*, 77.

112. Howell, *State Trials*, vol. 3: 1283; David A. Smith, *Constitutional Royalism and the Search for Settlement 1640–1649* (Cambridge: Cambridge UP, 1994) 69–70.

113. *House of Commons Journal*, vol. 2 (21 May 1642).

114. Smith, *A History of Modern British Isles*, 122–123; Tanner, *English Constitutional Conflicts of the Seventeenth Century*, 108–111.

115. Howell, *State Trials*, vol. 4: 122–123. Lord Kimbolton and his codefendants had been charged with high treason on January 3, 1641. Ibid., 83.

116. Ibid., 131–132.

117. Tanner, *English Constitutional Conflicts of the Seventeenth Century*, 15.

118. Howell, *State Trials*, vol. 4: 28; Cobbett, *Parliamentary History of England*, vol. 2: 861.

119. In 1642, two years after the impeachment of Wren, Laud himself was charged with high treason on the grounds the he had caused the King to dissolve Parliament in 1628, as well as for other actions he had taken in furtherance of his stated intention "to shake and alter the true Protestant Religion established in the Church of England." Laud was attainted and beheaded. Howell, *State Trials*, vol. 4: 315.

120. Ibid., 151; Cobbett, *Parliamentary History of England*, vol. 2: 1147.

121. Howell, *State Trials*, vol. 4: 159–166; Cobbett, *Parliamentary History of England*, vol. 2: 1406. Guerney was removed from office and imprisoned in the Tower of London.

122. Howell, *State Trials*, vol. 4: 167–170. No action by the Lords appears to have been taken.

123. Ibid., 171–172; Cobbett, *Parliamentary History of England*, vol. 2: 1407. It does not appear that any action was taken by the Lords.

124. Howell, *State Trials*, vol. 4: 914–916; Cobbett, *Parliamentary History of England*, vol. 3: 838. Maynard was committed to the Tower at the pleasure of the Commons. The proceedings against Maynard were later dropped and his seat in the Commons was restored.

125. Tanner, *English Constitutional Conflicts of the Seventeenth Century*, 217–218, 227–229. For example, in 1663, the Earl of Bristol charged Edward Hyde, Earl of Clarendon and lord high chancellor, with "High Treason and Other Crimes and Misdemeanors" for having accused the King of being inclined to "popery" and having assisted "papists" and thereby having attempted "to alienate from him the affections of his subjects." The impeachment was dismissed by the Lords on the grounds that an impeachment could not be brought by one peer against another. Howell, *State Trials*, vol. 4: 291–318; Cobbett, *Parliamentary History of England*, vol. 4: 276; Salmon, *Critical Review of the State Trials and Impeachments for High Treason*, vol. 1: 302. Hyde was subsequently blamed for England's humiliating defeat by the Dutch navy and the ensuing Treaty of Breda and was impeached for treason in 1667. The impeachment failed before the Lords but fearing trial before a special court of peers and realizing that he no longer enjoyed the protection of the King, Hyde fled England and died in exile at Rouen in December 1674. Smith, *A History of the Modern British Isles*, 218. In 1673, an attempt was made to impeach the Earl of Arlington for being a "promoter of popery and popish counsels." Commons rejected a motion to remove Arlington from his royal employments and no further action appears to have been taken. Howell, *State Trials*, vol. 6: 1053; Cobbett, *Parliamentary History of England*, vol. 4: 650.

126. The abuse of authority could be purely personal as it had been in the case of Lord Viscount Mordaunt, who was impeached in 1666 for high crimes and misdemeanors in connection with a personal vendetta against William Tayleur. Tayleur's daughter had rebuffed Mordaunt's advances and had threatened to inform Mordaunt's wife. In retaliation, Mordaunt ejected Tayleur from his residence, withdrew his employment, imprisoned him illegally for twenty weeks, and threatened to imprison him repeatedly for the rest of his life. The matter ended when the King prorogued Parliament. Howell, *State Trials*, vol. 6: 786; Cobbett, *Parliamentary History of England*, vol. 4: 348.

127. Harding, *A Social History of English Law*, 260. Frederick G. Marcham noted that in the late seventeenth and early eighteenth centuries the view had prevailed in the Commons that ministers should be held accountable for their actions even if the King could not. Between 1690 and 1715, eleven ministers and ex-ministers were impeached but the Commons did not proceed to trial before the Lords because it was recognized that the Lords were not amenable to impeachments for purely political purposes. Frederick G. Marcham, *A Constitutional History of Modern England 1485 to the Present* (New York: Harper) 210–211. Clayton Roberts made a similar observation in his reply to Raoul Berger in "The Law of Impeachment in Stuart England," *Yale Law Review* (1975) vol. 84: 1419.

128. Howell, *State Trials*, vol. 6: 866–868; Cobbett, *Parliamentary History of England*, vol. 4: 408–409. No action was taken by the Lords.

129. Howell, *State Trials*, vol.6: 869–878; Cobbett, *Parliamentary History of England*, vol. 4: 409–413. It does not appear that further action was taken by the Lords.

130. Cobbett, *Parliamentary History of England*, vol. 4: 693–695.

131. Smith, *A History of the Modern British Isles*, 252. Smith, *A Constitutional and Legal History of England*, 360.

132. Howell, *State Trials*, vol. 8: 127–136; and Cobbett, *Parliamentary History of England*, vol. 4: 1067–1074; Hatsell, *Precedents of Proceedings in the House of Commons*, vol. 4: 125; Salmon, *Critical Review of the State Trials and Impeachments for High Treason*, 330. It appears that Danby had been acting on behalf of Charles II and that the payments were to obtain England's neutrality. Lovell, *English Constitutional and Legal History*, 384. The Danby impeachment may also have been part of a larger contest between Parliament's control of finance and the King's prerogative in foreign affairs. Keir, *The Constitutional History of Modern Britain*, 255. In any event, the proceedings were brought to an end by the King's prorogation of Parliament on December 30, 1678 and the dissolution of Parliament on January 24, 1679. Tanner, *English Constitutional Conflicts of the Seventeenth Century*, 240, 241.

In the face of renewed impeachment proceedings, Danby was granted a royal pardon. However, the pardon was held not to bar impeachment and this was confirmed by the Act of Settlement of 1701. Smith, *A Constitutional and Legal History of England*, 369; Albert Thomas Carter, *Outlines of English Legal History* (London: Butterworth, 1899) 84–85. This exception to the pardoning power was later enshrined in Article II, Section 2(1) of the U.S. Constitution which grants the president authority to issue "pardons for offences against the United States, except in cases of impeachment."

133. Howell, *State Trials*, vol. 8: 127–137; Cobbett, *Parliamentary History of England*, vol. 4: 1222–1223. Parliament was dissolved before any action was taken by the Lords. Also in 1680, the lord chief justice, William Scroggs, was impeached of "High Treason and Other Great Crimes and Misdemeanors" for having obstructed the return of indictments against "many papists," including the Duke of York and for "absenting himself from church." Scroggs and other judges were also charged with "countenancing of popery, and discouragement of Protestants," by enjoining publication of a periodical "wherein the superstitions and cheats of the Church of Rome were from time to time exposed." The proceedings were abandoned in anticipation of the prorogation of Parliament. Howell, *State Trials*, vol. 8: 163–174; Cobbett, *Parliamentary History of England*, vol. 4: 1274–1277.

At this time, Commons asserted jurisdiction to impeach offenders for common law crimes. In 1688, Edward Fitzgerald was impeached for high treason for having advocated that Charles II be deposed. The Lords directed that the case be referred to the King's Bench for trial. Although the Commons disagreed, Parliament was dissolved and Fitzgerald was tried by the King's Bench and upon conviction was executed. W.W. Costin and J. Steven Watson, eds., *The Law and Working of the Constitution: Documents 1660–1914* (London: Adam and Charles Black, 1925) 185–186.

134. Howell, *State Trials*, vol. 14: 323. The Lords ordered the charges to be dismissed after the Commons in two successive Parliaments had failed to act.

135. Cobbett, *Parliamentary History of England*, vol. 5: 939.

136. Orford was also charged with mismanagement in his capacity as commander in chief of the Navy by procuring a commission and provisions for the privateer William Kidd and for allowing the escape of French naval forces. Howell, *State Trials*, vol. 14: 233–1259; Salmon, *Critical Review of the State Trials and Impeachments for High Treason*, 866.

137. Howell, *State Trials*, vol. 14: 250–261; 294–298; 311; 312; Cobbett, *Parliamentary History of England*, vol. 5: 1266–1277; 1299–1305; 1313. Orford, Sommers, and Halifax were ultimately acquitted by the Lords. Several years earlier in 1698, a group of merchants had been charged with high crimes and misdemeanors for engaging in commerce with France in violation of English Law. After confessing their guilt, they were fined and imprisoned at Newgate. Cobbett, *Parliamentary History of England*, vol. 5: 1175–1177.

138. Smith, *A History of the Modern British Isles*, 319.

139. Howell, *State Trials*, vol. 15: 39–40, 471–471, Cobbett, *Parliamentary History of England*, vol. 6: 809–812, 883–887; Hatsell, *Precedents of Proceedings in the House of Commons*, 256. Sacheverell was enjoined from preaching for three years and his sermons were ordered to be burned by the hangman.

140. The Committee of Secrecy in the Commons charged additionally that Oxford had weakened the army in Flanders by advising the Queen to send an expeditionary force to Canada, which proved to be a costly failure, and then had prevented the Commons from inquiring into the matter. Oxford was acquitted of all charges by the Lords. Howell, *State Trials*, vol. 15: 1046–1103, 1178; Cobbett, *Parliamentary History of England*, vol. 7: 74–103; Salmon, *Critical Review of the State Trials and Impeachments for High Treason*, 866.

141. Howell, *State Trials*, vol. 15: 1007–1014, Cobbett, *Parliamentary History of England*, vol. 7: 138–142.

142. Howell, *State Trials*, vol. 15: 994–1006; Cobbett, *Parliamentary History of England*, vol. 7: 143–155. Hallam described the impeachments of Oxford and Bolingbroke as "an intemperate excess of resentment at their scandalous dereliction of public honour and interest." Hallam, *The Constitutional History of England*, vol. 3: 312.

143. Howell, *State Trials*, vol. 15: 1013–1043; Cobbett, *Parliamentary History of England*, vol. 7: 143–155.

144. Howell, *State Trials*, vol. 16: 767–1395; and Cobbett, *Parliamentary History of England*, vol. 8: 420–453.

145. Stephen, *A History of the Criminal Law of England*, vol. 1: 160.

146. Holdsworth, *A History of English Law*, vol. 1: 381–382. F.W. Maitland drew this contrast with the Tudor period as well. Maitland, *The Constitutional History of England*, 246. Radcliff and Cross noted, however, that associating the grounds for impeachment with criminal conduct limited its effectiveness on controlling ministerial behavior. Geoffrey R.Y. Radcliffe and Geoffrey N. Cross, *The English Legal System*, ed. G.J. Hand and D.J. Bently, 6th ed. (London: Butterworths, 1977) 224.

147. Quoted in Marcham, *A Constitutional History of Modern England*, 210.

148. Bryce D. Lyon, *A Constitutional and Legal History of Medieval England* (New York: Norton, 1980) 558–559.
149. Ibid., 559.
150. Robert, Earl Russell, *An Essay on the History of English Government and Constitution: From the Reign of Henry VII to the Present Time* (New York: Kraus Reprint, 1971) 117.
151. Raoul Berger argued that to understand impeachment under the Constitution it was necessary to begin with English precedent. Berger contended that the meaning of high crimes and misdemeanors lay not in statutory or common law crime but was a crime "by the course of Parliament." Drawing on the impeachments of the seventeenth and eighteenth centuries, Berger concluded that in impeachment, Parliament had defined a category of political crimes that were distinct from known, ordinary criminal law offenses. These political offenses included: misapplication of funds; abuse of official power; neglect of duty; encroachment on or contempt of Parliament's prerogatives; and corruption in public office. Berger, *Impeachment: The Constitutional Problems*, 54–71. Selden and Holdsworth had the same view of Parliament's authority to pronounce the law. John Selden, *Table Talk of John Selden*, ed. Samuel Harvey Reynolds (Oxford: Clarendon, 1892) 100; Holdsworth, *A History of English Law*, vol. 1: 380–384.

   Berger's thesis concerning political crimes was criticized by Clayton Roberts, who faulted Berger for failing to give greater weight to those instances in which the Lords either acquitted the accused or took no action when offenses other than violations of known law were charged in an impeachment. In Roberts' view, while the Commons may have sought to define a category of offenses other than violations of known law, the Lords had opposed that effort. Roberts, "The Law of Impeachment in Stuart England," 1430–1436.

   Although Roberts' critique of Berger's thesis and of the meaning of high crimes and misdemeanors has weight, the relevance to the intent of the Framers of so fine an analysis of what the Lords found acceptable or unacceptable is at least questionable.
152. Quincy also noted in this regard that: "The Spencers, Father and Son, were Impeached, for that they prevented the great Men of the Realm from giving their Counsel to the King, except in their Presence," and "that they put good Magistrats out of Office, and advanced bad." *Boston Gazette and Country Journal*, January 4, 1768: 1.
153. Ibid.
154. Adams, *Works of John Adams*, vol. 10: 238–239. Adams also referred to his conversation with Major Hawley in his diary. Adams, *Works of John Adams*, vol. 2: 330.
155. Indeed, as Robert A. Rutland, the editor of George Mason's papers, noted, "Reports from England on the impeachment of Warren Hastings, the Viceroy of India, had an impact on Americans who were already convinced that corruption flourished throughout the British Empire. Hastings had been impeached for 'high crimes and misdemeanors' an expression

Mason soon borrowed." Rutland, *The Papers of George Mason*, ed. note, vol. 3: 980.

156. Alfred Lyall, *Warren Hastings* (Freeport: Books for Libraries Press, 1970, first published in 1889) 3.

157. Ibid., 29; and P.J. Marshall, ed., *The Oxford History of the British Empire: The Eighteenth Century* (Oxford: Oxford UP, 2001), 122, 165, 510, 513, 539–540 ("The Oxford History of the British Empire").

158. H.V. Bowen, "British India, 1765–1813: The Metropolitan Context," Marshall, *The Oxford History of the British Empire*, 540.

159. Ibid., 540–541.

160. Ibid., 541.

161. Conor Cruise O'Brien, "Warren Hastings in Burke's Great Melody," Geoffrey Carnal and Colin Nicholson, eds., *The Impeachment of Warren Hastings* (Edinburgh: Edinburgh UP, 1989) 61–62, 65. Lyall suggested that Burke may also have seen an attack on Hastings as serving a larger political objective in the contest with Pitt. Lyall, *Warren Hastings*, 186. Lord Macauley dismissed the contentions that Burke had personal or political motives for his pursuit of Hastings. Macauley found overreaching on Burke's part, however. Macauley also sensed that Burke may have been pushed forward by his own loss of standing. Thomas Babington Macauley, *Warren Hastings* (New York: Chautauqua Press, 1886) 143.

162. O'Brien, "Warren Hastings in Burke's Great Melody," 66.

163. Jeremy Bernstein, *The Dawning of the Raj: The Life and Trials of Warren Hastings* (Chicago: Ivan R. Dee, 2000) 209.

164. Ibid., 211–212. O'Brien has suggested that: "The main burden of Burke's charges against Hastings is that Hastings was in the habit of selling to the highest bidder the right to tax and that this practice resulted in vicious extortion and oppression." O'Brien, "Warren Hastings in Burke's Great Melody," 68.

165. Edmund Burke, *On Empire, Liberty, and Reform: Speeches and Letters of Edmund Burke*, ed. David Bromwich (New Haven: Yale UP, 2000), 388. With respect to the charges, Burke argued "It is by this tribunal that statesmen who abuse their power are accused by statesmen and tried by statesmen, not upon the niceties of a narrow jurisprudence, but upon the enlarged and solid principles of state morality." O'Brien, "Warren Hastings in Burke's Great Melody," 66–67. Here again, Burke made clear his view, and presumably that of the Commons whom he represented, that the high crimes and misdemeanors charged against Hastings were abuses of official power, not ordinary criminal offenses.

166. Earl Russell described the impeachment as "a long punishment." Russell, *An Essay on the History of the English Government and Constitution*, 119. Stephen described it as "a blot on the judicial history of the country." Stephen, *A History of the Criminal Law of England*, 160. Macauley noted that Hastings himself had remarked that "the arraignment had taken place before one generation, and the judgment was pronounced by another." Macauley, *Warren Hastings*, 170.

167. In his essay, "Personal Responsibility and Government—A Role for Impeachment?" A.W. Bradley has taken the opposite position that "[w]hat we can be sure of is that the framers were not influenced by the Hastings impeachment, since the convention in Philadelphia completed its work five months before the trial in Westminister Hall began." Carnall, *The Impeachment of Warren Hastings*, 173. Bradley is of course correct that the framers were not influenced by a trial that had not yet commenced. Nevertheless, the allegations against Hastings had been in the public record and the public press for at least a year before the convention convened and the Commons voted to impeach Hastings while the convention was in session. Thus, while the convention was not influenced by the trial, the circumstances coupled with Mason's reference to Hastings strongly suggest that the charges of misconduct lodged against Hastings directly influenced the delegates' decision to accept high crimes and misdemeanors as grounds for impeachment and removal.

168. The charges against Hastings are set forth in Edmund Burke, *The Works of the Right Honorable Edmund Burke*, 4th ed., vol. 3 (Boston: Little, 1871) 106.

169. A ninth state, New Jersey, provided in its constitution adopted on July 2, 1776, that judges could be removed who were "adjudged guilty of misbehavior, by the Council, on an impeachment of the Assembly." *Constitution of New Jersey*, Art. 12.

170. *The Constitution or Form of Government, Agreed to and Resolved Upon by the Delegates and Representatives of the Several Counties and Corporations of Virginia*, June 29, 1776.

171. *Constitution of the State of Delaware*, Art. 23.

172. *Constitution of North Carolina*, Art. 23 ("The Governor, and other offices, offending against the State, by violating any part of this constitution, maladministration, or corruption, may be prosecuted, on impeachment of the General Assembly.").

173. *Constitution of New York*, Art. 33 ("The power of impeaching the officers of the State, for mal and corrupt conduct in their respective offices, be vested in the representations of the people in Assembly.").

174. *Constitution of Vermont*, Sec. 20 ("Every officer of State, whether judicial or executive, shall be liable to be impeached by the General Assembly, either when in office, or after his resignation, or removal for maladministration.").

175. *Constitution of South Carolina*, Art. 23 ("That form of impeaching all officers of the State for mal and corrupt conduct in their respective offices, not amenable to any other jurisdiction, be vested in the House of Representatives.").

176. *Constitution of Georgia*, Art. 49.

177. *Constitution of Massachusetts*, Art. 8.

178. Hoffer and Hull, *Impeachment in America*, 78. Hoffer and Hull observed that the prospect of impeachment had curbed misuses of power such as intimidation of citizens, insubordination and overreaching. Impeachment had also posed a threat to incompetent officials.

179. Ibid., 79–83.

180. Ibid., 81–82.

181. Ibid., 83–85.

182. In contrast, debate over the presidency figured prominently in the debates. Fear of an elected monarch was a significant part of the Anti-Federalist critique. Jackson Turner Main, *The Anti-Federalists: Critics of the Constitution* (Chapel Hill: North Carolina UP, 1961) 141; Saul Cornell, *The Other Framers: Anti-Federalism and the Dissenting Tradition in America* (Chapel Hill: North Carolina UP, 1961) 31. Such fears were reflected in the November 6, 1787, letter of "An Officer of the Late Continental Army," Bailyn, *The Debates on the Constitution*, vol. 1: 100, and the November 22, 1787, letter of "Cato," ibid., 399. Patrick Henry warned the Virginia convention on June 7, 1787, that the president could become king by virtue of his command of the army. Henry questioned "by what law" the president would be punished. Ralph Ketchum, *The Anti-Federalist Papers and the Constitutional Debates* (New York: New American Library, 2003) 213–216. Thomas Jefferson also saw the risk that such an "officer for life" would be a target for the intrigues and bribery of a foreign power desirous of an executive who was sympathetic. David N. Mayer, *The Constitutional Thought of Thomas Jefferson* (Charlottesville, Virginia UP, 1994) 91–95, 224–226.

183. *Independent Gazetteer* (Philadelphia), September 28, 1787, Bernard Bailyn, ed., *The Debate on the Constitution*, vol. 1 (New York: The Library of America, 1993) 26–27 (emphasis original).

184. Noah Webster (writing as "A Citizen of America"), "An Examination into the Leading Principles of the Federal Constitution," Bailyn, *The Debate on the Constitution*, vol. 1: 141 (emphasis original). Contrary to Webster's view, however, as discussed in chapter 2, the Senate later concluded in the matter of Senator William Blount that members of Congress were not subject to impeachment.

185. George J. Graham, "Pennsylvania, Representation and the Meaning of Republicanism," Michael Allen Gillespie and Michael L. Lienesch, eds., *Ratifying the Constitution* (Lawrence: Kansas UP, 1989) 52.

186. "Dissent of the Minority of the Pennsylvania Convention," Pennsylvania Packet, December 18, 1787, Bailyn, *The Debate on the Constitution*, vol. 1: 546; Ketchum, *The Anti-Federalist Papers and the Constitutional Debates*, 235.

187. Bailyn, *The Debate on the Constitution*, vol. 2: 24.

188. Rakove suggests they were not. Rakove, *Original Meanings*, 132.

189. Alexander Hamilton ("Publius"), Federalist 65, Alexander Hamilton, James Madison, and John Jay, *The Federalist*, ed. Benjamin F. Wright (New York: Barnes, 1996) 426 (emphasis original). Hamilton continued his discussion of the impeachment power in Federalist 66. There, he answered the criticism of the Anti-Federalists concerning the Senate as the adjudicatory body for impeachments. With respect to the Anti-Federalists' argument that trial in the Senate contravened the principle of separation of powers, Hamilton noted that legislative impeachment was "an essential check in the hands

of that body upon the encroachments of the executive," and that dividing the authority between the two houses "avoids the inconvenience of making the same persons both accusers and judges." Ibid., 431. Hamilton also responded to the Anti-Federalist arguments that trial by the Senate allowed an undue accumulation of power by noting that the House was given the sole authority to institute impeachments. Ibid., 432–433. Hamilton answered the criticism raised by the Pennsylvania dissenters that the Senate would be called upon to judge the conduct of persons whose appointments it had approved by noting that in approving presidential appointments, the Senate exercised no choice and therefore, "it could hardly happen, that the majority of the Senate would feel any other complacency towards the object of an appointment than such as the appearances of merit might inspire, and the proofs of the want of it destroy." Ibid., 433–434. Finally, Hamilton addressed the contention raised in the Lowndes-Rutledge debate in South Carolina that involvement of the Senate in ratifying treaties "would constitute the senators their own judges, in every case of a corrupt or perfidious execution of that trust." Hamilton noted first that: "The *joint agency* of the Chief Magistrate of the Union, and of two-thirds of the members of a body selected by the collective wisdom of the legislatures of the several states, is designed to be the pledge for the fidelity of the national councils in this particular." In contrast, however, Hamilton argued, "so far as might concern the misbehavior of the Executive in perverting the instructions or contravening the views of the Senate, we need not be apprehensive of the want of a disposition in that body to punish the abuse of their confidence or to vindicate their own authority." Ibid., 434–436.

190. In his lectures on the law delivered many years later, Wilson wrote that "impeachments are confined to political characters, to political crimes and misdemeanors, and to political punishments." James Wilson, *The Works of James Wilson*, ed. Robert McCloskey (Cambridge, MA: Harvard UP, 1967) vol. 1: 246.

191. Gillespie and Lienesch, *Ratifying the Constitution*, 349. After adoption of the Bill of Rights, North Carolina became the twelfth state to ratify the constitution. Ibid., 364.

192. Bailyn, *The Debate on the Constitution*, vol. 2: 873.

193. Ibid., 877. Iredell explained that while the consequences of conviction were removal from office and disqualification from holding "any place of honor, trust, or profit," the person would nevertheless remain subject to criminal trial and to receive "such common-law punishment as belongs to a description of such offenses, if it be punishable by that law." Philip B. Kurland and Ralph Lerner, eds., *The Founders' Constitution* (Chicago: Chicago UP, 1987) vol. 4: Article II, Section 2, Clause 2, Document 22.

194. Bailyn, *The Debate on the Constitution*, vol. 2: 880.

195. Ibid., 882.

196. Ibid., 883.

197. Ibid., 383. In this, Iredell's views coincided with the Anti-Federalist writing under the name "Brutus," who in a letter to the *New York Journal* on March

20, 1788, said with respect to the removal of judges that "Errors in judgment, or want of capacity to discharge the duties of the office, can never be supposed to be included in these words, *high crimes and misdemeanors. A man may mistake a case in giving judgment, or manifest that he is incompetent to the discharge of the duties of a judge, and yet give no evidence of corruption or want of integrity. To support the charge, it will be necessary to give in evidence some facts that will show, that the judges committed the error from wicked and corrupt motives.*" Ibid., 375 (emphasis original).

198. Ibid., 883. Iredell argued, as Hamilton had in Federalist 66 that in either instance, the Senate would be the appropriate forum in which to try a charge of misdemeanor.

## 2   The Impeachment and Trial of Andrew Johnson

1.  The extent of the president's removal power would be the gravamen of the complaint against President Andrew Johnson.
2.  Joseph Gales, ed., *The Debates and Proceedings in the Congress of the United States*, vol. 1 (Washington, DC: Gales and Seaton, 1834) 495.
3.  Ibid., 496.
4.  Buckner F. Melton, Jr., *The First Impeachment: The Constitution's Framers and the Case of Senator William Blount* (Macon: Mercer UP, 1998) 61–63.
5.  Madison's notes of the convention reflect that at the time of the signing of the proposed constitution on September 17, "Mr. Blount said he had declared that he would not sign, so as to pledge himself in support of the plan, but he was relieved by the form proposed and would without committing himself attest the fact that the plan was the unanimous act of the States in convention." Madison, *Notes*, 657.
6.  Melton, *The First Impeachment*, 64–66.
7.  Ibid., 64–66.
8.  Ibid., 74–76.
9.  Ibid., 86–95. The Neutrality Act is codified at 18 U.S.C. § 960.
10. Francis Wharton, *State Trials of the United States during the Administration of Washington and Adams* (Philadelphia: Adams, Carey and Heart, 1849) 200.
11. Ibid., 217–218.
12. Ibid., 201. The House had debated the impeachment on July 6. A legal opinion was secured to the effect that Blount's correspondence constituted a crime for which Blount could be impeached. Elenore Bushnell, *Crimes, Follies, and Misfortunes: The Federal Impeachment Trials* (Urbana: Illinois UP, 1992) 27–28; and Melton, *The First Impeachment*, 106.
13. Wharton, *State Trials of the United States*, 251–252.
14. Bushnell, *Crimes, Follies, and Misfortunes*, 29; Melton, *The First Impeachment*, 126–127, 131–132.
15. In essence, the articles of impeachment charged that between February and June 1797, Blount had conspired to invade Florida and Louisiana in order

to capture the territory for Britain, which was then at war with Spain. In furtherance of the conspiracy, the Creek and Cherokee Nations were to be incited to take hostile action against the settlers in the territory in violation of the Neutrality Act. Wharton, *State Trials of the United States*, 253–255.

16. Ibid., 257.
17. United States Senate, *Extracts from the Journal of the United States Senate in all Cases of Impeachment 1798–1904*, Senate Document No. 876 (Washington, DC: U.S. Government Printing Office, 1912) 9 ("Senate Document no. 876").
18. Wharton, *State Trials of the United States*, 261.
19. In his answer to the articles of impeachment, Blount argued impeachment could only be grounded on charges of treason, bribery, or other high crimes and misdemeanors "alleged to have been committed by the president, vice president, or any civil officer of the United States in the execution of their offices held under the United States." *Senate Document No. 876*, 10. Blount further contended that he had not been "a civil officer of the United States" at the time of the alleged misconduct and that he had not been charged in the articles "with having committed any crime or misdemeanor in the execution of any civil office held under the United States, nor with any malconduct in a civil office or abuse of any public trust in the execution thereof." *Senate Document No. 876*, 10.
20. Wharton, *State Trials of the United States*, 277.
21. Ibid., 290–291.
22. Ibid., 313.
23. *Senate Document No. 876*, 13.
24. Ibid., 14.
25. Ibid., 14. For that reason, the case is viewed as establishing the immunity of members of Congress from impeachment. Walter Ehrlich, *Presidential Impeachment: An American Dilemma* (Saint Charles: Forum Press, 1974) 36; Michael J. Gerhardt, *The Federal Impeachment Process: A Constitutional and Historical Analysis*, 3d ed. (Chicago: Chicago UP, 2000) 48–50; Philip B. Kurland, *Watergate and the Constitution* (Chicago: Chicago UP, 1978) 116.
26. Wharton, *State Trials of the United States*, 315–316; *Senate Document No. 876*, 15.
27. Alfred H. Kelly, Winfred A. Harbison, and Herman Belz, *The American Constitution: Its Origins and Development*, 7th ed., vol. 1 (New York: Norton 1991) 162–163.
28. *Marbury v. Madison*, 5 U.S. (1 Cranch) 137 (1803).
29. Bushnell, *Crimes, Follies, and Misfortunes*, 43; Hoffer and Hull, *Impeachment in America*, 207. As noted by Lynn W. Turner, Pickering's impeachment "would have seemed less brutal" had Pickering not had such a distinguished career in public service. Lynn W. Turner, "The Impeachment of John Pickering," *American Historical Review* (1949): vol. 54: 487–488.
30. Hoffer and Hull, *Impeachment in America*, 207.
31. Bushnell, *Crimes, Follies, and Misfortunes*, 43. Interestingly, just ten years earlier, in 1794, the Congress had removed jurisdiction from the District Court of New Hampshire to the Circuit Court because the district judge, John

Sullivan, had been similarly incapacitated by drunkenness and dementia. David P. Currie, "The Constitution in Congress: The Most Endangered Branch, 1801–1805," *Wake Forest Law Review,* 33 (1998): 236.

32. Bushnell, *Crimes, Follies, and Misfortunes,* 45; Hoffer and Hull, *Impeachment in America,* 208, Turner, "The Impeachment of John Pickering," 491.

33. Andrew C. McLaughlin, *A Constitutional History of the United States* (New York: D. Appleton-Century, 1935) 320. Jefferson had earlier expressed the view that impeachment was a criminal proceeding. Thomas Jefferson, *Jefferson's Parliamentary Writings,* ed. Wilbur Samuel Howell (Princeton: Princeton UP, 1987) 11. This being so, it is not clear what crime, other than public intoxication, Jefferson thought that Pickering had committed.

34. Hoffer and Hull, *Impeachment in America,* 208.

35. The ship had been seized by the collector of customs, a Republican, in Portsmouth for nonpayment of duties. The ship's owner, a prominent Federalist, was granted release of the ship by Judge Pickering without evidencing payment. The customs collector libeled the ship and its cargo and the owner's suit for their return was heard by Judge Pickering. Turner, "Impeachment of John Pickering," *American Historical Review,* vol. 54: 489. The impeachment articles charged that the ship and contents had been returned without proof of payment and that Pickering had refused to hear testimony on behalf of the United States during trial. Following the trial, Pickering had refused to allow the appeal of the U.S. attorney contrary to the Judiciary Act. Lastly, Pickering was charged with intoxication during the trial and with invoking the name of the "Supreme Being" in a "most profane and indecent manner." All of these actions were "contrary to his trust and duty as a judge in violation of the laws of the United States," and therefore were high crimes and misdemeanors. Emily Field Van Tassell and Paul Finkelman, eds., *Impeachable Offenses: A Documentary History from 1787 to the present,* (Washington, DC: Congressional Quarterly, 1999) 93–95.

36. *Senate Document No. 876,* 19–22.

37. Ibid., 29; Van Tassell and Finkelman, *Impeachable Offenses,* 95–96; Currie, "The Constitution in Congress," *Wake Forest Law Review,* vol. 33: 240.

38. Turner, "The Impeachment of John Pickering," 494.

39. Ibid., 504.

40. Ibid., 499.

41. Rollin M. Perkins, *Criminal Law,* 2d ed. (Mineola: Foundation Press, 1969) 857; Currie, "The Constitution in Congress," 244–245.

42. William Plumer, *William Plumer's Memorandum of Proceedings in the United States Senate 1803–1807,* ed. Everettt Somerville Brown (New York: Macmillan, 1923) 160–161.

43. Turner, "The Impeachment of John Pickering," 504–505. The Republican tactic has been characterized as a "subterfuge." Jerry W. Knudson, "The Jeffersonian Assault on the Federal Judiciary," *American Journal of Legal History* (1970) vol. 14: 61; McLaughlin, *A Constitutional History of the United States,* 320–321. Currie referred to the Senate's verdict as "pretty disreputable." Currie, "The Constitution in Congress," 244–245.

44. *Annals of Congress, Senate, 8th Cong., 1st Sess.*, 365.

45. *Senate Document No. 876*, 33–34.

46. Adams, *History of the United States of America*, vol. 2: 158.

47. Albert J. Beveridge, *The Life of John Marshall*, vol. 3 (Boston: Houghton, 1916) 169.

48. Ibid., 184 n.5.

49. Ibid.; Richard B. Lillich, "The Chase Impeachment," *American Journal of Legal History*, vol. 4 (1960): 52–53; Knudson, "The Jeffersonian Assault," 62–63; Richard Ellis, "The Impeachment of Samuel Chase," Michael Belknap, ed., *American Political Trials* (Westport: Greenwood Press, 1981) 58–59.

50. Fries had opposed the enforcement of federal revenue laws by force. He had been convicted on undisputed facts and condemned to death. A new trial had been granted and assigned to Justice Chase and Judge Peters (who had presided at the earlier trial). On the day of the trial, Justice Chase distributed his opinion. Although Chase later agreed to withdraw the opinion, the counsel for Fries refused to proceed with the case. Fries was again convicted and condemned to death. He was later pardoned by President Adams. R.W. Carrington, "The Impeachment Trial of Samuel Chase," *Virginia Law Review* (1923) vol. 9: 487.

51. Callender had published pamphlets accusing Washington and Adams of corruption. Chase's handling of the trial had been criticized, particularly his belittling of Callender's counsel, his refusal to seat several sympathetic Republicans on the jury, and his statement that he would "punish" Callender. Carrington, "The Impeachment Trial of Samuel Chase," 487.

52. Charles Warren, *The Supreme Court in United States History*, 273, quoted in Lillich, "The Chase Impeachment," 53; Belknap, *American Political Trials*, 61. As was observed in this connection, "It was not by his judicial capacity alone that Samuel Chase had earned his reputation. For years he had been known as a pugnacious lawyer and politician who sought quarrels and delighted in them. Indeed, his entire career had been marked by such intemperance of word and action that he seemed to be perpetually with a mob at his heels, which sometimes pursued but quite often followed him." Frederick T. Hill, *Decisive Battles of the Law*, 6–7, quoted in Lillich, "The Chase Impeachment," 51, n.6. Sean Wilentz wrote that following his confirmation in 1795, Chase "turned into a single-minded enforcer during the Alien and Sedition crisis" and had "presided belligerently over several of the most sensational sedition trials and punished those convicted to the limits the law allowed." Wilentz observed that "Chase was, in 1804, the most powerful conservative Federalist in the federal government, and the Republicans' loathing for him ran deep." Sean Wilentz, *The Rise of American Democracy: Jefferson to Lincoln* (New York: Norton, 2005) 126.

53. 5 U.S. (1 Cranch) 137 (1803).

54. Adams, *History of the United States of America*, vol. 2: 148–149. Chase told the grand jurors that passage of the Judiciary Act and the establishment of universal suffrage under the state constitution would "take away all security for property and personal liberty." Chase warned that the Constitution "will

sink into a mobocracy—the worst of all possible governments" and that the "modern doctrines by our late reformers, that all men…are entitled to enjoy equal liberty and equal rights," had "brought this mischief upon us." Chase said that he feared "it will rapidly progress until peace and order, freedom and prosperity, shall be destroyed."

55. Adams, *History of the United States of America*, vol. 2: 150.

56. Ibid., 150–51.

57. Beveridge, *The Life of John Marshall*, vol. 3: 171.

58. Adams, *History of the United States of America*, vol. 2: 151. Adams wrote that: "Randolph was no lawyer; but this defect was a trifling objection compared with his greater unfitness in other respects. Ill-balanced, impatient of obstacles, incapable of sustained labor or of a methodical arrangement, illogical to excess, and egotistic to the verge of madness, he was sparkling and formidable in debate or on the hustings, where he could follow the wayward impulse of his fancy running in the accustomed channels of his thought; but the qualities that helped him in debate were fatal to him at the bar." Ibid., 151–152.

59. Chase was charged with a variety of instances of misconduct in the Fries and Callender trials. Chase was also charged with having refused to discharge a grand jury after having harangued them concerning the "seditious" writings of a local newspaper editor. Lastly, Chase was charged with misconduct in regard to his remarks to the Baltimore grand jury that had prompted his impeachment in the first instance. Plumer, *William Plumer's Memorandum*, 216–218.

60. *Senate Document No. 864*, 35–36.

61. Adams, *Writings of John Quincy Adams*, vol. 3: 115. John Quincy Adams further noted that these articles, apparently the fifth and sixth articles, "afford the most unequivocal proofs of a determination to establish the principle that judges are removable by impeachment for any mistake on the point of law" and "contained in themselves a virtual impeachment not only of Mr. Chase, but of all the judges of the Supreme Court from the first establishment of the national judiciary." Ibid.,116.

62. In conversation with Adams, Giles had "treated with the utmost contempt the idea of an *independent* judiciary" and had expressed the view that other than the lone Republican justice, "All other Judges of the Supreme Court…must be impeached and removed." With obvious reference to *Marbury v. Madison*, Giles told Adams, "The power of impeachment was given without limitation to the House of Representatives" and "the power of trying impeachments was given equally without measure to the Senate." Accordingly, if the justices of the Supreme Court were to declare a law unconstitutional, "it was the undoubted right of the House of Representatives to remove them for giving such opinions, however honest or sincere they may have been in entertaining them." Giles flatly stated, "*we want your offices*, for the purpose of giving them to men who will fill them better." John Quincy Adams, *Memoirs of John Quincy Adams*, ed. Charles Francis Adams (Philadelphia: Lippincott, 1874) vol. 1: 322 (emphasis original).

63. Ibid. The Federalist position was diametrically opposed. As William Plumer wrote in his journal, "Incapacity in the officer is a misfortune, but no cause for impeachment…to impeach, convict and remove a judge from office, for

having formed an erroneous opinion, is a doctrine pregnant with ruin to the Judiciary." Plumer, *William Plumer's Memorandum of Proceedings,* 232.

64. *Senate Document No. 876,* 44.

65. Keith Whittington observed that Chase's insistence that the Senate proceedings mirror a criminal trial, with the attendant legal standards and procedures, ensured that the grounds for impeachment would be construed narrowly. Keith E. Whittington, *Constitutional Construction: Divided Powers and Constitutional Meaning* (Cambridge, MA: Harvard UP, 1999) 27.

66. *Annals of Congress,* Senate, 8th Cong., 2d Sess., 101–150.

67. Belknap, *American Political Trials,* 70.

68. Adams, *History of the United States of America,* vol. 2: 223.

69. Plumer, *William Plumer's Memorandum,* 281–295; Beveridge, *The Life of John Marshall,* vol. 3: 189.

70. *Annals of Congress,* Senate, 8th Cong., 2d Sess., 331–332.

71. Ibid., 562. Beveridge described Nicholson's statement as an "irretrievable blunder" that rendered the Senate "dumbfounded." Beveridge, *The Life of John Marshall,* vol. 3: 207–208.

72. Knudson, "The Jeffersonian Assault," 65.

73. *Annals of Congress,* Senate, 8th Cong., 2d Sess., 359 (emphasis original).

74. Ibid., 433.

75. *Senate Document No. 864,* 55–60; *William Plumer's Memorandum,* 309–310. As to the issue of an impeachable act, Adams observed that "The question whether impeachment could be had for acts not violating any law was discussed and sifted, until the managers themselves were compelled to abandon it, at least in its application to the cause." John Quincy Adams, *The Writings of John Quincy Adams,* ed. Worthington Chauncy Ford (New York: Macmillan, 1914) 112–113.

76. Beveridge, *The Life of John Marshall,* vol. 3: 219.

77. Peck was a U.S. District Judge in Missouri. Following the publication of an article by a lawyer, Luke E. Lawless, in a suit before Peck that was highly critical of Peck's handling of the case, Peck held Lawless in contempt of court and ordered that Peck be jailed for twenty-four hours and be suspended from law practice. Complaint was made to Congress and attempts were made in 1826 and 1828 to impeach Peck. Finally, in 1830, the House Judiciary Committee recommended that Peck be impeached on one charge of high crime and misdemeanor for the imprisonment of Lawless, which the Committee said had been an "abuse of judicial authority" and a "subversion of the liberty of the people." At trial before the Senate, the House Managers argued that Peck could be removed for committing an illegal act with bad intent or an otherwise legal act that was not warranted by the circumstances. Thus, one of the managers argued that "any official act committed or omitted by a judge, which is in violation of the condition upon which he holds his office, is an impeachable offense under the Constitution." Peck's defense argued that both the "illegality of the act" and the "guilt of the intention" were necessary for removal. Peck was acquitted and continued to serve until his death in 1836. Bushnell, *Crimes, Follies, and Misfortunes,* 91–92.

78. West H. Humphreys was a District Judge in Tennessee. In 1862, Judge Humphreys absented from the District Court in order to accept appointment as a judge by Jefferson Davis, president of the Confederacy. However, because Judge Humphreys had not resigned from the federal bench, President Lincoln was not able to appoint a successor. This anomaly could only be resolved by the removal of Judge Humphreys and on May 22, 1862, the House of Representatives adopted seven articles of impeachment regarding Judge Humphreys. Judge Humphreys did not respond to the charges and after a brief evidentiary hearing, he was convicted of high crimes and misdemeanors. The judge was thereafter removed from office by the Senate. Bushnell, *Crimes, Follies, and Misfortunes*, 115–124.
79. Lois Fisher, *Constitutional Conflicts between Congress and the President* (Lawrence: Kansas UP, 1997) 55.
80. Rhenquist, *Grand Inquests*, 257–258.
81. William Rawle, *A View of the Constitution of the United States of America*, 2d ed. (Philadelphia: Phillip H. Nicklin, 1829) 211.
82. Ibid., 215.
83. James Wilson, *The Works of James Wilson*, ed. Robert Green McCloskey, vol. 1 (Cambridge, MA: Harvard UP, 1967) 324
84. Ibid., 426.
85. Story, *Commentaries on the Constitution of the United States*, vol. 2: 167–169.
86. Ibid., 171.
87. Ibid., 217.
88. Ibid., 220.
89. Ibid., 263–264.
90. Ibid., 270–272.
91. Ibid., 264.
92. Ibid., 267.
93. James Kent, *Commentaries on American Law*, 9th ed., vol. 1 (Boston: Little, 1858) 311.
94. George Ticknor Curtis, *History of the Origin, Formation and Adoption of the Constitution of the United States*, vol. 2 (New York: Harper, 1858) 260–261.
95. Theodore W. Dwight, "Trial by Impeachment," *American Law Register*, 15 (1867) vol. 15: 257.
96. Ibid., 268–269.
97. Ibid.
98. William Lawrence, "The Law of Impeachment," *American Law Register*, 15 (1867): 641.
99. Ibid., 647.
100. Ibid., 644 (emphasis original).
101. Ibid., 647.
102. Ibid., 649.
103. Ibid., 645–646.
104. Ibid., 665.
105. Ibid., 666.
106. Ibid., 680.

107. David Miller Dewitt, *The Impeachment and Trial of Andrew Johnson* (New York: Macmillan, 1903) 1; and Michael Les Benedict, *The Impeachment and Trial of Andrew Johnson* (New York: Norton, 1973) 1.

108. Dewitt, *The Impeachment and Trial of Andrew Johnson*, 2. Nevertheless, there were profound differences between Lincoln and the Radical Republicans. Foner noted that to Lincoln, Reconstruction was part of his strategy to win the war and to achieve emancipation through establishing state governments that would include Southerners who took a loyalty oath and who pledged to uphold abolition. The Radical Republicans viewed Reconstruction as a broader plan to reform Southern society. Eric Foner, *Reconstruction: America's Unfinished Revolution 1863–1877* (New York: Harper & Row, 1988) 61–62.

109. Dewitt, *The Impeachment and Trial of Andrew Johnson*, 5. Benedict, *The Impeachment and Trial of Andrew Johnson*, 3; David O. Stewart, *Impeached: The Trial of President Andrew Johnson and the Fight for Lincoln's Legacy* (New York: Simon & Schuster, 2009) 7; Lloyd Paul Stryker, *Andrew Johnson* (New York: Macmillan, 1929) 1–129; Robert W. Winston, *Andrew Johnson: Plebian and Patriot* (New York: Holt, 1928) 3–257. By the time Johnson succeeded Lincoln, the Republican Party was in disarray. William A. Dunning, "More Light on Andrew Johnson," *American Historical Review*, 11 (1906): 574.

110. Whittington, *Constitutional Construction*, 114. Benedict described Johnson as having been "[i]ntent on wrecking the Republican Reconstruction program irrevocably." Michael Les Benedict, *A Compromise of Principle: Congressional Republicans and Reconstruction 1863–1869* (New York: Norton, 1974) 294. Benedict observed that from the beginning of his administration Johnson had worked to vitiate the Reconstruction program of the Radical Republicans. Benedict, *The Impeachment and Trial of Andrew Johnson*, 39–40. Richard M. Valelly suggested a direct political purpose in Johnson's efforts to undo reconstruction, that of building a coalition of Southern conservatives and northern democrats in anticipation of the 1868 election. Richard M. Valelly, *The Two Reconstructions: The Struggle for Black Enfranchisement* (Chicago: Chicago UP, 2004) 27.

111. Dewitt, *The Impeachment and Trial of Andrew Johnson*, 5–6.

112. Stewart, *Impeached*, 50–51; Dewitt, *The Impeachment and Trial of Andrew Johnson*, 45–48; Stryker, *Andrew Johnson*, 273; Gene Smith, *High Crimes and Misdemeanors: The Impeachment and Trial of Andrew Johnson* (New York: Morrow, 1977) 143–144; William H. Rehnquist, *Grand Inquests: The Historic Trials of Justice Samuel Chase and President Andrew Johnson* (New York: Morrow, 1992) 205. Benedict attributed the vetoes of both the Freedman's Bureau Act and the Civil Rights Act to Johnson's view of limited federalism. Benedict, *The Impeachment and Trial of Andrew Johnson*, 12. Milton Lomask had also suggested that Johnson feared the concentration of power in the Executive. Milton Lomask, *Andrew Johnson: President on Trial* (New York: Farrar, 1960) 142. However, Hans Trefousse found a racial motive for Johnson's veto of the Freedman's Bureau Act. Hans L. Trefousse, *Impeachment of a President* (New York: Fordham UP, 1999) 15. Benedict

similarly observed that Johnson's policies clearly favored Southern whites to the detriment of the black population. Michael Les Benedict, "A New Look at the Impeachment of Andrew Johnson," *Political Science Quarterly*, 113 (1998): 494–495.

113. Dewitt, *The Impeachment and Trial of Andrew Johnson*, 49; Lomask, *Andrew Johnson: President on Trial*, 163–164. Benedict wrote that the Radical Republicans reacted against the veto with "frustrated outrage," the intensity of which had shocked Johnson. Benedict, *The Impeachment and Trial of Andrew Johnson*, 12–13. Sir Frederick Bruce described their reaction as "venom and defeat." Smith, *High Crimes and Misdemeanors*, 144. Sumner Welles, the secretary of the Navy, shared this view as well. Welles wrote: "The effect of this veto will probably be open rupture between the President and a portion of the Republican members of Congress." Stryker, *Andrew Johnson*, 270.

114. Dewitt, *The Impeachment and Trial of Andrew Johnson*, 51–52; Stryker, *Andrew Johnson*, 280–281; Smith, *High Crimes and Misdemeanors*, 158–159; Stewart, *Impeached*, 51–52. In that speech, Johnson referred to the Republican Radicals as being "a common gang of cormorants and blood suckers, who have been fattening upon the country." Benedict, *The Impeachment and Trial of Andrew Johnson*, 13. The president's rhetoric was condemned in the popular press as well as by supporters of the Republican Radicals. An article in *Harper's Weekly* described the president's remarks as being "something so unprecedented and astounding that, while every generous man will allow for the excitement of passion, there is no self-respecting American citizen who will not feel humiliated that the chief citizen of the Republic, in such a place, on such a day, should have been utterly mastered by it." *Harper's Weekly*, March 10, 1866: 147.

115. Dewitt, *The Impeachment and Trial of Andrew Johnson*, 51–54. Dewitt viewed Johnson's speech on Washington's Birthday as being the benchmark date of the movement to impeach Johnson. To Foner, Johnson's Washington's Birthday speech "displayed Johnson at his worst." Foner, *Reconstruction*, 249.

116. Stewart, *Impeached*, 53; Dewitt, *The Impeachment and Trial of Andrew Johnson*, 67–82; Stryker, *Andrew Johnson*, 287–291. Johnson again vetoed the legislation as being an improper invasion of rights reserved to the states. He also objected to the criminal provisions. Lomask, *Andrew Johnson: President on Trial*, 157–160. Trefousse suggested a racial motivation underlying Johnson's veto of the Civil Rights Act. Trefousse wrote that "The entire bill seemed to him a violation of states' rights. Beyond that, it offended his racial sensibilities since it proposed to outlaw all discrimination between the races. Would it not enable Congress to repeal state laws forbidding interracial marriage, he argued. And quoting Chancellor Kent, was not such a prospect 'revolting and…offensive against public decorum?'" Trefousse, *Impeachment of a President*, 26.

117. Dewitt, *The Impeachment and Trial of Andrew Johnson*, 87–97; Stryker, *Andrew Johnson*, 299–300. According to Trefousse, Johnson's objection to

the Fourteenth Amendment centered on black suffrage and the "enormous power" that would be conferred upon Congress by the due process clause. Trefousse, *Impeachment of a President*, 36–38. However, as Rehnquist noted, while Johnson had no constitutional authority to block ratification of the Fourteenth Amendment, Johnson nevertheless opposed ratification. Johnson sought the views of his cabinet, and whether due to his ambivalence or duplicity, Stanton indicated that he disapproved of it. Rehnquist, *Grand Inquests*, 207. Bruce Ackerman suggested that Johnson's opposition to the Fourteenth Amendment was a decisive cause of Johnson's impeachment. Bruce Ackerman, *We The People: Foundations*, vol. 1 (Cambridge, MA: Harvard UP, 1991) 83.

118. Stryker, *Andrew Johnson*, 317–319; Trefousse, *Impeachment of a President*, 37–38; Winston, *Andrew Johnson: Plebian and President*, 358–363; Stewart, *Impeached*, 54–55.

119. Johnson's comments to the delegates may have been intended to serve his political aspirations for the 1868 general election as an appeal to the National Union Party. Whittington, *Constitutional Construction*, 125.

120. Dewitt, *The Impeachment and Trial of Andrew Johnson*, 113; and Stryker, *Andrew Johnson*, 324–325.

121. Dewitt, *The Impeachment and Trial of Andrew Johnson*, 113.

122. Ibid., 115–118; and Stryker, *Andrew Johnson*, 353–358; Stewart, *Impeached*, 67.

123. Dewitt, *The Impeachment and Trial of Andrew Johnson*, 119–120; Winston, *Andrew Johnson: Plebian and Patriot*, 363–370.

124. Dewitt, *The Impeachment and Trial of Andrew Johnson*, 120.

125. Ibid., 180.

126. Foner, *Reconstruction*, 333.

127. Valelly observed that the Tenure of Office Act and the Command of the Army Act was Congress's attempt to control both the cabinet and the army. Valelly, *The Two Reconstructions*, 31. The Tenure of Office Act was not repealed until 1887. In *Myers v. United States*, 272 U.S. 52 (1926), the Supreme Court held a similar statute requiring senatorial approval for the removal of certain federal officers to be unconstitutional.

128. Stewart, *Impeached*, 75; Dewitt, *The Impeachment and Trial of Andrew Johnson*, 199–203; Stryker, *Andrew Johnson*, 437–439. Johnson's cabinet unanimously recommended that Johnson veto the Act as being an unconstitutional interference with the president's appointment power. Ironically, Stanton assisted Secretary of State Seward in drafting Johnson's veto message. Rehnquist, *Grand Inquests*, 210. During the cabinet's deliberation on the constitutionality of the Act, Stanton had declared: "No man of a proper sense of honor would remain in the cabinet when invited to resign." Hearing that, Johnson asked Stanton to draft the veto message. Lomask, *Andrew Johnson: President on Trial*, 248. Also at this time, Johnson vetoed the First Reconstruction Act, which declared that there were no legal governments in the South and, accordingly, the reestablishment of military governments was authorized. Civil governments were only to be restored after a constitution was ratified by

universal male suffrage. In his veto message, Johnson again stated his opposition to federal intervention into issues of state governance and his opposition to mandatory black suffrage. Trefousse, *Impeachment of a President*, 47.

129. Stryker, *Andrew Johnson*, 447.

130. Ibid., 477–478.

131. Ibid., 479. Ackerman has argued that the support of the army was crucial to the ratification of the Fourteenth Amendment in the South, as well as to the Republican Party garnering votes for the general election in 1868. For Republicans, time was of the essence. Johnson's interests were served by delay and to the extent that provisional state governments were loyal to him, those states could delay the registration and convention process, thus thwarting ratification. Ackerman, *We The People*, vol. 2: 210–214. To counter such a tactic, Congress enacted the Command of the Army Act, which prevented removal of Ulysses S. Grant as general of the army without express consent of the Senate and which required the president to issue all military orders through General Grant. Charges that Johnson had violated the Tenure Act and the Command of the Army Act comprised the majority of the counts in the bill of impeachment.

132. Stryker, *Andrew Johnson*, 480–481; Benedict, *The Impeachment and Trial of Andrew Johnson*, 22. The response of the Radical Republicans to the veto was to call for Johnson's impeachment. In direct contravention of their caucus, Congressman James Ashley and others brought impeachment resolutions to the floor. The resolutions were referred to the Judiciary Committee where they were subject to "the long and tedious job of collecting evidence and taking testimony." Benedict, *The Impeachment and Trial of Andrew Johnson*, 23. Ashley charged Johnson with usurpation of his constitutional powers and corruption in his use of the appointment, pardon, and veto powers. On November 25, 1867, the Judiciary Committee issued a report by a 5 to 4 vote favoring impeachment. The chairman of the Committee, James Wilson, filed a minority report in which he argued that none of the acts complained of by the majority constituted a basis for impeachment because they were not indictable offenses. After two days of debate in December 1867, the resolution to impeach Johnson failed by a vote of 108 to 57. Rehnquist, *Grand Inquests*, 214.

133. Ibid., 212.

134. Stryker, *Andrew Johnson*, 483–484; Dewitt, *The Impeachment and Trial of Andrew Johnson*, 271–272. Sheridan was finally relieved of command in August after he removed twenty-two New Orleans aldermen, the city treasurer, and the chief of police. Sheridan was reassigned to the Department of Missouri. Stryker, *Andrew Johnson*, 500.

135. Both incidents emerged from the trial in June 1867 of the one remaining assassination conspirator, John H. Surratt. In the course of the trial, an issue was raised concerning Johnson's signing of the death warrant for Surratt's mother, Mary E. Surratt, after five members of the military commission that convicted her had recommended clemency. Johnson believed that he had not been shown the clemency recommendation drawn up by

Judge Advocate Joseph Holt. Johnson directed Stanton to provide him with the original record, which he did on August 5. Examining it, Johnson was convinced that Holt and Stanton had obscured the document and it was on that day that Johnson informed Stanton of his removal. Dewitt, *The Impeachment and Trial of Andrew Johnson*, 272–276. On the same day, a critical prosecution witness against John Surratt, Sanford Conover, informed Johnson that Ashley and William Butler, two leading Radicals in Congress, had contrived to create evidence linking Johnson with Jefferson Davis and John Wilkes Booth in the assassination of Lincoln. This information also had come to light on August 5. Stryker, *Andrew Johnson*, 486–488; Dewitt, *The Impeachment and Trial of Andrew Johnson*, 272–276; Trefousse, *Impeachment of a President*, 80–81; Smith, *High Crimes and Misdemeanors*, 210–212.

136. Dewitt, *The Impeachment and Trial of Andrew Johnson*, 276–277, Stryker, *Andrew Johnson*, 488–489.

137. Rehnquist, *Grand Inquests*, 212–213.

138. Dewitt, *The Impeachment and Trial of Andrew Johnson*, 283–284; Stryker, *Andrew Johnson*, 489–490; Smith, *High Crimes and Misdemeanors*, 212–214. Upon receiving Stanton's reply, Johnson remarked that "The turning point has at last come. The Rubicon is crossed." Lomask, *Andrew Johnson: President on Trial*, 250.

139. Dewitt, *The Impeachment and Trial of Andrew Johnson*, 309–314; Stryker, *Andrew Johnson*, 517–518.

140. Dewitt, *The Impeachment and Trial of Andrew Johnson*, 314–316; Stryker, *Andrew Johnson*, 519–520.

141. Dewitt, *The Impeachment and Trial of Andrew Johnson*, 322–324; Stryker, *Andrew Johnson*, 536–537; Lomask, *Andrew Johnson: President on Trial*, 261; Smith, *High Crimes and Misdemeanors*, 221–222.

142. Stryker, *Andrew Johnson*, 559–561; Dewitt, *The Impeachment and Trial of Andrew Johnson*, 343–345; Smith, *High Crimes and Misdemeanors*, 226–227. Stanton was encouraged by the reaction in both the House and the Senate. Among the expressions of support, Senator Sumner transmitted a famously brief one-word message: "Stick." Benedict, *A Compromise of Principle*, 297–298; Dewitt, *The Impeachment and Trial of Andrew Johnson*, 347; Trefousse, *Impeachment of a President*, 134–135; Smith, *High Crimes and Misdemeanors*, 228; Lomask, *Andrew Johnson: President on Trial*, 266.

143. Stryker, *Andrew Johnson*, 565–568; Smith, *High Crimes and Misdemeanors*, 230–233.

144. Stryker, *Andrew Johnson*, 569–570; Dewitt, *The Impeachment and Trial of Andrew Johnson*, 351–357.

145. Whittington observed that Stanton's removal had implications for the Radicals beyond the loss of any ally. In removing Stanton, Johnson had openly defied the will of Congress. Whittington, *Constitutional Construction*, 136–137.

146. Stryker, *Andrew Johnson*, 572–578; Dewitt, *The Impeachment and Trial of Andrew Johnson*, 357–374; Smith, *High Crimes and Misdemeanors*, 234–235;

Trefousse, *Impeachment of a President*, 137; Winston, *Andrew Johnson: Plebian and Patriot*, 419–424; and Lomask, *Andrew Johnson: President on Trial*, 269–274; Rehnquist, *Grand Inquests*, 217–218.

147. Ibid., 219. Nevertheless, as Foner pointed out, taken as a whole, the articles were predicated on the premise that only a clear violation of a statute would warrant Johnson's removal; which was also the central premise of Johnson's defense. Additionally, Foner noted, Chief Justice Chase "steered the proceedings in a narrowly legalistic direction," and as a consequence, the managers were compelled to focus on violations of the Tenure Act and the Command of the Army Act rather than raising the broader policy issues of Johnson's frustration of Congress. Foner, *Reconstruction*, 335.

148. Smith, *High Crimes and Misdemeanors*, 236.

149. Johnson was charged with having violated the Tenure of Office Act by removing Stanton without obtaining the consent of the Senate; by appointing General Thomas as secretary of war ad interim without first having obtained the advice and consent of the Senate; and by appointing General Thomas "without authority," there having been "no vacancy in the said office at the time" (Article 1–3). *Trial of Andrew Johnson on Impeachment*, vol. 1: 8.

150. Johnson was charged with violating the Command of the Army Act by advising the commander of the military forces in Washington on February 22, 1868, that the Act was unconstitutional and therefore was not binding upon him (Article 9). *Trial of Andrew Johnson on Impeachment*, vol. 1: 8.

151. Johnson was charged with various acts of conspiracy with General Thomas to violate the Tenure of Office Act including: preventing Stanton from holding office as secretary of war by "intimidation and threats;" by attempting to prevent Stanton from holding office "by force;" by taking possession of U.S. property at the War Department "by force" through attempts to prevent Stanton from holding office; and by taking possession of U.S. property at the War Department, although not by force (Articles 4–8). These offenses were characterized either as a "high crime" (Articles 4 and 6) or a "high misdemeanor" (Articles 5, 7 and 8). *Trial of Andrew Johnson on Impeachment*, vol. 1: 7–8.

152. Johnson was alleged to have endeavored to bring Congress "into disgrace, ridicule, hatred, contempt and reproach" and to "impair and destroy Congress" in statements made in Washington and during Johnson's "swing around the circle." It was charged that Johnson had made these statements "unmindful of the high duties of his high office and the dignity and proprieties thereof," and as a consequence Johnson had brought the presidency "into contempt, ridicule and disgrace, to the great scandal of all good citizens," a "high misdemeanor in office" (Article 10). Lastly, Johnson was cited for his comment in his August 18 speech at the White House (which also formed part of Article 10) that the Congress was not properly authorized under the Constitution because it was "Congress of only part of the States." The House characterized Johnson's statement as "intending to deny that the legislation of said Congress was valid or obligatory on him" and that the

Congress lacked authority "to propose amendments to the Constitution." It was a charge that as a consequence of his denial of Congress' authority, Johnson had attempted "to contrive means" by which to violate the Tenure of Office Act and to prevent the execution of the Command of the Army Act and the Second Reconstruction Act (Article 11). These actions too were alleged to constitute a "high misdemeanor in office." *Trial of Andrew Johnson on Impeachment*, vol. 1: 10.

153. U.S. Congress, *The Impeachment and Trial of Andrew Johnson, President of the United States* (New York: Dover Publications, 1974) 22.

154. Trefousse, *Impeachment of a President*, 150.

155. With respect to Articles 1–3, grounded on violation of the Tenure of Office Act, Johnson contended that replacing Stanton was a lawful exercise of the removal power and that, in any event, as a hold-over from the Lincoln administration, Stanton was not covered by the Act. Johnson further contended that the appointments of Grant and Thomas had only been ad interim until a permanent appointment could be made. With respect to the conspiracy charged in Articles 4–7, Johnson denied conspiring with anyone to hinder execution of the Tenure Act and specifically denied contemplating the use of force to remove Stanton. Johnson stated that his "sole intent" had been "to vindicate his authority as President" and, "by peaceful means," to bring the question of Stanton's removal before the Supreme Court. With regard to violation of the Command of the Army Act, Johnson noted his objection that the Act "virtually deprives the President of his constitutional functions as Commander-in-Chief of the Army." Johnson contended that he had expressed his opinion on the constitutionality of the Act when he spoke with the Washington commander. With respect to the complaints about Johnson's criticism of Congress, Johnson argued that his statements had been protected by the First Amendment. *Trial of Andrew Johnson on Impeachment*, vol. 1: 37–53; *The Impeachment and Trial of Andrew Johnson*, 36–42.

156. *Trial of Andrew Johnson on Impeachment*, vol. 1: 87–88; *The Impeachment and Trial of Andrew Johnson*, 47.

157. In support of the House position, Butler entered in the record a document entitled *A Brief of the Authorities upon the Law of Impeachable Crimes and Misdemeanors* written by Congressman Lawrence, which substantially paralleled Lawrence's article in the *American Law Register*. Lawrence noted that "misdemeanor" in parliamentary usage was equivalent to "maladministration" or "misconduct." Lawrence also noted that in light of the writings of Rawle, Story, and Curtis, it was "clear that impeachments are not necessarily limited to acts indictable by statute or common law" but that it was not possible "to define in advance by statute the necessary subjects of impeachment." Instead, the Senate was to be the "sole judge" of what constituted "high crimes and misdemeanors." *Trial of Andrew Johnson on Impeachment*, vol. 1: 123–137.

158. *Trial of Andrew Johnson on Impeachment*, vol. 1: 88–89; *The Impeachment and Trial of Andrew Johnson*, 47.

159. *Trial of Andrew Johnson on Impeachment*, vol. 1: 409; *The Impeachment and Trial of Andrew Johnson*, 110.
160. *Trial of Andrew Johnson on Impeachment*, vol. 1: 409; *The Impeachment and Trial of Andrew Johnson*, 110.
161. *Trial of Andrew Johnson on Impeachment*, vol. 1: 410–411; *The Impeachment and Trial of Andrew Johnson*, 110–111.
162. *Trial of Andrew Johnson on Impeachment*, vol. 2: 22–23. Logan noted that a president incapacitated by insanity could be removed not because insanity is a crime but because every act "almost necessarily would be a misdemeanor in office."
163. *Trial of Andrew Johnson on Impeachment*, vol. 2: 219–220; *The Impeachment and Trial of Andrew Johnson*, 214.
164. *Trial of Andrew Johnson on Impeachment*, vol. 2: 220; *The Impeachment and Trial of Andrew Johnson*, 215.
165. *Trial of Andrew Johnson on Impeachment*, vol. 2: 139; *Impeachment and Trial of Andrew Johnson*, 197.
166. *Trial of Andrew Johnson on Impeachment*, vol. 2: 140; *Impeachment and Trial of Andrew Johnson*, 198. Nelson requested that the Chief Justice provide a "judicial exposition of the meaning of the Constitution," but the Chief Justice declined.
167. *Trial of Andrew Johnson on Impeachment*, vol. 2: 286–287; *Impeachment and Trial of Andrew Johnson*, 236–237. Evarts noted that inclusion of "high misdemeanor" in the Tenure of Office Act was an unnecessary qualification since the seriousness of the offense could be ascertained from the attendant punishment.
168. The Senate's vote was not without drama. Johnson's conviction had been in doubt since Senator William P. Fessenden, leader of the conservative Republicans, had signaled his support of acquittal. Benedict, *A Compromise of Principle*, 310. Nevertheless, the issue of Johnson's conviction and removal remained unresolved well into the first call of the roll. Fessenden was the first of Senators considered to be "undecided" to vote for acquittal. Senator Joseph S. Fowler had been subjected to intense lobbying by the Radicals. When he first announced his vote, it was thought that he had said "guilty," but when Sumner asked him to repeat what he had said, Fowler shouted "Not guilty." Senator James W. Grimes had suffered a paralyzing stroke two days earlier. His body covered by blisters and unable to walk, Grimes was helped to stand and informed the Senate of his vote for acquittal. John B. Henderson had been subjected to such pressure from the Radicals that he had offered to resign in order to allow the governor of Missouri to appoint another Senator. The Radicals had sent spies to watch his every movement. Nevertheless, Henderson too voted for acquittal, setting the stage for the climactic vote of Edward G. Ross. There were 35 votes committed to conviction. Only 1 additional vote was needed for conviction and removal of Johnson. His fellow Kansas Senator, Samuel C. Pomeroy, a Radical Republican, showed him purported head-counts assuring conviction and dined with Ross the night before the vote urging conviction.

Stanton sent General Daniel Sickles to Ross' lodgings. General Sickles waited until 4:00 a.m. but was not permitted to see Ross. When Ross rose to announce his decision, he later told friends that he felt as though he was looking into his own grave. Nevertheless, he pronounced his decision, "not guilty," thereby breaking the impeachment effort. Smith, *High Crimes and Misdemeanors*, 285–293. With Senators Peter G. Van Winkle and Lyman Trumbull, Fessenden, Fowler, Grimes, Henderson, and Ross came to be known as the "Recusants." *Impeachment of a President*, 167.

169. *Trial of Andrew Johnson on Impeachment*, vol. 2: 484–487; *Impeachment and Trial of Andrew Johnson*, 288–289.
170. *Trial of Andrew Johnson on Impeachment*, vol. 2: 496–498.
171. *Trial of Andrew Johnson on Impeachment*, vol. 3: 56 (Johnson), 163 (Davis), 203 (Fowler) and 297 (Henderson)
172. *Trial of Andrew Johnson on Impeachment*, vol. 3: 24 (Fessenden), 54 (Johnson), 100 (Hendricks), 118 (Vickers), 149 (Van Winkle), 170 (Davis), 202–203 (Fowler), 226 (Buckalew), 326–327 (Trumbull), and 353 (Grimes).
173. *Trial of Andrew Johnson on Impeachment*, vol. 3: 26 (Fessenden), 57 (Johnson), 96–97 (Hendericks), 119 (Vickers), 150 (Van Winkle), 177–178 (Davis), 205 (Fowler), 227 (Buckalew), 305 (Henderson), and 335 (Grimes).
174. *Trial of Andrew Johnson on Impeachment*, vol. 3: 206 and the views of the individual Senators: 28 (Fessenden), 50 (Johnson), 96 (Hendericks), 119–120 (Vickers), 150 (Van Winkle), 160 (Davis), 227–228 (Buckalew), 244 (Doolittle), 306 (Handerson), 327 (Trumbull), and 339 (Grimes).
175. *Trial of Andrew Johnson on Impeachment*, vol. 3: 307.
176. *Trial of Andrew Johnson on Impeachment*, vol. 3: 29 (Fessenden), 50 (Johnson), 96 (Hendericks), 120 (Vickers), 152 (Van Winkle), 161 (Davis), 206–207 (Fowler), 229 (Buckalew), 246 (Doolittle), 308 (Henderson), and 327 (Trumbull).
177. *Trial of Andrew Johnson on Impeachment*, vol. 3: 340 (Grimes), 175 (Davis).
178. *Trial of Andrew Johnson on Impeachment*, vol. 3: 7 (Sherman), 110 (Yates), 271 (Sumner), 313 (Patterson), 341 (Pomeroy).
179. *Trial of Andrew Johnson on Impeachment*, vol. 3: 15–16 (Sherman), 49–50 (Howard), 80–81 (Howe), 94 (Edmunds), 114 (Yates), 126 (Ferry), 135 (Morrill of Maine), 142–143 (Morrill of Vermont), 193 (Tipton), 217 (Wilson), 279 (Sumner), and 346 (Pomeroy).
180. *Compare, Trial of Andrew Johnson on Impeachment*, vol. 3 12 (Sherman), 46–47 (Howard), 92–93 (Edmonds), 121 (Ferry), 140–141 (Morrill), 278 (Sumner).
181. *Compare, Trial of Andrew Johnson on Impeachment*, vol. 3: 15 (Sherman), 48 (Howard), 77 (Howe), 93 (Edmonds), 141–142 (Morrill), 192 (Tipton), 212 (Ferry), 278 (Sumner), 345 (Pomeroy).
182. *Trial of Andrew Johnson on Impeachment*, vol. 3: 15 (Sherman), 94 (Edmonds), 122 (Ferry), 142 (Morrill).
183. *Trial of Andrew Johnson on Impeachment*, vol. 3: 49 (Howard), 78–79 (Howe), 193 (Tipton), 278–279 (Sumner), 346 (Pomeroy).
184. *Trial of Andrew Johnson on Impeachment*, vol. 3: 29–30 (Fessenden), 51 (Johnson), 120 (Vickers), 157–159 (Davis), 194 (Fowler), 231 (Buckalew).

185. *Trial of Andrew Johnson on Impeachment*, vol. 3: 3 (Sherman), 144 (Morrill), 250 (Sumner), 352 (Williams).
186. *Trial of Andrew Johnson on Impeachment*, vol. 3: 68 (Howe), 94 (Edmunds), 213 (Frelinghuysen), 215 (Wilson).
187. *Trial of Andrew Johnson on Impeachment*, vol. 3: 3 (Sherman), 113 (Yates), 249–253 (Sumner).
188. Thus, although the impeachment was not successful in removing Johnson, the impeachment may have served Congress' broader Reconstruction objectives of blunting Johnson's resistance. Valelly, *The Two Reconstructions*, 44.
189. Dewitt, *The Impeachment and Trial of Andrew Johnson*, 613–629; Lomask, *Andrew Johnson: President on Trial*, 344–347; Smith, *High Crimes and Misdemeanors*, 300–302; Noel B. Gerson, *The Trial of Andrew Johnson* (Nashville: Thomas Nelson, 1977) 127–147.
190. Rehnquist, *Grand Inquests*, 246; Trefousse, *Impeachment of a President*, 214–215; Benedict, *A Compromise of Principle*, 300 and 307.
191. Ibid., 311; Rehnquist, *Grand Inquest*, 247.
192. Benedict, *The Impeachment and Trial of Andrew Johnson*, 180.
193. Ackerman, *We the People,* vol. 1: 83; Whittington, *Constitutional Construction*, 139.

## 3    The Proceedings against Richard M. Nixon

1. Belknap resigned his position when he learned that he would be impeached by the House of Representatives. On April 4, 1876, five Articles of Impeachment charging Belknap with high crimes and misdemeanors were presented to the Senate. Interestingly, Belknap was not charged with bribery despite each of the articles being grounded on Belknap's relationship with Marsh. Bushnell, *Crimes, Follies, and Misfortunes*, 167–189. Three years earlier, allegations of bribery and conflict of interest against Vice President Schuyler Colfax arising from his involvement with Credit Moblier while Colfax had been speaker of the House were referred to the Committee on the Judiciary, which, after reviewing the record, concluded that there was no factual basis for impeachment. Committee on the Judiciary, *Impeachment: Selected Materials*, 93d Cong., 1st Sess. (Washington, DC: U.S. Government Printing Office, 1973) 601–615.
2. Charles Swayne was appointed to the U.S. District Court in Florida by President Benjamin Harrison in 1890. Almost immediately, Judge Swayne antagonized the Florida Democratic Party when he presided over cases of election fraud allegedly perpetrated by the Democrats. After the Florida legislature twice requested Judge Swayne's removal by Congress, by a vote of 198 to 61 the House determined that Judge Swayne should be impeached. However, when the articles of impeachment were presented by the Judiciary Committee, a lengthy and heated debate ensued. Ultimately articles of impeachment were adopted by a close majority that followed party lines. The first three articles charged Swayne with having overcharged the

government for expenses in connection with service outside his judicial district. Two articles charged that Swayne had used a private railroad car belonging to a bankrupt railroad without having compensated the company. Two articles charged that Swayne illegally resided outside the judicial district in which he served. The final five articles charged Swayne with having imposed unlawful punishments for contempt of court on three individuals, including the disbarment of two attorneys for a period of two years. Swayne's trial in the Senate lasted from February 10 to February 27, 1905. Swayne was acquitted by a vote that reflected the partisan division of the Senate. Bushnell, *Crimes, Follies, and Misfortunes*, 191–214.

3. On January 13, 1913, Circuit Judge Robert W. Archbald became only the third federal official to be convicted by the Senate following impeachment by the House. Archbald was convicted of five of the thirteen articles lodged against him by the House. Two of the articles charged that Archbald had acquired properties from railroads and other companies that had cases pending in the Commerce Court on which he served. One article charged that Archbald had received $500 from a friend on whose behalf Archbald had attempted, unsuccessfully, to secure a lease of property from a coal company. The fourth article on which he was convicted charged that Archbald had improper ex parte communications with a litigant in a case pending in his court. The fifth article alleged a pattern of self-dealing over the entire course of his eleven-year judicial career. Archbald's acquittal on the other articles appears to have resulted from the view of some senators that Archbald was not subject to impeachment for acts committed while he was a district judge prior his appointment to the Circuit Court. Bushnell, *Crimes, Follies, and Misfortunes*, 217–242.

   One of Archbald's attorneys in the trial before the Senate, Alexander Simpson, published the brief he had prepared for Judge Archbald, which he titled, *A Treatise on Federal Impeachments*. In his treatise, Simpson concluded with respect to high crimes and misdemeanors that "notwithstanding the interesting arguments to the contrary,…the House in prosecuting and the Senate in trying impeachments are not limited to offenses which are indictable." Nevertheless, Simpson argued that "the offence must be one of a serious character" and although not necessarily indictable, impeachable offenses "must be of such a 'high' character as might properly be made criminal, and must be one against the United States." Further, Simpson wrote, "the offense must be one in some way affecting the administration of the office from which it is sought to exclude the offender." Although in Simpson's view, it was not necessary that the offense be committed in the performance of the office, "the character of the offence, or that which flows there from, must tend to bring the office…into ignominy and disgrace." Alexander Simpson, *A Treatise on Federal Impeachments* (Philadelphia: Law Association of Philadelphia, 1916) 49–53.

4. Judge English was impeached on a variety of colorful charges. Article 1 charged English with "tyranny and oppression" as a result of his having summarily disbarred two lawyers appearing before him and having summoned state officials and a mayor to his courtroom and threatening to remove them

from their offices "in a loud angry voice, using improper, profane and indecent language." Judge English was also charged with having threatened newspaper reporters and editors with incarceration if they published articles concerning his court, and having admonished a jury "if he told them a man was guilty and they found him not guilty that he would send them to jail." Article 2 charged that English had colluded with the bankruptcy referee in order to serve "their own interests and profit and that of relatives and friends." Article 4 charged that English and the referee had caused funds to be deposited in a bank of which they were shareholders and had borrowed funds equal to the assets and capital of the bank at low interest with no security. Lastly, Article 5 charged that English had used his position to secure employment for his son. Van Tassel and Finkelman, *Impeachable Offenses*, 144–152.

5. On May 24, 1932, the Bar Association of San Francisco petitioned the House of Representatives to investigate the conduct of District Court Judge Harold Louderback. It was alleged that Judge Louderback had appointed friends and political allies to serve as receivers for companies in distressed circumstances. The House empanelled an investigative committee, which held hearings in San Francisco and Washington, DC. The committee recommended to the Judiciary Committee that Louderback be impeached. The Judiciary Committee rejected the recommendation by a vote of 17 to 5 and recommended instead that Judge Louderback be censured. The House disregarded the Judicial Committee's recommendation and voted to impeach him. The Senate, however, voted to acquit Judge Louderback. Bushnell, *Crimes, Follies, and Misfortunes*, 245–266.

6. Within days of the acquittal by the Senate of Judge Louderback, the House commenced an investigation into allegations of misconduct on the part of Halstead L. Ritter, a district judge in the Southern District of Florida. The allegations against Judge Ritter involved his conduct in connection with the bankruptcy and receivership of a resort hotel; inaccuracies in reporting of the judge's income; and Ritter's having continued to practice law after his appointment to the federal bench. As had occurred in the Louderback proceedings, the Judiciary Committee rejected the investigating subcommittee's recommendation that Ritter be impeached, but then reversed that decision and recommended impeachment by the House.

The principal charge against Ritter was that he had shared in the fees paid to a former law partner in a lawsuit over which Ritter presided. Ritter was impeached on six articles. The first two articles charged him with offenses arising from his acceptance of money from his former partner. Articles 3 and 4 charged him with having accepted $7500 from a friend to whom Ritter had given legal advice. Articles 5 and 6 charged that Ritter had failed to pay taxes on income in 1928 and 1930. Ritter was acquitted of each of these substantive offenses. However, notwithstanding the Senate's acquittals on these charges, Ritter was convicted, by 1 vote, of the seventh article, which was in essence a restatement of the first six articles. The Senate then unanimously voted against a permanent disqualification from holding office.

Following the Senate's action, Ritter filed suit in the Court of Claims ostensibly to compel payment of his salary. Ritter argued that the charges did not constitute the high crimes and misdemeanors contemplated by the Constitution. Ritter also challenged the validity of his conviction on an article that only restated the charges on which he was acquitted. The Court of Claims held, however, that only the Senate had jurisdiction over impeachments, and therefore the court had no jurisdiction over Ritter's claim. Bushnell, *Crimes, Follies, and Misfortunes*, 269–287.

7. After efforts to reach a compromise between steel producers and the United Steel Workers failed in April 1952, President Truman directed the Secretary of Commerce, Charles Sawyer, in effect to nationalize steel production under authority of the president's war powers. In May 1953, the Supreme Court declared that seizure to be unconstitutional. *Youngstown Sheet and Tube Co. v. Sawyer*, 343 U.S. 937 (1952); Melvin I. Urofsky, *A March of Liberty: A Constitutional History of the United States* (New York: Knopf: 1988) 760–761. While the action was pending in the courts, on April 22, 1952, Representative Noah M. Mason called for the institution of impeachment proceedings, calling the president's actions "illegal, high-handed, arbitrary and un-necessary," and stating that "such action is extremely drastic and extremely dangerous; and as such, warrants drastic counter-action." Resolutions of impeachment were offered by Mason's Republican colleagues, George H. Bender and Paul W. Schafer. *Congressional Record*, vol. 98, 82nd Cong., 2d Sess. (1942) 4220–4221. Shafer also cited the commitment of troops in Korea without congressional approval; the dismissal of General Douglas MacArthur (which Shafer called a "grave act of mal-administration"); the withholding of information from Congress; and presidential statements that jeopardized "the good name, the peace, and the security" of the country. *Congressional Record*, vol. 98, 4518–4519. No action was taken by Congress.

8. The first attempt to impeach Justice Douglas was in June 1953 after he had granted a stay of the execution of Julius and Ethel Rosenberg, who had been convicted of espionage for procuring information concerning the atomic bomb for the Soviet Union. Despite vacation of the stay by the Supreme Court, Congressman William M. Wheeler pressed for impeachment on the grounds that Douglas' loyalty to "left-wing so-called liberals" had resulted in conduct unbecoming a justice that tended to bring the court into disrepute; moral turpitude (Douglas had been named a correspondent in adultery); conspiracy; and treason. *Congressional Record*, vol. 99, 83rd Cong., 1st Sess. (1953) 7586–7589. No action was taken on Wheeler's proposed resolution. William O. Douglas, *The Court Years 1939–1975* (New York: Random House, 1980) 78–82.

A second effort at impeachment was led by Congressman Gerald R. Ford in 1970, on grounds of Douglas' extrajudicial employments. Ford charged that Douglas had breached the standard of "good behavior" by failing to recuse himself from ruling on a libel suit against Ralph Ginzburg after accepting payment for two articles published in magazines controlled by Ginzburg. Ford further charged that Douglas had been compensated for service as president of the Parvin Foundation (which Ford contended had ties to organized crime) and for serving as a consultant and executive committee member of the "leftish" Center for the Study of Democratic Institutions (which according to

Ford was also supported by the Parvin Foundation), which had fostered planning for "the violent disruptions" of the 1960's. Ford suggested that Douglas' publication of his book, *Points of Rebellion* (New York: Random House, 1970), although constitutionally protected, "at a critical time in our history when peace and order is what we need —is less than judicial good behavior." Although hearings were held on these charges, no action was taken by Congress. *Congressional Record*, vol. 116, 91st Cong. 2d Sess. (1970) 11912–1197.

9. Ibid., 11913; Walter Ehrlich, *Presidential Impeachment: An American Dilemma* (Saint Charles: Forum Press, 1974) 91–92.

10. Richard Reeves, *President Nixon: Alone in the White House* (New York: Simon & Schuster, 2001) 11–12.

11. Theodore H. White, *Breach of Faith: The Fall of Richard Nixon* (New York: Atheneum, 1975) 62.

12. See Vanmik D. Volkan, Norman Itzkowitz, and Andrew W. Dod, *Richard Nixon: A Psychobiography* (New York: Columbia UP, 1997) 91; Stanley I. Kutler, *The War of Watergate: The Last Crisis of Richard Nixon* (New York: Norton, 1990) 617; Fawn M. Brodie, *Richard Nixon: The Shaping of his Character* (Cambridge: Harvard UP, 1983) 23–25; David Abrahamson, *Nixon v. Nixon: An Emotional Tragedy* (New York: Farrar, 1977) 34; James David Barber, *The Presidential Character: Predicting Performance in the White House* (Englewood Cliffs: Prentice-Hall, 1972) 347.

13. Brodie, *Richard Nixon: The Shaping of His Character*, 37; Stephen E. Ambrose, *Nixon: The Education of Politician* (New York: Simon & Schuster, 1987) 34–84.

14. Brodie, *Richard Nixon: The Shaping of His Character*, 170–184; Ambrose, *Nixon: The Education of a Politician*, 117–140; White, *Breach of* Faith, 63.

15. Ambrose, *Nixon: The Education of a Politician*, 208–224; Brodie, *Richard Nixon: The Shaping of His Character*, 232–245; White, *Breach of Faith*, 63–64.

16. Ambrose, *Nixon: the Education of a Politician*, 258–260.

17. Ibid., 584–607.

18. Ibid., 1597–600, 651; Brodie, *Richard Nixon: The Shaping of His Character*, 435–441. It has been suggested that Nixon's connection to Hughes may have been a motivating factor in the later Watergate burglary. Kutler, *The Wars of Watergate*, 203–204.

19. White, *Breach of Faith*, 71–72.

20. Reeves, *President Nixon: Alone in the White House*, 74–75. Committee on the Judiciary, *Report: Impeachment of Richard M. Nixon President of the United States*, Report No. 93–1305, U.S. House of Representatives, 93rd Cong., 2d Sess. (Washington, DC: U.S. Government Printing Office, 1974) 147 ("Report No. 93–1305").

21. *Report No. 93–1305*, 148–153

22. Ibid., 151–152. In his memorandum, Huston acknowledged that use of "surreptitious entries" would be "clearly illegal."

23. Ibid., 152; Fred Emery, *Watergate: The Corruption of American Politics and the Fall of Richard Nixon* (New York: Simon & Schuster, 1995) 25. Keith W. Olson, *Watergate*, 17. The report of the Senate Select Committee on Presidential Campaign Activities, chaired by Senator Samuel J. Ervin, noted that in a pubic statement issued on May 22, 1973, Nixon had represented that the Huston plan had been rescinded on July 28. However, in a top secret memorandum to Attorney General Mitchell dated September 18, 1970, John Dean stated that steps should be taken "to commence our domestic intelligence operation as quickly as possible." Dean recommended the formation of an interagency domestic intelligence unit, "which had been an integral part of the Huston Plan." Dean suggested that the attorney general monitor the progress closely to ensure that "we are moving this program as quickly as possible." Senate Select Committee on Presidential Campaign Activities, *The Senate Watergate Report: The Final Report of the Senate Select Committee on Presidential Campaign Activities* (New York: Carroll & Graf, 1974) 55–57. ("Senate Select Committee Report").

24. David Rudenstine, *The Day the Presses Stopped* (Berkeley: California UP, 1996) 20–27; Sanford S. Ungar, *The Papers and the Papers: An Account of the Legal and Political Battle over the Pentagon Papers* (New York: Dutton, 1972) 19–31.

25. Rudenstine, *The Day the Papers Stopped*, 46–47; Ungar, *The Papers and the Papers*, 85.

26. Ibid., 150–160. This litigation was eventually resolved in the U.S. Supreme Court, which held that the attempt by the U.S. Government to stop publication of the Pentagon Papers had been an unconstitutional "prior restraint" on the exercise of rights secured by the First Amendment. *New York Times Company v. United States*, 403 U.S. 713 (1971).

27. Kutler, *The Wars of Watergate*, 110, quoting Richard M. Nixon, *Memoirs*, 629–634.

28. Keith W. Olson: *Watergate: The Presidential Scandal that Shook America* (Lawrence: Kansas UP, 2003) 18.

29. Kutler, *The Wars of Watergate*, 112. According to Charles W. Colson, special counsel to the president, creation of the Plumbers was "the pivotal moment…when we crossed the line." Leon Friedman and William F. Levantrosser, eds., *Watergate and Afterward* (Westport: Greenwood Press, 1992) 87–88.

30. *Report No. 93-1305*, 158–161; Kutler, *The Wars of Watergate*, 112; Olson, *Watergate*, 18–19; Emery, *Watergate: The Corruption of American Politics*. At the time of their arrest following the Watergate burglary, Colson described both Hunt and Liddy as "good healthy right wing exuberants." Stanley I. Kutler, ed., *Abuse of Power: The New Nixon Tapes* (New York: Free Press, 1997) 43.

31. *Report No. 93-1305*, 161. Olson, *Watergate*, 19. As an example of this desire to discredit Ellsberg, Nixon told Haldeman and Mitchell on June 30, 1971, "Just get everything out. Try him in the press. Try him in the press. Everything John

[Mitchell], that there is on the investigation get it out, leak it out. We want to destroy him in the press. Press. Is that clear?" Kutler, *Abuse of Power*, 6.

32. *Report No. 93–1305*, 163.

33. *Senate Select Committee Report*, 199; Reeves, *President Nixon Alone in the White House*, 353; Emery, *Watergate: The Corruption of American Politics*, 62.

34. *Senate Select Committee Report*, 200–201; Kutler, *Wars of Watergate*, 115; Emery, *Watergate: The Corruption of American Politics*, 66–67; Olson, *Watergate*, 19.

35. *Report No. 93–1305*, 164–165; Reeves, *President Nixon: Alone in the White House*, 369. On September 8, Ehrlichman alluded to the Fielding burglary in a conversation with Nixon. Ehrlichman told Nixon that "We had one little operation. It's been aborted out in Los Angeles which, I think, is better that you don't know about. But we've got some dirty tricks underway. It may pay off." Kutler, *Abuse of Power*, 28. Another target of the White House's covert operations unit was the Brookings Institution in Washington, DC, and in particular, the files of Leslie Gelb, a former consultant to the National Security Council, who was believed to have been engaged in a Pentagon Papers-like study of the Vietnam War after 1967. After Haldeman told Nixon about the files, Nixon told Haldeman, "Now do you remember Huston's plan? Implement it….I want it implemented…Goddamn it, get in and get those files. Blow the safe and get it." In another recorded conversation with Haldeman on June 30, Nixon reiterated his order that the Brookings Institution be burglarized. Nixon told Haldeman, "I want Brookings, I want them just to break in and take it. Do you understand?…You talk to Hunt. I want the break in…You're to break into the place, rifle the files, and bring them in." Kutler, *Abuse of Power*, 6.

36. Kutler, *The Wars of Watergate*, 105; Reeves, *President Nixon: Alone in the White House*, 370. In a conversation recorded on September 13, 1971, Nixon told Haldeman "Now here's the point. Bob, *please* get me the names of the Jews, you know, the big Jewish contributors of the Democrats….All right. Could we please investigate some of the cocksuckers? That's all." Kutler, *Abuse of Power*, 31. In another conversation with Haldeman on September 14, Nixon said to Haldeman, "What about the rich Jews?…You see, IRS is full of Jews, Bob…That's what I think. I think that's the reason they're after Graham, is the rich Jews." Kutler, *Abuse of Power*, 32.

37. Kutler, *Wars of Watergate*, 105.

38. *Report No. 93–1350*, 141–142; Reeves, *President Nixon: Alone in the White House*, 228. Information was obtained from the IRS concerning a journalist investigating a fundraising event and several prominent entertainers. IRS also provided information concerning a candidate for a position with the Committee to Re-Elect the President (CRP). *Report No. 93–1350*, 142; *Senate Select Committee Report*, 220–221.

39. *Report No. 93–1305*, 142–143; Kutler, *The Wars of Watergate*, 204–205.

40. *Senate Select Committee Final Report*, 74–75.

41. Reeves, *President Nixon: Alone in the White House*, 429–430; *Senate Select Committee Report*, 74–75. A predecessor of the Gemstone Project was Operation Sandwedge, a creation of John Caulfield, involving "offensive intelligence and

defensive—security" operations. Caulfield's plan called for covert penetration of the Democratic nominee's organization and headquarters; burglary; surveillance; and publication of derogatory information. Kutler, *Wars of Watergate*, 199.

42. This was the so-called Diamond plan. Emery, *Watergate: The Corruption of American Politics*, 89.

43. The prostitutes on the boat were designated as the "Sapphire" plan, and the communications center, to which compromising conversations would be transmitted, was denominated the "Crystal" plan. Emery, *Watergate: The Corruption of American Politics*, 90.

44. *Senate Select Committee Report*, 75; Reeves, *President Nixon: Alone in the White House*, 430. These were designated as "Opal" plans I–IV. In addition, under the "Topaz" plan, document copying teams were to be sent to the Muskie and McGovern headquarters in Washington and other locations to be determined. Emery, *Watergate: The Corruption of American Politics*, 90. Mitchell told Liddy to come back with a less expensive and more realistic plan.

45. Reeves, *President Nixon: Alone in the White House*, 430–431. At that, Dean interjected that he didn't think that "this kind of conversation should go on in the Attorney General's Office."

46. *Senate Select Committee Report*, 79–80; Kutler, *Wars of Watergate*, 199; Olson, *Watergate*, 38.

47. Kutler, *Wars of Watergate*, 365–366. Mitchell told the Senate Select Committee that the purpose of the cover-up was to conceal the White House Horrors from public disclosure rather than simply concealing the involvement of the White House in the Watergate burglary. Kutler, *Wars of Watergate*, 366; Olson, *Watergate*, 99.

48. *Senate Select Committee Report*, 83–86; Reeves, *President Nixon: Alone in the White House*, 493; Emery, *Watergate: The Corruption of American Politics*, 118–122; Olson, *Watergate*, 38–39. According to Magruder, the objective of the phone taps was to learn what information O'Brien had concerning the Hughes-Nixon relationship. Friedman and Levantrosser, *Watergate and Afterward*, 40–45.

49. *Senate Select Committee Report*, 85–86.

50. Ibid., 51.

51. Reeves, *President Nixon: Alone in the White House*, 449.

52. *Senate Select Committee Report*, 51–52; Reeves, *President Nixon: Alone in the White House*, 449.

53. *Senate Select Committee Report*, 52, 88; Reeves, *President Nixon: Alone in the White House*, 499–500; Emery, *Watergate: the Corruption of American Politics*, 132–135.

54. Kutler, *Wars of Watergate*, 187–188. Caddy had been contacted by Hunt and the wife of one of the Miami burglars.

55. *Senate Select Committee Report*, 88; Kutler, *Wars of Watergate*, 187.

56. Ibid., 188.

57. *Senate Select Committee Report*, 88.

58. Reeves, *President Nixon: Alone in the White House*, 501.

59. *Report No. 93-1305*, 42–43.

60. Dean eventually destroyed Hunt's notebooks that had been in the safe. *Senate Select Committee Report*, 93.
61. *Report No. 93–1305*, 44–45. *Senate Select Committee Report*, 90–91; Reeves, *President Nixon: Alone in the White House*, 501; Kutler, *Wars of Watergate*, 216; Olson, *Watergate*, 48–49.
62. Dean met with Liddy the day before and had been told by Liddy that the burglary had been "a CRP Operation." Dean apprised Echrlichman of his conversation with Liddy.
63. Haldeman's notes indicated that it would be necessary to prevent the FBI from going "beyond what's necessary in developing evidence and we can keep a lid on that." The record of this meeting was subsequently destroyed in what became known as the "18 ½ minute gap." Kutler, *Abuse of Power*, 47. However, in another conversation between Nixon and Haldeman on June 20, Haldeman told Nixon that the investigators did not have a case against Hunt because they could not put him at the scene of the burglary. Nixon replied, "We know where he was, though." Reeves, *President Nixon: Alone in the White House*, 507.
64. *Report No. 93–1305*, 47. The House Judiciary Committee concluded in regard to the president's June 22 statement that "When the President issued this statement, he knew or should have known that Howard Hunt, Gordon Liddy and other CRP personnel were responsible for the burglary, and that some of these persons had previously engaged in covert activities, as members of the Plumbers unit, on the President's behalf." *Report No. 93–1305*, 47.
65. Ibid., 49; Kutler, *Abuse of Power*, 67–70; Kutler, *Wars of Watergate*, 218.
66. Reeves, *President Nixon: Alone in the White House*, 508–509; Emergy, *Watergate: The Corruption of American Politics*, 190–192.
67. *Report No. 93–1305*, 48–54; *Senate Select Committee Report*, 96.
68. *Report No. 93–1305*, 55–57.
69. Ibid., 57–58.
70. Ibid., 67; *Senate Select Committee Report*, 103–106.
71. *Report No. 93–1305*, 59–60; *Senate Select Committee Report*, 107.
72. *Report No. 93–1305*, 60; Kutler, *Wars of Watergate*, 222–223.
73. *Report No. 93–1305*, 60.
74. Ibid. In fact, as the Judiciary Committee noted, "Dean testified that he first heard of his 'complete' investigation in the President's announcement." Ibid., 82.
75. Ibid., 83–84; *Senate Select Committee Report*, 107.
76. *Report No. 93–1305*, 84–85.
77. Ibid., 87; *Senate Select Committee Report*, 159–160.
78. Prior to the burglary, Hunt received $10,000 in cash from Liddy. This money was given to the attorney Caddy within hours of the arrests. *Report No. 93–1305*, 66.
79. Ibid., 50, 66–67; *Senate Select Committee Report*, 112–116; Reeves, *President Nixon: Alone in the White House*, 511; Kutler, *Wars of Watergtate*, 248–250.
80. *Report No. 93–1305*, 67; *Wars of Watergate*, 249.
81. *Report No. 93–1305*, 67–68; *Senate Select Committee Report*, 117–118; Kutler, *Wars of Watergate*, 250.

82. *Report No. 93–1305*, 68–69; Kutler, *Abuse of Power*, 247; Reeves, *President Nixon: Alone in the White House*, 577. Later, prosecutors would advise Nixon to retain criminal counsel after they heard the tape of this conversation that they believed established Nixon's culpability as a coconspirator. Emery, *Watergate: The Corruption of American Politics*, 261–263.
83. Kutler, *Abuse of Power*, 248–252.
84. *Report No. 93–1305*, 69.
85. Kutler, *Abuse of Power*, 253–254; *Senate Select Committee Report*, 120.
86. Kutler, *Abuse of Power*, 254; Reeves, *President Nixon: Alone in the White House*, 578.
87. Kutler, *Abuse of Power*, 254; *Senate Select Committee Report*, 119–120; Reeves, *President Nixon: Alone in the White House*, 578; *Watergate: The Corruption of American Politics*, 263.
88. *Report No. 93–1305*, 69–70; Kutler, *Wars of Watergate*, 274–278.
89. *Report No. 93–1305*, 73.
90. Ibid., 74.
91. *United States v. George Gordon Liddy*, Cr. No. 1872–72 (D.D.C.); Kutler, *Wars of Watergate*, 212.
92. Ibid., 253–254; Emery, *Watergate: The Corruption of American Politics*, 238–239.
93. Kutler, *Wars of Watergate*, 260.
94. Letter dated March 19, 1973, from James W. McCord, Jr. to Judge Sirica.
95. Kutler, *Wars of Watergate*, 261.
96. *Report No. 93–1305*, 91–92.
97. Ibid., 92.
98. Ibid., 100–101; Kutler, *Wars of Watergate*, 264, 286. Kutler, *Watergate: The Corruption of American Politics*, 276–277.
99. Strachan was considered the critical witness in establishing Haldeman's culpability. At this time, Mardian was also preparing witnesses to testify before the grand jury. In a colloquy on April 15, 1973, cited by the Judiciary Committee, Ehrlichman informed Nixon that Mardian had coached the witnesses to give false testimony. Nixon asked Ehrlichman, "Well, is there anything wrong with that?" When Ehrlichman replied that there was a problem, Nixon asked whether the problem was that "He was not their attorney." Ehrlichman replied that the problem was that "He asked them to say things that weren't true." *Report No. 93–1305*, 92.
100. Ibid., 92–93, 103; *Senate Select Committee Report*, 160; Kutler, *Wars of Watergate*, 284.
101. *Report No. 92–1305*, 94–95.
102. Ibid., 96–97.
103. Ibid., 97.
104. *Senate Select Committee Report*, 39–40.
105. *Report No. 93–1305*, 116–117. Kutler, *Wars of Watergate*, 258.
106. *Report No. 93–1305*, 122–123. John Dean later admitted that the White House strategy had been to thwart the Senate's inquiry while adopting a public posture of cooperation. Kutler, *Wars of Watergate*, 258.

107. *Report No. 93–1305*, 121; Reeves, *President Nixon: Alone in the White House*, 602; Emery, *Watergate: The Corruption of American Politics*, 350–357.

108. *Report No. 93–1305*, 121–122; Emery, *Watergate: The Corruption of American Politics*, 355–367.

109. *Report No. 93–1305*, 123, Kutler, *Wars of Watergate*, 389; Emery, *Watergate: The Corruption of American Politics*, 368–369, 371–373.

110. *Nixon v. Sirica*, 487 F.2d 800 (D.C. Cir. 1973); *Report No. 93–1305*, 123; Kutler, *Wars of Watergate*, 389–390.

111. *Report No. 93–1305*, 123–124; Kutler, *Wars of Watergate*, 401–402.

112. *Report No. 93–1305*, 124; Emery, *Watergate: The Corruption of American Politics*, 385–399.

113. Kutler, *Wars of Watergate*, 402–406.

114. *Report No. 93–1305*, 124; Kutler, *Wars of Watergate*, 426–429.

115. *Report No. 93–1305*, 125–126.

116. *United States v. Nixon*, 418 U.S. 683 (1974).

117. *Report No. 93–1305*, 126–127; Emery, *Watergate: The Corruption of American Politics*, 409–418; Olson, *Watergate*, 127. Subsequent analysis of the "18 ½ minute gap" revealed that it had resulted from a series of five to nine manual operations. *Report No. 93–1305*, 127; Kutler, *Wars of Watergate*, 429–431.

118. Kutler, *Wars of Watergate*, 478. David E. Kyvig noted that Congress had been slow to consider impeachment seriously until the Saturday Night Massacre. David E. Kyvig, *The Age of Impeachment: American Constitutional Culture Since 1960* (Lawrence, Kansas UP, 2008) 141–142.

119. *Report No. 93–1305*, 6.

120. Ibid., 187, 234–278.

121. Ibid., 188.

122. Ibid., 9–10; Kutler, *Wars of Watergate*, 490–492; Emery, *Watergate: The Corruption of American Politics*, 425–427; Olson, *Watergate*, 137–138.

123. Impeachment Inquiry Staff, Committee on the Judiciary of the United States House of Representatives, *Constitutional Grounds for Presidential Impeachment* (Washington, DC: Public Affairs Press, 1974) ("Staff Report").

124. *Staff Report*, 29. With respect to whether "other high crimes and misdemeanors" referred to criminal conduct, the staff noted that the Framers could simply have written "or other crimes" as they had in other provisions.

125. Ibid., 29–35.

126. Ibid., 35–37.

127. Ibid., 41–42; John R. Labovitz, *Presidential Impeachment* (New Haven: Yale UP, 1978) 126–131. The staff observed that unlike the criminal law, impeachment is a "remedial process," which is intended "primarily to maintain constitutional government."

128. *Staff Report*, 42–43.

129. Ibid., 47.

130. James D. St. Clair and Charles Alan Wright, *"An Analysis of the Constitutional Standard for Presidential Impeachment"* (Washington, DC: U.S. Government Printing Office, 1974) 32, 34–38.

131. In an apparent reference to the Staff Report, the defense dismissed reliance on the impeachments of federal judges "to support the proposition that impeachment will lie for conduct which does not of itself constitute an indictable offense" as being "mostly appealing to those broad constructionists who favoring a severely weakened Chief Executive argue that certain non-criminal 'political' offenses may justify impeachment." Ibid., 39. The defense also cited a statement by the House of Managers of the Archbald trial in the Senate as establishing the precedential principal that because different standards for removal apply to judges, misbehavior may warrant removal of a federal judge but not other civil officers, including the president. Ibid., 45–47.

132. Ibid., 53–59. The Department of Justice, Office of Legal Counsel submitted a memorandum that offered no conclusive view of the nature of impeachable conduct. United States Department of Justice, Office of Legal Counsel, "Legal Aspects of Impeachment: An Overview" (Washington DC: Office of Legal Counsel, 1974).

133. Committee on the Judiciary, *Debate on Articles of Impeachment: Hearings Before the Committee on the Judiciary of the House of Representatives*, 93d Cong., 2d Sess. (Washington, DC: U.S. Government Printing Office, 1974) 133 (*Debate on Articles of Impeachment*).

134. Ibid., 7.

135. *Report No. 93–1305*, 1–3.

136. *Debate on Articles of Impeachment*, 329–331.

137. *Report No. 93–1305*, 3–4.

138. *Debate on Articles of Impeachment*, 335–336.

139. Ibid., 337.

140. Ibid., 341–342.

141. Ibid., 426.

142. Ibid., 442.

143. Ibid., 445–447.

144. *Report No. 93–1305*, 188.

145. *Debate on Articles of Impeachment*, 470.

146. Ibid., 476.

147. Ibid., 477.

148. Ibid., 487.

149. Ibid., 488–489. Two additional articles were considered by the Committee. The first charged that Nixon had "authorized, ordered, and ratified the concealment from the Congress of the facts and the submissions to the Congress of false and misleading statements concerning the existence, scope and nature of American bombing operations in Cambodia in derogation of the power of the Congress to declare war, to make appropriations and to raise and support armies." These charges arose from the conduct of a secret bombing campaign, including the "Menu Operation," the disclosure of which had resulted in a series of illegal telephone interceptions and eventually in the creation of the Plumbers unit. The Committee declined to report these charges to the House by a vote of 26 to 12. *Report No. 93–1305*, 217–219.

The second article involved allegations that Nixon had received compensation in excess of that permitted under the Constitution and that he had underreported his income in violation of the Internal Revenue Code. In this regard, it was alleged that Nixon had benefited personally from federal expenditures for renovations and improvements to his properties in Key Biscayne, Florida, and San Clemente, California. The Joint Committee on Internal Revenue estimated this personal income to be $92,000 and the Internal Revenue Service calculated the income to be $67,000. The second article also involved allegations that Nixon had improperly and fraudulently claimed deductions from his personal income tax, including a $576,000 deduction for the gift of his personal papers that had allegedly been back dated. The Committee voted 26 to 12 not to refer this Article to the House as well. *Report No. 93–1305*, 220–223.

150. Ibid., 303.
151. Ibid., 362–371.
152. Ibid., 495–496.
153. White, *Breach of Faith*, 28–29; Kutler, *Wars of Watergate*, 538–548; Emery, *Watergate: The Corruption of American Politics and the Fall of Richard Nixon*, 473–477.
154. White, *Breach of Faith*, 349–350; Kutler, *Wars of Watergate*, 548. Twelve days later, on August 20, by a vote of 412 to 3, the full House voted to accept the report of the Judiciary Committee. Kutler, *Wars of Watergate*, 557.
155. Emery, *Watergate: The Corruption of American Politics and the Fall of Richard Nixon*, 482.
156. Brant, *Impeachment: Trials and Errors*, 181–182.
157. Berger, *Impeachment: The Constitutional Problems*, 61–63 (emphasis original).
158. Committee on Federal Legislation, Association of the Bar of the City of New York, *The Law of Presidential Impeachment* (New York: Harper, 1974) 6, 18–19.
159. Charles L. Black, Jr., *Impeachment: A Handbook* (New Haven: Yale UP, 1974) 33–37.
160. Kurland, *Watergate and the Constitution*, 107.
161. Ibid., 111–112.
162. Ibid., 114.
163. Ibid., 119.
164. Friedman and Levantrosser, *Watergate and Afterward*, 202.
165. *Report No. 93–1305*, 217–219; Kutler, *Wars of Watergate*, 136–137.


## 4   The Impeachment and Trial of William Jefferson Clinton

1. Peter Baker, *The Breach: Inside the Impeachment and Trial of William Jefferson Clinton* (New York: Scribner, 2000) 18; Kyvig, *The Age of Impeachment*, 352.
2. Federalist 65, Hamilton, Madison, and Jay, *The Federalist*, 426.
3. 28 U.S.C. §§ 591–599.
4. Starr was appointed independent counsel by order of the Special Court, a three judge panel of the Court of Appeals for the District of Columbia Circuit, in the case of *In re: Madison Guaranty Savings and Loan Association*, Division No.

94–1. In appointing Starr, the panel of judges rejected the request of the attorney general that Robert B. Fiske, Jr., be reappointed because of a perceived conflict of interest. It has been suggested that the appointment of Starr to replace Fiske was the result of congressional influence. Nicol C. Rae and Colton C. Campbell, *Impeaching Clinton: Partisan Strife on Capital Hill* (Lawrence: Kansas UP, 2004) 21.

5. *Paula Corbin Jones v. William Jefferson Clinton*, Civil Action No. LR-C-094-290 (E.D. Arkansas, 1994), ¶¶ 6–13 ("*Jones* Complaint").

6. Ibid., ¶ 38.

7. Ibid., ¶¶ 58–74.

8. Ibid., ¶¶ 75–79

9. Ibid., ¶¶ a–d. From its inception, the *Jones* suit was as much a vehicle, or a strategem, for political conservatives to attack and embarrass Clinton as it was to vindicate purported violations of Jones' civil rights. Prior to filing her suit, Jones had appeared at a convention of the Conservative Political Action Committee in Washington, DC. Jones' expenses had been paid by another conservative group, the Legal Affairs Council. Following the decision of the U.S. Supreme Court allowing the *Jones* case to proceed against Clinton, an offer was made to Jones to settle the case for $700,000, the amount of damages sought in her complaint. Joe Conason and Gene Lyons, *The Hunting of the President: The Ten Year Campaign to Destroy Bill and Hillary Clinton* (New York: St. Martin's Press, 2000) 120–121, 304; Kyvig, *The Age of Impeachment*, 323–326. Despite what her attorneys considered to be a "complete victory" in view of the weaknesses in her case on the merits (by that point her defamation claim had been dismissed and there was virtually no evidence that Jones had lost either income or status at her job), Jones rejected the president's offer. Conason and Lyons, *The Hunting of the President*, 304–306. Jones' decision was based largely on advice from her media advisor, Susan Carpenter MacMillan, and conservative lawyer and media personality, Ann Coulter. Jones's lawyers, Joseph Cammarata and Gilbert Davis, withdrew from the case and were replaced with lawyers working for another conservative organization, the Rutherford Institute. David Brock, *Blinded by the Right: The Conscience of an Ex-Conservative* (New York: Crown Publishers, 2002) 184; Rae and Campbell, *Impeaching Clinton*, 2.

10. 72 F.3d 1354 (8th Cir. 1996).

11. *Clinton v. Jones*, 500 U.S. 681 (1997).

12. Kenneth W. Starr, *The Starr Report: The Findings of Independent Counsel Kenneth W. Starr on President Clinton and the Lewinsky Affair* (New York: Public Affairs, 1998) 48–74 ("Starr Report"); Baker, *The Breach*, 28–33; William J. Clinton, *My Life*, 773.

13. Starr, *Starr Report*, 62–65; Bob Woodward, *Shadow: Five Presidents and the Legacy of Watergate* (New York: Simon & Schuster, 1999) 424; Conason and Lyons, *The Hunting of the President*, 280–281.

14. Woodward, *Shadow*, 359. Tripp reportedly recorded her conversations with Lewinsky at the suggestion of her literary agent, who had close ties to conservative opponents of Clinton. Conason and Lyons, *The Hunting of a President*, 290, 323–332.

15. Committee on the Judiciary, *Impeachment of William Jefferson Clinton, President of the United States: Report of the Committee on the Judiciary of The House of Representatives*, 105th Cong., 2d Sess., Report No: 105–830, (Washington, DC: U.S. Government Printing Office, 1998) 8–9 ("Report No. 105–830").

16. Starr, *Starr Report*, 95–98. Jordan's efforts to assist Lewinsky in finding employment was specified by the House as one of the means by which Clinton had sought to obstruct justice. It had been Linda Tripp who suggested Vernon Jordan to Lewinsky. Woodward, *Shadow*, 359.

17. *Report No. 105–830*, 11; Starr, *Starr Report*, 102–104.

18. Jordan met Clinton on December 19 and told Clinton that Lewinsky had received a subpoena in the *Jones* case. *Report No. 105–830*, 14; Starr, *Starr Report*, 117–120. During his deposition in the *Jones* case, Clinton had been asked "Did anyone other than your attorneys ever tell you that Monica Lewinsky had been served with a subpoena in this case?" And Clinton replied, "I don't think so." Later, in his testimony at the grand jury, Clinton was questioned about his testimony at the *Jones* deposition. Clinton stated that he "knows now" that he spoke with Jordan but that his memory was not "clear." The Committee majority considered Clinton's testimony in this regard to be false and misleading. It was the Committee majority's opinion that "When one considers the nature of the conversation between President Clinton and Mr. Jordan, the suggestion that President Clinton forgot it defies common sense." *Report No. 105–830*, 14.

    The subpoena served on Lewinsky also directed her to produce any gifts that she had received from Clinton. When Lewinsky met with Clinton at the White House on December 28, Lewinsky suggested that she return the gifts to him in order to avoid producing them. Clinton replied, "I don't know" or "let me think about that." Several hours later, Betty Currie called Lewinsky and arranged to retrieve the gifts. *Report No. 105–830*, 16; Starr, *Starr Report*, 117, 122–124. The Committee majority called these actions "one of the most blatant efforts to obstruct justice and conceal evidence." The Committee majority said that the fact that Currie and Lewinsky had spoken several hours after Lewinsky had met with Clinton and the fact that Currie had simply taken the items from Lewinsky without questioning her, "strongly suggests that President Clinton directed her to do so." *Report No. 105–830*, 16.

19. Starr, *Starr Report*, 120–121.

20. Ibid., 121.

21. *Report No. 105–830*, 19. Starr, *Starr Report*, 128–130.

22. *Report No. 105–830*, 18; Starr, *Starr Report*, 132–133. The Committee majority characterized the offer of employment by Revlon as Lewinsky's "reward for signing the false affidavit." *Report No. 105–830*, 18.

23. Clinton later testified that he had not "focused" on Bennett's "exact words." The Committee majority considered his statement to be "critical," and noted that "[t]he videotape of the deposition shows clearly that President Clinton was paying close attention and that he followed his lawyer's argument." *Report No. 105–830*, 20.

24. Ibid., 21.

25. Woodward, *Shadow*, 371.

26. Ibid., 372–373.

27. Ibid., 375–376; Conason and Lyons, *The Hunting of the President*, 359–361. While she was being held by the FBI and Starr's staff, Lewinsky had also asked to speak with her mother. One of Starr's lawyers told her "You're old enough. You don't need to call your mommy." Her request was refused. Conason and Lyons, *The Hunting of the President*, 361.

28. *Report No. 105–830*, 20–21; Starr, *Starr Report*, 138–139.

29. Memorandum and Order, *Jones v. Clinton*, Civil Action No. LR-C-94–290 (E.D. Ark., January 29, 1998).

30. Memorandum and Order, *Jones v. Clinton*, Civil Action No. LR-C-94–290 (E.D. Ark., March 9, 1998) (emphasis original); 933 F. Supp. 1217.

31. With respect to the proffered evidence of Clinton's other relationships, Judge Wright stated that "Whether other women may have been subjected to workplace harassment, and whether such evidence has allegedly been suppressed, does not change the fact that Plaintiff has failed to demonstrate that she has a case worthy of submitting to a jury." Memorandum and Order, *Jones v. Clinton*, Civil Action No. LR-C-94–290 (E.D. Ark., April 1, 1998), ("Memorandum Opinion")

32. With respect to this statement, the Committee majority opined that "President Clinton carefully crafted his statements to give the appearance of being candid, when actually he intended the opposite." *Report No. 105–830*, 29. According to the Committee majority, "his reading of the definition was an afterthought conceived while preparing for his grand jury testimony. His explanation to the grand jury then, was also false and misleading." Ibid., 21.

33. Baker, *The Breach*, 433.

34. Ibid., 70.

35. Office of the Independent Counsel, *Communication from Kenneth W. Starr Independent Counsel Transmitting a Referral to the United States House of Representatives in Conformity with the Requirements of Title 28, United States Code, Section 595(c)*, Committee on the Judiciary, U.S. House of Representatives, 105th Cong., 2d Sess., House Document 105–310 (Washington, DC: U.S. Government Printing Office, 1998).

36. Starr, *Starr Report*, 154–155.

37. David E. Kendall, et al., *The Preliminary Memorandum of the President of the United States Concerning the Referral of the Office of the Independent Counsel and the Initial Response of the President of the United States to the Referral of the Office of the Independent Counsel*, Committee on Judiciary of The House of Representatives, 105th Cong., 2d Sess., House Document No. 104–317 (Washington, DC: U.S. Government Printing Office, 1998) 1–6.

38. Committee on the Judiciary, *Authorization of an Inquiry into Whether Grounds Exist for the Impeachment of William Jefferson Clinton, President of the United States, Meeting of the House Committee on the Judiciary Held October 5, 1998, Presentation by Inquiry Staff, Consideration of Inquiry Resolution, Adoption of Inquiry Procedures*, House of Representatives, 105th Cong., 2d Sess. (Washington, DC: U.S. Government Printing Office, 1998) 58.

39. Ibid., 58–81.
40. Ibid., 82–99.
41. Ibid., 120–122.
42. *Report No. 105–830*, 308.
43. Judiciary Committee, *Committee on the Judiciary, Requests for Admissions of the President of the United States Related to House Resolution 581 submitted by the Honorable Henry J. Hyde, Chairman, Committee on the Judiciary, U.S. House of Representatives*, Report No. 105–830, 400–440.
44. It was the majority's conclusion that Clinton's responses had "added obstruction of an inquiry of the Legislative Branch to his obstructions of justice before the Judicial Branch." Ibid., 32.
45. A copy of the letter from the "Historians in Defense of the Constitution" was attached as an exhibit to *Background and History of Impeachment: Hearing Before the Subcommittee on the Constitution of the Committee on the Judiciary*, U.S. House of Representatives, 106th Cong., 1st Sess., House Document No. 106–3 (Washington, DC: U.S. Government Printing Office, 1999) ("Background and History of Impeachment").
46. A copy of the law professors' letter was also attached was an exhibit to *Background and History of Impeachment*, 374–383.
47. The law professors characterized Starr's allegations of obstruction of justice based on Clinton's declining to testify voluntarily and asserting testimonial privileges as being "not remotely impeachable." Ibid., 375.
48. Ibid., 375.
49. Testimony of Professor Sean Wilentz, *Presentation on Behalf of the President*; Committee on the Judiciary, *Hearing Before the Committee on the Judiciary of the House of Representatives*, 105th Cong., 2d Sess. (December 8 and 9, 1998) (Washington, DC: US Government Printing Office, 1998) 20.
50. *Background and History of Impeachment*, 78.
51. Ibid., 95.
52. Jonathan Turley of George Washington University contended that the allegations of misconduct had put into issue Clinton's "political legitimacy to govern" and for that reason, irrespective of whether the House believed that he would be convicted by the Senate, it was incumbent on the House to impeach Clinton and refer the case for trial by the Senate so that Clinton could gain "constitutional redemption." Ibid., 254.
53. Ibid., 118.
54. Ibid., 219. Matthew Holden of the University of Virginia similarly warned that adoption of "sexual morality" as a criterion for impeachment would "convert the impeachment process into a referendum on the Presidency." Ibid., 71.
55. Ibid., 231.
56. Ibid., 203.
57. Ibid., 128.
58. Ibid., 109.
59. Ibid., 228.
60. Ibid., 231.

61. Ibid., 231.
62. In 1984, Judge Harry E. Claiborne of the U.S. District Court for the District of Nevada was convicted of making false statements on his income tax returns for 1979 and 1980. On March 16, 1986, Judge Claiborne began serving a two year sentence in federal prison. Judge Claiborne had not resigned his position as District Judge and continued to receive his annual salary of $78,700. Claiborne stated his intention to return to the bench following his release. Faced with Claiborne's intransigence, the Judiciary Committee reported, and the House immediately adopted, four articles of impeachment charging that: 1) Claiborne had made false statements in failing accurately to report his income for 1979; 2) Claiborne had made false statements in failing accurately to report his income for 1980; 3) Claiborne had been convicted of making false income tax returns for 1979 and 1980 and he was therefore "guilty of misbehavior and was and is guilty of high crimes"; and 4) Claiborne had "betrayed the trust of the people of the United States and reduced confidence in the integrity and impartiality of the Judiciary, thereby bringing disrepute on federal courts and the administration of justice by the courts." The Senate designated a committee to hear evidence and report to the full Senate. After hearing arguments on behalf of the House and of Claiborne, the Senate voted to convict and remove Claiborne from office based on Articles 1, 2, and 4. By a vote of 46 to 17, the Senate rejected the article charging that conviction and imprisonment was a "high crime." Van Tassell and Finkelman, *Impeachable Offenses*, 168–172.
63. In 1983, Judge Alcee L. Hastings, of the United States District Court for the Southern District of Florida, was charged with having conspired with an attorney, William Borders, to solicit bribes totaling $150,000 from the defendants in a criminal case, over which Judge Hastings was presiding, in order to secure sentences that did not include incarceration. At the conclusion of his trial on February 4, 1983, Hastings was acquitted by a jury. However, notwithstanding his acquittal, by a vote of 417 to 3, the House adopted seventeen articles of impeachment. As it had in the Claiborne matter, the Senate referred the Hastings case to a committee to hear evidence and report to the full Senate. When the case came for trial before the full Senate, Articles 10 through 15 were not considered by agreement. Hastings was acquitted by the Senate of Article 6 (alleging that Hastings had testified falsely at his criminal trial concerning a meeting with Borders in Hastings' hotel room); Article 16 (alleging that Hastings had obstructed a criminal investigation by revealing confidential information from a wire tap); and Article 17 (alleging that Hastings had undermined the integrity and impartiality of the Judiciary and had brought disrepute on the federal courts as a result of his corrupt relationship with Borders, his false testimony and fabrication of documentary evidence at this trial, and his disclosure of confidential information). Nevertheless, the Senate voted to convict Hastings of the remaining eight articles (alleging a corrupt conspiracy with Borders and various incidents of false testimony by Hastings at this trial). Although Hastings was removed from his position on the District Court, he was not disqualified from future

public office and three years after his impeachment and conviction, Hastings was elected to Congress. Van Tassel and Finkelman, *Impeachable Offenses*, 172–180.

64. As the Senate was preparing for the trial of Judge Hastings, the House adopted three articles of impeachment charging Judge Walter L. Nixon, of the United States District Court for the Southern District of Mississippi, with having given false testimony to a grand jury investigating the business dealings between Judge Nixon and Willey Fairchild and the judge's involvement in the criminal prosecution of Fairchild's son (Articles 1 and 2); and with having brought the judiciary into disrepute by giving false testimony (Article 3). Although several senators who had served on the evidentiary committee voted to acquit him, Nixon was convicted by the Senate of Articles 1 and 2 and removed from office. Van Tassel and Finkelman, *Impeachable Offenses*, 180–185. Nixon challenged the Senate's procedure, claiming that delegation to a committee of the evidentiary function, under Senate Rule 81, violated the Constitution's directive that the Senate was to "try" all impeachments. The Supreme Court held that his claim was not justiciable by the federal courts. *Nixon v. United States*, 506 U.S. 224 (1993).

65. *Background and History of Impeachment*, 77

66. Ibid., 104.

67. Ibid., 201.

68. Ibid., 82.

69. Ibid., 233.

70. Ibid., 56. Gerhardt illuminated his views on impeachable offenses in his book, *The Federal Impeachment Process: A Constitutional and Historical Analysis*, 2d ed. (Chicago: Chicago UP, 2000) 106.

71. *Background and History of Impeachment*, 83, 90.

72. Ibid., 58.

73. Ibid., 224

74. Ibid., 235.

75. Ibid., 99.

76. Ibid., 244.

77. Ibid., 116.

78. Ibid., 112. In the same vein, Daniel H. Pollit of the University of North Carolina described the impeachment remedy as being "like the atom bomb…a weapon to be used only on very rare and specific occasions." Ibid., 207.

79. Ibid., 90. At best, Arthur Schlesenger said, Starr's charges, even if proven, "would perhaps be defined as low crimes and misdemeanors." Ibid., 100–101.

80. Ibid., 208–209.

81. Ibid., 90.

82. Ibid., 246. Schlesenger too told the Committee that Starr's charges did not rise to the level of impeachable conduct because they did not reflect acts committed by Clinton "in his role as public official," and they did not "involve grave breaches of official duties." Ibid., 100–101.

83. Committee on the Judiciary, *Constitutional Grounds for Presidential Impeachment, Report of the Staff of the Impeachment Inquiry*, U.S. House of Representatives, 105th Cong., 2d Sess. (Washington, DC: U.S. Government Printing Office, 1998) ("Majority Staff Report").

84. Committee on the Judiciary, *Constitutional Grounds for Presidential Impeachment, Report of the Staff of the Impeachment Inquiry*, U.S. House of Representatives, 105th Cong., 2d Sess. (Washington, DC: U.S. Government Printing Office, 1998) ("Minority Staff Report").

85. *Majority Staff Report*, 2.

86. Ibid., 3.

87. Ibid., 4–14.

88. Ibid., 14–16.

89. Ibid., 16–17.

90. *Minority Staff Report*, 2–3.

91. Ibid., 6–7.

92. Ibid., 16–19. The Minority Staff took exception to the Majority Staff's characterization of the Claiborne, Nixon, and Hastings judicial impeachments and concluded that the impeachments were predicated on misconduct, not abuse of official power. Ibid., 20–23.

93. *Background and History of Impeachment*, 29–30 (Testimony of Gary L. McDowell of the University of London).

94. Ibid., 237–238 (Testimony of William Van Allstyne of Duke University).

95. Committee on the Judiciary, *The Consequences of Perjury and Related Crimes: Hearing Before the Committee on the Judiciary*, House of Representatives, 105th Cong., 2d Sess. (Washington, DC: U.S. Government Printing Office, 1998).

96. Ibid., 6–9.

97. Ibid., 76–84.

98. Ibid., 60–74. Two of the panelists, Judge Gerald B. Tjoflat and Charles E. Wiggins, stated that the allegations against Clinton constituted impeachable offenses. The third panelist, Judge A. Leon Higginbotham, agreed with the earlier testimony of professors Drinan, Holden, Schlesenger, and Sunstein that the allegations did not reach "the narrow category of egregious or large scale abuses of authority that comes from the exercise of distinctly presidential power."

99. Ibid., 74–101.

100. Committee on the Judiciary, *Appearance of Independent Counsel: Hearing before the Committee on the Judiciary of The House of Representatives*, 105th Cong., 2d Sess. (Washington, DC: U.S. Government Printing Office, 1998) ("Starr Hearing").

101. Committee on the Judiciary, *Impeachment Inquiry: Presentation on Behalf of the President: Hearing before the Committee on the Judiciary of The House of Representatives*, 105th Cong., 2d Sess. (Washington, DC: U.S. Government Printing Office, 1998).

102. Ibid., 14–46. A third witness, Bruce Ackerman of Yale University, questioned whether an expiring Congress had authority under the Twentieth Amendment to the Constitution to send an impeachment to a new Senate.

103.  Ibid., 118–137.

104.  Ibid., 212–227.

105.  Ibid., 283–333.

106.  Ibid., 406–419.

107.  Committee on the Judiciary, *Impeachment Inquiry: Presentations by Investigative Counsel*, Committee on the Judiciary of The House of Representatives, 105th Cong., 2d Sess. (Washington, DC: U.S. Government Printing Office, 1999).

108.  *Report No. 105–830*, 32–106.

109.  Ibid., 128–135. Rae and Campbell commented on the strongly partisan nature of the Judiciary Committee. Rae and Campbell, *Impeaching Clinton*, 53–54.

110.  As to Article 1, the House voted 228 in favor and 206 opposed, 5 members of each party voted with the other party. Article 2 was rejected in the House by a vote of 229 opposed and 205 in favor, 28 Republicans having voted in opposition to the article. Article 3 was adopted by a vote of 221 in favor of the article and 212 opposed. Finally, Article 4 was rejected, overwhelmingly, by a vote of 285 opposed and 148 in favor. *Congressional Record*, vol. 144, 12040–12042 (December 19, 1998); Baker, *The Breach*, 251–252. Rae and Campbell similarly viewed the House debate and vote as "an essentially partisan, political proceeding." Rae and Campbell, *Impeaching Clinton*, 118.

111.  United States Senate, *Proceedings of the United States Senate in the Impeachment Trail of President William Jefferson Clinton*, Senate, 106th Cong., 1st Sess., vol. 1 (Washington, DC: U.S. Government Printing Office, 2000) 17–20, ("Proceedings of the Senate"), vol. 1, 17–20.

112.  Ibid., 445–47.

113.  Ibid., 58–70.

114.  Ibid., 735–739.

115.  Ibid., 1151–1152.

116.  *Proceedings of the Senate*, vol. 2: 1162–1163.

117.  Ibid., 1171–1176.

118.  Ibid., 1188–1192.

119.  Ibid., 1195–1204.

120.  Ibid., 1205–1206.

121.  Ibid., 1210–1225.

122.  Ibid., 1237–1274.

123.  Ibid., 1274–1290.

124.  Ibid., 1292–1324.

125.  Ibid., 1324–1335.

126.  Ibid., 1356–1358.

127.  Ibid., 1358.

128.  Ibid., 1402–1403, 1410–1411.

129.  Ibid., 1412–1413.

130.  Ibid., 1582–1583, 1687–1797; vol. 3: 2027–2533.

131.  Ibid., 1800–1873.

132.  Ibid., 1882–1954.

133. Ibid., 1970–1971, 1984.
134. Ibid., 1986.
135. *Proceedings of the Senate*, vol. 4: 3051.
136. The senators that considered perjury and obstruction to be high crimes and misdemeanors were Samuel Brownback, Susan Collins, Larry E. Craig, William Frist, John F. Kerry of Massachusetts, Patty Murray, and Charles S. Robb. Senators Collins, Kerry, Murray, and Robb voted to acquit Clinton. Ibid., 2563 (Senator Murray), 2655 (Senator Robb), 2678 (Senator Fitzgerald), 2701 (Senator Frist), 2812 ( Senator Collins), 2870 (Senator Craig), 2912 (Senator Brownback), 2943 (Senator Kerry).
137. Ibid., 2987–2989.
138. Ibid., 2971–2972. Other senators who considered Clinton's conduct to have violated his oath were: John McCain, 2656; Senator Peter V. Domenici, 2630; Senator Conrad Burns, Senator Wayne Allard, 2794; Senator Ted Stevens, 2980; Senator Orrin G. Hatch, 3066.
139. Ibid., 2570 (Senator Richard D. Lugar); 2616 (Senator Spencer Abraham); 2701 (Senator William Frist); 2794; (Senator Wayne Allard); 2948 (Senator Michael DeWine).
140. Ibid., 2551 (Senator Kay Bailey Hutchinson); 2561 (Senator Tim Hutchinson); 2683; (Senator William V. Roth); 2977 (Senator Frank H. Murkowski).
141. Ibid., 2718–2719. Senator Frank R. Lautenberg also expressed the view that removal required consideration of the national interest. Ibid., 2643.
142. Ibid., 2650 (Senator Kent Conrad); 2639 (Senator J. Robert Kerry); 2653 (Senator Charles S. Robb); 2689 (Senator Max Cleland); 2789 (Senator Daniel Patrick Moynihan); 2884 (Senator Paul Wellstone); 2891 (Senator Ted Stevens); 2892 (Senator Joseph I. Lieberman); 2916 (Senator Richard H. Bryan); 2939 (Senator Byron L. Dorgan).
143. Ibid., 3106–3107 (Senator John F. Reed).
144. Ibid., 3001.
145. Ibid., 2577. Senator Snowe similarly observed that the high crimes or misdemeanors "must be of such a magnitude that the American people need protection…by the extraordinary act of removal of their duly elected President." Ibid., 3001. Other senators as well were of the view that the misconduct had to affect the nation in order to warrant impeachment and removal. Ibid., 2560 (Senator Kent Conrad); 2567 (Senator Timothy Johnson); 2622 (Senator Barbara Mikulski); 2639 (Senator J. Robert Kerry); 2791 (Senator Daniel Patrick Moynihan); 2794 (Senator Robert Graham); 2884 (Senator Paul Wellstone); 2891 (Senator Ted Stevens); 2897 (Senator Joseph I. Lieberman); 2913 (Senator Richard H. Bryan).

Finally, a number of senators were critical of the proceedings, particularly in the House. There were concerns expressed for the separation of powers. Ibid., 2558 (Senator Kent Conrad); 2575 (Senator Joseph R. Biden); 2691 (Senator Max Cleland); 2791 (Senator Patrick Moynihan). Other senators derided the politically partisan nature of the proceedings in the House. Ibid., 2560 (Senator Kent Conrad); 2573 (Senator Joseph R. Biden); 2706–2707 (Senator Richard J. Durbin); 2807 (Senator Edward M. Kennedy); 2814

(Senator Thomas Harkin); 2826 (Senator Harry Reid); 2944 (Senator John F. Kerry); 2985 (Senator Robert C. Byrd), 3023 (Senator Jeffrey Bingham). Still other senators concluded that because, as Congressman Graham had said, reasonable people could disagree whether the president's conduct merited impeachment, the president should not be removed in any event. Ibid., 2832 (Senator John Edwards); 2876 (Senator Christopher Dodd); 2916 (Senator Richard H. Bryan); 2962 (Senator Ernest F. Hollings).

146. Ibid., 1994–2000.

147. William C. Berman, *From the Center to the Edge* (Lanham: Rowman & Littlefield, 2000) 87.

148. Indeed, according to Sidney Blumenthal, the party of the incumbent president had gained seats in Congress only during the presidencies of Franklin Roosevelt in 1934 and James Monroe in 1822. Sidney Blumenthal, *The Clinton Wars* (New York: Penguin, 2003) 494.

149. Several commentators have pointed to Congressman Tom Delay, who had succeeded Congressman Newt Gingrich as majority leader, having been the moving force behind the Clinton impeachment. For example, according to Blumenthal, Republican Congressman Peter King told him "coming out of the election, everyone thought impeachment was dead. I didn't hear anyone discuss impeachment. It was over. Then Delay assumed control." Ibid., 539. Peter Baker wrote that, beginning with Clinton's August 18 statement, Delay led to the drive to oust Clinton from office. Baker, *The Breach*, 44. The centrality of Delay's role in moving the impeachment effort forward in the House was also noted by Rae and Campbell. Rae and Campbell, *Impeaching Clinton*, 103–104. On November 9, 1998, Chairman Hyde told the Republican members of the Judiciary Committee that despite the midterm returns, he had been told by the Republican leadership that the articles of impeachment were to go to the House for a vote before the Christmas recess. Blumenthal, *The Clinton Wars*, 502.

150. John J. Janssen, *Constitutional Equilibria: The Partisan Contingency of American Constitutional Law from the Jeffersonian "Revolution" to the Impeachment of Bill Clinton* (Lanham: University Press of America, 2000) 147.

151. Baker, *The Breach*, 77–78; Brock, *Blinded by the Right*, 127.

152. Richard A. Posner, *An Affair of State: The Investigation, Impeachment, and Trial of President Clinton* (Cambridge, MA: Harvard UP, 1999) 204–205. So, for example, Delay told the Congregation of the First Baptist Church of Pearland, Texas that Delay believed he was an instrument of God's will to promote "a biblical world view" and that Clinton had been impeached because he had "the wrong world view." Blumenthal, *The Clinton Wars*, 501.

153. *Proceedings of the Senate*, vol. 4: 2942.

154. For example, a poll conducted by the *Washington Post* and *ABC News* on December 15 revealed that 56 percent of those polled had an "unfavorable impression of Clinton as a person." Baker, *The Breach*, 225.

155. After Clinton's public statement following his grand jury appearance on August 17, a public opinion poll taken by *ABC News* showed that 69

percent of those polled favored an immediate end to the Starr investigation. Blumenthal, *The Clinton Wars*, 465. On September 21, the day that Clinton's grand jury testimony was released to the public, the Pew Research Center found that 70 percent of their sample approved of Clinton's performance in office. Blumenthal, *The Clinton Wars*, 484. The poll conducted by the *Washington Post* and *ABC News* on December 15 revealed that 60 percent of those in the survey opposed impeachment. Baker, *The Breach*, 224.

## 5   Conclusion

1. Madison, *Notes*, 331.
2. Proponents of the criminal law interpretation of high crimes and misdemeanors cite the text of several provisions of the Constitution in support of their reading of Article II, Section 4. Berger, *Impeachment: The Constitutional Problems*, 78–79. For example, Article II, Section 2, Clause 1, authorizes the president to "grant reprieves and pardons for offenses against the United States, except in cases of impeachment." This provision had its historical origins in the Act of Settlement of 1700. Additionally, when the Framers considered the pardoning power, concerns were expressed that a president could evade discovery and impeachment by pardoning those "coadjutors" who had conspired with the president to engage in impeachable conduct. Mason expressed this view both at the convention, Farrand, *The Records of the Federal Convention*, vol. 2: 639, and in the Virginia ratification debates, *The Founders' Constitution*, vol. 4, Article II, Section 2, Clause 1, Document 6. Randolph had also sought to exclude treason from the pardoning power for that reason, with which both Mason and Morris agreed. Madison, *Notes*, 646. Thus, rather than suggesting that impeachment was a proceeding to adjudicate crimes, the exclusion of impeachment from the president's prerogatives of reprieve and pardon served to ensure that the impeachment power would not be thwarted thereby.

   Proponent's of the criminal law interpretation also cite Article III, Section 2, Clause 3, which provides that "The Trial of All Crimes, Except Cases of Impeachment, Shall be By Jury." However, Article I, Section 3, Clause 7, makes clear that following conviction by the Senate, "the party convicted shall nevertheless be liable and subject to indictment, trial, judgment and punishment, according to law." Thus, impeachment is a proceeding independent of judicial adjudication, as Iredell explained in his previously cited comments. In any event, there appears to be no dispute that conduct violating the criminal laws may also support impeachment. Indeed, treason and bribery are criminal offenses in addition to being abuses or violations of the public trust, as Hamilton said in Federalist 65. Hamilton, Madison, and Jay, *The Federalist*, 426.
3. This argument was first made in the defense of Andrew Johnson. In 1798, the Supreme Court held, in *Calder v. Bull*, 3 U.S. 386, 393 (1798) that the prohibition against ex post facto laws applied only to penal and criminal statutes. John Dickinson had also cited Blackstone's *Commentaries* during debate

to the effect that ex post facto laws related to criminal cases only. Madison, *Notes*, 547. Impeachment is neither a penal nor criminal proceeding. Indeed, Article I, Section 3, Clause 6 provides that "Judgment in cases of impeachment shall not extend further than to removal from office, and disqualification to hold and enjoy any office of honor, trust or profit under the United States." Accordingly, under the express terms of the Constitution, a conviction by the Senate following impeachment is not an attainder or ex post facto law.

4. U.S. Constitution, Article IV, Section 2, Clause 2.
5. U.S. Constitution, Article I, Section 6, Clause 1.
6. Madison, *Notes*, 605.
7. Hugh Williamson, Madison, *Notes*, 58; Committee of the Whole, Ibid., 150, 331; Referral to the Committee on Detail (July 26), Ibid., 383.
8. Gunning Bedford, Madison, *Notes*, 49.
9. Madison, *Notes*, 332.
10. Randolph, Madison, *Notes*, 334.
11. Hamilton Plan, Madison, *Notes*, 139; Mason, Ibid., 331–332; Morris, Ibid., 332, 355; Report of the Committee of Detail (August 6), Ibid., 393 (treason, bribery or corruption); Report of the Committee of Eleven (September 4), Ibid., 575.
12. One of the mysteries of the constitutional convention was the elimination of references to the United States in conjunction with high crimes and misdemeanors. As proposed by Mason and initially adopted by the delegates, removal of the president was to result from conviction after impeachment for "treason, bribery or other high crimes and misdemeanors against the State." Madison, *Notes*, 605. Almost immediately, United States was substituted for State "in order to remove ambiguity." Ibid., 551–552. However, in the report issued by the Committee on Style and Arrangement on September 19 just four days later, the reference to the United States had been deleted. Ibid., 624. This committee had been constituted "to revise the stile [*sic*] of and arrange the articles which had been agreed to by the House," Ibid., 608, not to make substantive changes. Thus, it has been assumed that it was implicit in the meaning of high crimes and misdemeanors that they were to be offenses against the United States.

    It should be noted that during the debate in the House on the removal power on May 19, 1789, both Congressman Madison and Congressman Livermore of New York referred to high crimes and misdemeanors against "the United States" or against "the Government" as the basis for impeachment. Gales, *The Debates and Proceedings in the Congress of the United States*, vol. 1: 387 (Madison), 393–394 (Lawrence).
13. Rawle, *A View of the Constitution of the United States of America*, 211.
14. Federalist 65, Hamilton, Madison, and Jay, *The Federalist*, 426.
15. Wilson, *The Works of James Wilson*, vol. 1: 426.
16. Story, *Commentaries on the Constitution of the United States*, vol. 2: 217.
17. Ibid., 263.
18. Ibid., 270.
19. Ibid., 272.
20. Selden, *The Table Talk of John Selden*, 99.
21. Black, *Impeachment: A Handbook*, 35–36.

22. Ibid., 33–34; Richard M. Pius, "Impeaching the President: The Intersection of Constitutional and Popular Law," *St. Louis Law Journal*, (1999) vol. 43: 871; Laurence H. Tribe, "Defining 'High Crimes and Misdemeanors': Basic Principles," *George Washington Law Review* (1999) vol. 67: 2.

23. Black, *Impeachment: A Handbook*, 35.

24. Kurland, *Watergate and the Convention*, 111–112; Daniel H. Pollitt, "Sex in the Oval Office and Cover-Up under Oath: Impeachable Offense?" *North Carolina Law Review* (1998) vol. 77: 262; Tribe, "Defining 'High Crimes and Misdemeanors,'" 720.

25. Tribe, "Defining 'High Crimes and Misdemeanors,'" 720.

26. Mason noted that unlike presidents, judicial appointments are not for a limited term, thus it was "necessary…that a forum should be created for trying misbehavior." Madison, *Notes*, 333. In Federalist No. 79, Hamilton argued under the Constitution for "malconduct" by judges and for disqualification by reason of insanity. *The Federalist*, 498–499.

27. Judge Pickering was removed on the basis of his insanity despite his incapacity to form the mens rea required for criminality. Judge Humphreys was removed in 1862 for his support of the armed rebellion against the United States. Judge Swayne was removed for having obtained funds from the United States by false pretense, despite his counsel's argument that only acts "in the actual administration of justice" would support impeachment. David Y. Thomas, "The Law of Impeachment in the United States," *American Political Science Review* (1908) vol. 2: 381–382. Judge Archbald was removed for "misbehavior" and "misdemeanors in office" relating to his dealings with railroads over which his court had jurisdiction. Judge Ritter was found by the Senate to be "unfit to serve as a judge." Judge Claiborne was removed on the basis of his conviction for tax fraud. Judge Nixon was removed on the basis of his conviction for perjury. Judge Hastings was removed for making false statements at his criminal trial, notwithstanding his acquittal.

28. In essence, conviction and removal of a judge is the withdrawal of senatorial consent required for judicial appointment while removal of a president would effectively undo the national election that installed the president in the first instance. Additionally, impeachment proceedings distract the president from the duties of office, encumber the executive and legislative branches, and undermine the foreign relations of the United States.

29. Berger, *Impeachment: The Constitutional Problems*, 295; Rehnquist, *Grand Inquests*, 271; Gerhardt, *The Federal Impeachment Process*, 191.

30. Kurland, *Watergate and the Constitution*, 119; Rehnquist, *Grand Inquests*, 274; Gerhardt, *The Federal Impeachment Process*, 192.

31. Gerhardt, *The Federal Impeachment Process*, 185.

32. Whittington, "Bill Clinton was no Andrew Johnson," 422.

33. Frank O. Browman and Stephen L. Sepinuck, "High Crimes and Misdemeanors": Defining the Constitutional Limits on Presidential Impeachment," *Southern California Law Review*, vol. 72 (1999) 1532.

34. Federalist 65, Hamilton, Madison, and Jay, *The Federalist*, 427.

35. Berger, *Impeachment: The Constitutional Problems*, 298.

36. Sunstein, "Impeaching the President," 315.

# Selected Bibliography


Abrahamsen, David. *Nixon v. Nixon: An Emotional Tragedy.* New York: Farrar, 1997.

Ackerman, Bruce. *The Failure of the Founding Fathers: Jefferson, Marshall, and the Rise of Presidential Democracy.* Cambridge, MA: Harvard UP, 2005.

———. *We the People.* 2 vols. Cambridge, MA: Harvard UP, 1991.

Adams, George Burton. *Constitutional History of England.* New York: Holt, 1926.

Adams, John. *Diary and Autobiography of John Adams.* Ed. L.H. Butterfield. 4 vols. Cambridge, MA: Belknap-Harvard UP, 1961.

———. *Papers of John Adams.* Ed. Robert J. Taylor. 8 vols. Cambridge, MA: Belknap Harvard UP, 1977.

———. *The Works of John Adams, Second President of the United States: With a Life of the Author, Notes and Illustrations, By His Grandson Charles Francis Adams.* Ed. Charles Francis Adams. 10 vols. Boston, 1856.

Adams, John Quincy. *The Diary of John Quincy Adams, 1794–1845; American Political, Social, and Intellectual Life from Washington to Polk.* Ed. Allan Nevins. New York: Longmans, Green, 1928.

———. *Memoirs of John Quincy Adams, Comprising Portions of His Diary from 1795 to 1848.* Ed. Charles Francis Adams. 10 vols. Philadelphia, 1874.

———. *Writings of John Quincy Adams.* Ed. Worthington Chauncey Ford. 7 vols. New York: Macmillan, 1917.

Amar, Akhil Reed. *America's Constitution: A Biography.* New York: Random House, 2005.

Ambrose, Stephen E. *Nixon.* 3 vols. New York: Simon & Schuster, 1991.

Association of the Bar of the City of New York, Committee on Federal Legislation, *The Law of Presidential Impeachment.* New York: Harper, 1974.

Bailyn, Bernard, ed. *The Debates on the Constitution.* New York: the Library of America, 1993.

———. *The Ordeal of Thomas Hutchinson.* Cambridge, MA: Belknap-Harvard UP, 1974.

Baker, Peter. *The Breach: Inside the Impeachment and Trial of William Jefferson Clinton.* New York: Scribner, 2000.

Barber, James David. *The Presidential Character: Predicting Performance in the White House.* Englewood Cliffs: Prentice-Hall, 1972.

Belknap, Michael R., ed. *American Political Trials.* Westport: Greenwood, 1981.

Benedict, Michael Les. *A Compromise of Principle: Congressional Republicans and Reconstruction 1863–1869.* New York: Norton, 1974.

———. *The Impeachment and Trial of Andrew Johnson.* New York: Norton, 1973.

Benedict, Michael Les. "A New Look at the Impeachment of Andrew Johnson." *Political Science Quarterly* 113 (1998): 493–511.

Berger, Raoul. *Impeachment: The Constitutional Problems.* Cambridge, MA: Harvard UP, 1973.

Berkins, Carol. *A Brilliant Solution: Inventing the American Constitution.* New York: Harvest-Harcourt, 2002.

Berman, William C. *From the Center to the Edge: The Politics & Policies of the Clinton Presidency.* Lanham: Rowman & Littlefield, 2001.

Berstein, Jeremy. *The Dawning of the Raj: The Life and Trials of Warren Hastings.* Chicago: Ivan R. Dee, 2000.

Beveridge, Albert J. *The Life of John Marshall.* 4 vols. Boston: Houghton, 1916.

Black, Charles L. *Impeachment: A Handbook.* New Haven: Yale UP, 1974.

Blackstone, William. *Commentaries on the Laws of England.* 4 vols. Chicago: Chicago UP, 1979.

Blumenthal, Sidney. *The Clinton Wars.* New York: Penguin, 2003.

Bowman, Frank O. and Stephen L. Sepinuck. "'High Crimes and Misdemeanors': Defining the Constitutional Limits on Presidential Impeachment." *Southern California Law Review* 72 (1999): 1517–1600.

Brant, Irving. *Impeachment: Trials and Errors.* New York: Knopf, 1972.

Brock, David. *Blinded by the Right: The Conscience of an Ex-Conservative.* New York: Crown, 2002.

Brodie, Fawn M. *Richard Nixon: The Shaping of His Character.* Cambridge, MA: Harvard UP, 1983.

Burke, Edmund. *On Empire, Liberty and Reform: Speeches and Letters of Edmund Burke.* Ed. David Bromwich. New Haven: Yale UP, 2002.

——. *The Works of the Right Honorable Edmund Burke.* 4th ed. 10 vols. Boston: 1871.

Bushnell, Elenore. *Crimes, Follies and Misfortunes: The Federal Impeachment Trials.* Urbana: Illinois UP, 1992.

Carnall, Geoffrey, and Colin Nicholson, eds. *The Impeachment of Warren Hastings.* Edinburgh: Edinburgh UP, 1989.

Carrington, R.W. "The Impeachment Trial of Samuel Chase." *Virginia Law Review* 9 (1923): 485–500.

Carter, Albert Thomas. *Outlines of English History.* London: 1899.

Clarke, M.V. "The Origin of Impeachment." *Oxford Essays in Medieval History.* Ed. Herbert Edward Salter. 1934. Freeport: Books for Libraries Press, 1968. 164–189.

Cobbett, William. *The Parliamentary History of England.* 10 vols. London: 1806.

Coke, Edward. *The Golden Passage in the Great Charter of England Called Magna Carta.* London: 1775.

Colburn, H. Trevor. *The Lamp of Experience: Whig History and the Intellectual Origins of the American Revolution.* Indianapolis: Liberty Fund, 1998.

Conason, Joe, and Gene Lyons. *The Hunting of the President: The Ten Year Campaign to Destroy Bill and Hillary Clinton.* New York: St. Martin, 2000.

Cong. Rec. April 22. 1952: 4220–4221. Washington, D.C.: U.S. Government Printing Office.

——. April 23. 1952: 4325.

——. April 28. 1952: 7424.

Cong. Rec. June 29. 1953: 7586–7590.

———. April 15. 1970: 11912–11927.

———. December 19. 1998: 12040–12042.

Cornell, Saul. *The Other Framers: Anti-Federalism and the Dissenting Tradition in America, 1788–1828.* Chapel Hill: North Carolina UP, 1961.

Costin, W.W., and J. Steven Watson, eds. *The Law and Working of the Constitution: Documents 1660–1914.* London: Adam and Charles Black, 1952.

Currie, Davie P. "The Constitution in Congress: The Most Endangered Branch 1801–1805," *Wake Forrest Law Review* 33 (1998): 219–256.

Curtis, George Ticknor. *History of the Origin, Formation and Adoption of the Constitution of the United States.* 2 vols. New York: 1858.

Dewitt, David Miller. *The Impeachment and Trial of Andrew Johnson.* New York: Macmillan, 1903.

Domer, Thomas. "The Role of George S. Boutwell in the Impeachment and Trial of Andrew Johnson." *New England Quarterly* 49 (1967): 596–617.

Douglas, William O. *The Court Years 1939–1975: The Autobiography of William Douglas.* New York: Random, 1980.

Dunning, William A. "More Light on Andrew Johnson." *American Historical Review* 11 (1906): 574–594.

Dwight, Theodore W. "Trial by Impeachment." *American Law Register* 15 (1867): 257–283.

Ehrlich, Walter. *Presidential Impeachment: An American Dilemma.* Saint Charles: Forum, 1974.

Ellis, Richard. "The Impeachment of Samuel Chase." *American Political Trials.* Ed. Michael R. Belknap. Westport: Greenwood, 1981, 57–78.

Emery, Fred. *Watergate: The Corruption of American Politics and the Fall of Richard Nixon.* New York: Simon and Schuster, 1995.

Farrand, Max. *The Framing of the Constitution of the United States.* 1913. New Haven: Yale UP, 1972.

———. *The Records of the Federal Convention of 1787.* 3 vols. 1911. New Haven: Yale UP, 1966.

Fisher, Louis. *Constitutional Conflicts between Congress and the President.* 4th ed. Lawrence: Kansas UP, 1997.

Foner, Eric. *Reconstruction: America's Unfinished Revolution 1863–1877.* New York: Harper & Row, 1988.

Friedman, Leon, and William F. Levantrosser, eds. *Watergate and Afterward: The Legacy of Richard M. Nixon.* Westport: Greenwood, 1992.

Gales, Joseph, ed. *The Debates and Proceedings in the Congress of the United States.* 10 vols. Washington, DC: 1834.

Gerhardt, Michael J. *The Federal Impeachment Process: A Constitutional and Historical Analysis.* 2d ed. Chicago: Chicago UP, 2000.

Gerson, Noel B. *The Trial of Andrew Johnson.* Nashville: Thomas Nelson, 1977.

Gillespie, Michael Allen, and Michael Lienesch, eds. *Ratifying the Constitution.* Lawrence: Kansas UP, 1989.

Hale, Matthew. *The History of the Common Law of England.* Ed. Charles M. Gray. Chicago: Chicago UP, 1971.

Hale, Matthew. *Pleas of the Crown: A Methodical Summary.* Ed. P.R. Glazebrook. London: Professional Books, 1972.

Hallam, Henry. *Constitutional History of England: From the Accession of Henry VII to the Death of George II.* 3 vols. London: 1854.

Hamilton, Alexander, James Madison, and John Jay. *The Federalist.* Ed. Benjamin F. Wright. New York: Barnes, 1996.

Harding, Allan. *A Social History of English Law.* Gloucester: Peter Smith, 1973.

Hatsell, John. *Precedents of Proceedings in the House of Commons: With Observations.* 4 vols. London: 1818.

Hirst, Derek. "The Defection of Sir Edward Dering, 1640–1641." *The English Civil War: The Essential Readings.* Ed. Peter Gaunt. Oxford: Blackwell, 2000. 207–225.

Hoffer, Peter Charles, and N.E.H. Hull. *Impeachment in America, 1635–1805.* New Haven: Yale UP, 1984.

Holdsworth, W.S. *A History of English Law.* 3 vols. London: Methuen, 1909.

Howell, Thomas Bayly. *A Complete Collection of State Trials and Proceedings for High Treason and Other Crimes and Misdemeanors from the Earliest Period to the Year 1783.* 34 vols. London: 1809.

Jefferson, Thomas. *Jefferson's Parliamentary Writings: Parliamentary Pocket Book and a Manual on Parliamentary Practice.* Ed. Wilbur Samuel Howell. Princeton: Princeton UP, 1987.

*Journals of the House of Representatives of Massachusetts: 1773–1774.* Boston: Massachusetts Historical Society, 1981.

Keir, David Lindsay. *The Constitutional History of Modern Britain Since 1845.* 9th ed. London: Adam & Charles Black, 1966.

Kelly, Alfred H., Winfred Harbison, and Herman Belz. *The American Constitution: Its Origins and Development.* 7th ed. 2 vols. New York: Norton, 1991.

Kent, James. *Commentaries on American Law.* 9th ed. 4 vols. Boston: 1858.

Kethcham, Ralph, ed. *The Anti-Federalist Papers and the Constitutional Convention Debates: The Clashes and Compromises that Gave Birth to Our Form of Government.* New York: New American Library, 2003.

Knappen, M.M. *A Constitutional and Legal History of England.* Hamden: Archon Books, 1964.

Knudson, Jerry W. "The Jeffersonian Assault on the Federal Judiciary, 1802–1805: Political Forces and Press Reaction." *American Journal of Legal History* 14 (1970): 55–75.

Kurland, Philip B., and Ralph Lerner, eds. *The Founder's Constitution.* 5 vols. Chicago: Chicago UP, 1987.

Kurland, Philip B. *Watergate and the Constitution.* Chicago: Chicago UP, 1978.

Kutler, Stanley I., ed. *Abuse of Power: The New Nixon Tapes.* New York: Free Press, 1997.

———. *The Wars of Watergate: The Last Crisis of Richard Nixon.* New York: Norton, 1990.

Kyvig, David E. *The Age of Impeachment: American Constitutional Culture since 1960.* Lawrence: Kansas UP, 2008.

Labovitz, John R. *Presidential Impeachment.* New Haven: Yale UP, 1978.

Lawrence, William. "The Law of Impeachment." *American Law Register* 15 (1867): 641–680.

Levy, Leonard W. *Original Intent and the Framer's Constitution.* Chicago: Ivan R. Dee, 1988.

Lillich, Richard B. "The Chase Impeachment." *American Journal of Legal History* 4 (1960): 49–72.

Lomask, Milton. *Andrew Johnson: President on Trial.* New York: Farrar, 1960.

Lovell, Colin Rhys. *English Constitutional and Legal History: A Survey.* New York: Oxford UP, 1962.

Lyall, Alfred. *Warren Hastings.* 1889. Freeport: Books for Libraries Press, 1970.

Lyon, Bryce D. *A Constitutional and Legal History of Medieval England.* 2d ed. New York: Norton, 1980.

MacAuly, Thomas Babington. *Warren Hastings.* New York: 1886.

Madison, James. *Notes of Debates in the Federal Convention.* 1893. New York: Norton, 1987.

Main, Jackson Turner. *The Anti-Federalists: Critics of the Constitution, 1781–1788.* Chapel Hill: North Carolina UP, 1961.

Maitland, F.W. *The Constitutional History of England.* Cambridge: Cambridge UP, 1911.

Malone, Dumas. *Jefferson and His Life.* 6 vols. Boston: Little, Brown, 1981.

Marcham, Frederick George. *A Constitutional History of Modern England, 1485 to the Present.* New York: Harper, 1960.

Marshall, P.J., ed. *The Oxford History of the British Empire: The Eighteenth Century.* Oxford: Oxford UP, 2001.

Mason, George. *The Papers of George Mason.* Ed. Robert A. Rutland. 3 vols. Chapel Hill: North Carolina UP, 1970.

Mayer, David N. *The Constitutional Thought of Thomas Jefferson.* Charlottesville: Virginia UP, 1994.

McDonald, Forrest. *The American Presidency.* Lawrence: Kansas UP, 1994.

McLaughlin, Andrew C. *A Constitutional History of the United States.* New York: D. Appleton-Century, 1995.

Melton, Buckner F. *The First Impeachment: The Constitution's Framers and the Case of Senator William Blount.* Macon: Mercer UP, 1998.

Morrison, Samuel Eliot, Henry Steele Commager and William E. Leuchtenburg. *The Growth of the American Republic.* 6th ed. 2 vols. New York: Oxford UP, 1969.

Norton, Thomas James. *The Constitution of the United States: Its Sources and Its First Application.* Cleveland: World, 1943.

Olson, Keith W. *Watergate: The Presidential Scandal that Shook America.* Lawrence: Kansas UP, 2003.

Perkins, Rollin M. *Criminal Law,* 2d ed. Mineola: Foundation Press, 1969.

Pious, Richard M. "Impeaching the President: The Intersection of Constitutional and Popular Law." *St. Louis Law Journal* 43 (1999): 859–904.

Plucknett, T.F.T. *Studies in English Legal History.* London: Hambledon, 1983.

Plummer, William. *William Plumer's Memorandum of Proceedings in the United States Senate 1803–1807.* Ed. Everett Somerville Brown. New York: Macmillan, 1923.

Pollitt, Daniel H. "Sex in the Oval Office and Cover-up under Oath: Impeachable Offense?" *North Carolina Law Review* 77 (1998): 259–282.

Posner, Richard A. *An Affair of State: The Investigation, Impeachment and Trial of President Clinton.* Cambridge, MA: Harvard UP, 1999.

Prescott, Arthur Taylor. *Drafting the Federal Constitution: A Rearrangement of Madison's Notes, Giving Consecutive Developments of Provisions in the Constitution of the United States, Supplemented by Documents Pertaining to the Philadelphia Convention and to Ratification Processes and Including Insertions by The Compiler.* Baton Rouge: Louisiana State UP, 1941.

Quincy, John. "Causes for Impeachment." *Boston Gazette and Country Journal* January 4, 1768: 1.

Radcliffe, Geoffrey R.Y., and Geoffrey N. Cross. *The English Legal System.* Ed. G.J. Hand and D.J. Bentley. 6th ed. London: Butterworths, 1977.

Rae, Nicol C., and Colton C. Campbell. *Impeaching Clinton: Partisan Strife on Capital Hill.* Lawrence: Kansas UP, 2004.

Rakove, Jack N. *Original Meanings: Politics and Ideas in the Making of the Constitution.* New York: Knopf, 1996.

Rawle, William. *A View of the Constitution of the United States of America.* Philadelphia: 1829.

Reeves, Richard. *President Nixon: Alone in the White House.* New York: Simon & Schuster, 2001.

Rehnquist, William H. *Grand Inquests: The Historic Impeachments of Justice Samuel Chase and President Andrew Johnson.* New York: Morrow, 1992.

Roberts, Clayton. "The Law of Impeachment in Stuart England: A Reply to Raoul Berger." *Yale Law Review* 84 (1975): 1419–1439.

Russell, Robert. *An Essay on the History of the English Government and Constitution from the Reign of Henry VII to the Present Time.* 1865. New York: Kraus Reprint, 1971.

Salmon, Thomas. *Critical Review of the State Trials and Impeachments for High Treason.* London: 1730.

Schwartz, Bernard. *A Commentary on the Constitution of the United States.* 2 vols. New York: Macmillan, 1963.

Selden, John. *The Table Talk of John Seldon.* Ed. Samuel Harvey Reynolds. Oxford: 1892.

Sharp, James Roger. *American Politics in the Early Republic: The New Nation in Crisis.* New Haven: Yale UP, 1993.

Simpson, Alexander. *A Treatise on Federal Impeachments.* Philadelphia: Law Association of Philadelphia, 1916.

Smith, David A. *Constitutional Royalism and the Search for Settlement, 1640–1649.* Cambridge: Cambridge UP, 1994.

———. *A History of the Modern British Isles 1603–1707.* Oxford: Blackwell, 1998.

Smith, Gene. *High Crimes and Misdemeanors: The Impeachment and Trial of Andrew Johnson.* New York: Morrow, 1977.

Smith, Goldwin. *A Constitutional and Legal History of England.* New York: Scribner, 1955.

Starr, Kenneth W. *The Starr Report: The Findings of Independent Counsel Kenneth W. Starr on President Clinton and the Lewinsky Affair.* New York: Public Affairs, 1998.

St. Clair, James D., and Charles Alan Wright. "An Analysis of the Constitutional Standard for Presidential Impeachment." Washington, DC: U.S. Government Printing Office, 1974.

Stephen, James Fitzgerald. *A History of the Criminal Law of England.* 3 vols. London: 1883.

Stewart, David O. *Impeached: The Trial of President Andrew Johnson and the Fight for Lincoln's Legacy.* New York: Simon & Schuster, 2009.

Story, Joseph. *Commentaries on the Constitution of the United States.* 3 vols. Boston: 1833.

Stryker, Lloyd Paul. *Andrew Johnson.* New York: Macmillan, 1929.

Sunstein, Cass R. "Impeaching the President." *University of Pennsylvania Law Review* 147 (1998): 279–315.

Tanner, J.R. *English Constitutional Conflicts of the Seventeenth Century.* Cambridge: Cambridge UP, 1966.

Thomas, David Y. "The Law of Impeachment in the United States." *American Political Science Review* 2 (1908): 378–395.

Trefousse, Hans L. *Impeachment of a President.* New York: Fordham UP, 1999.

Tribe, Lawrence A. "Defining 'High Crimes and Misdemeanors': Basic Principles." *George Washington Law Review* 67 (1999): 712–734.

Turner, Lynn W. "The Impeachment of John Pickering." *American Historical Review* 54 (1949): 485–507.

Ungar, Sanfords. *The Papers and the Papers: An Account of the Legal and Political Battle over the Pentagon Papers.* New York: Dutton, 1972.

United States Department of Justice. Office of Legal Counsel. *Legal Aspects of Impeachment Inquiry: An Overview.* Washington, DC: U.S. Department of Justice, 1974.

United States Cong. House. Committee on the Judiciary. *Appearance of the Independent Counsel: Hearing Before the Committee on the Judiciary of the House of Representatives.* Washington, DC: U.S. Government Printing Office, 1998.

———. *Authorization of an Inquiry into Whether Grounds Exist for the Impeachment of William Jefferson Clinton, President of the United States, Meeting of the House Committee on Judiciary Held on October 5, 1998, Presentation by the Inquiry Staff, Consideration of Inquiry Resolution, Adoption of Inquiry Procedures.* Washington, DC: U.S. Government Printing Office, 1998.

———. *Background and History of Impeachment: Hearing Before the Subcommittee on the Constitution of the Committee on the Judiciary, House of Representatives.* Washington, DC: U.S. Government Printing Office, 1998.

———. *Communication from Kenneth W. Starr, Independent Counsel, Transmitting a Referral to the United States House of Representatives in Conformity with the Requirements of Title 28, United States Code, Section 595(c).* Washington, DC: U.S. Government Printing Office, 1998.

———. *The Consequences of Perjury and Related Crimes: Hearing Before the Committee on the Judiciary of the House of Representatives.* Washington, DC: U.S. Government Printing Office, 1998.

United States Cong. House. *Constitutional Grounds for Presidential Impeachment.* Washington, DC: Public Affairs Press, 1974.

United States Cong. House. *Constitutional Grounds for Presidential Impeachment: Modern Precedents, Report by the Staff of the Impeachment Inquiry.* Washington, DC: U.S. Government Printing Office, 1998.

———. *Debate on Articles of Impeachment: Hearings Before the Committee on the Judiciary of the House of Representatives.* Washington, DC: U.S. Government Printing Office, 1974.

———. *Impeachment: Selected Materials.* Washington, DC: U.S. Government Printing Office, 1973.

———. 1998.

———. *Impeachment Inquiry: Presentations by Investigative Counsel.* Washington, DC: U.S. Government Printing Office, 1998.

———. *Impeachment Inquiry: Presentations on Behalf of the President: Hearing Before the Committee on the Judiciary of the House of Representatives.* Washington, DC: U.S. Government Printing Office, 1998.

———. *Impeachment of William Jefferson Clinton, President of the United States: Report of the Committee on the Judiciary of the House of Representatives:* Washington, DC: U.S. Government Printing Office, 1998.

———. *The Preliminary Memorandum of the President Concerning the Referral of the Office of the Referral of the Office of the Independent Counsel Independent Counsel and the Initial Response of the President of the United States to the Referral of the Office of the Independent Counsel.* Washington, DC: U.S. Government Printing Office, 1998.

———. *Report: Impeachment of Richard M. Nixon President of the United States.* Washington, DC: U.S. Government Printing Office, 1974.

United States Cong. House. *The Impeachment and Trial of Andrew Johnson, President of the United States.* 1868. New York: Dover, 1974.

United States Cong. House. Senate. *Extracts from the Journal of the United States Senate in all Cases of Impeachment, 1798–1904.* Washington, DC: U.S. Government Printing Office, 1912.

———. *Proceedings of the United States Senate in the Impeachment Trial of President William Jefferson Clinton.* Washington, DC: U.S. Government Printing Office, 2000.

———. Select Committee on Presidential Campaign Activities. *The Senate Watergate Report: The Final Report of the Senate Select Committee on Presidential Campaign Activities.* New York: Carroll & Graff, 1974.

———. *Trial of Andrew Johnson President of the United States Before the Senate of the United States on Impeachment by the House of Representatives for High Crimes and Misdemeanors.* 3 vols. 1868. New York: Dacappo Press, 1970.

Urofsky, Melvin I. *A March of Liberty: A Constitutional History of the United States.* New York: Knopf, 1988.

Valelly, Richard M. *The Two Reconstructions: The Struggle for Black Enfranchisement.* Chicago: Chicago UP, 2004.

Van Tassel, Emily Field, and Paul Finkleman, eds. *Impeachable Offenses: A Documentary History from 1787 to President.* Washington, DC: Congressional Quarterly, 1999.

Volkan, Vamik, Norman Itzkowitz, and Andrew W. Dod. *Richard Nixon: A Psychobiography.* New York: Columbia UP, 1997.

Wharton, Francis. *State Trials of the United States during the Administration of Washington and Adams.* Philadelphia: 1849.

White, Theodore H. *Breach of Faith: The Fall of Richard Nixon.* New York: Athenuem, 1975.

Whittington, Keith E. *Constitutional Construction: Divided Powers and Constitutional Meaning.* Cambridge, MA: Harvard UP, 1999.

———. "Bill Clinton was no Andrew Johnson: Comparing Two Impeachments." *University of Pennsylvania Journal of Constitutional Law* 2 (2000): 422–465.

Wood, Gordon S. *The Creation of the American Republic 1776–1787.* Chapel Hill: North Carolina UP, 1998.

Wilentz, Sean. *The Rise of American Democracy: Jefferson to Lincoln.* New York: Norton, 2005.

Wilson, Bradford P., and Peter W. Schramm. *Separation of Power and Good Government.* Lanham: Rowman & Littlefield, 1994.

Wilson, James. *The Works of James Wilson.* Ed. Robert Green McCloskey. 2 vols. Cambridge, MA: Belknap-Harvard UP, 1967.

Winston, Robert W. *Andrew Johnson: Plebian and Patriot.* New York: Holt, 1928.

Wood, Gordon S. *The Creation of the American Republic 1776–1787.* Chapel Hill: North Carolina UP, 1998.

Wooddeson, Richard. *A Systematic View of the Laws of England; As Treated of in a course of Vinerian Lectures, Read at Oxford, During a Series of Years, Commencing in Michaelmas Term, 1777.* 2 vols. Dublin: 1792.

Woodward, Bob. *Shadow: Five Presidents and the Legacy of Watergate.* New York: Touchstone-Simon & Schuster, 1999.

# Index